Grammar Practice
for Pre-intermediate Students

with key

live
LANGUAGE
live-language.com

Vicki Anderson,
Gill Holley and Rob Metcalf
with Elaine Walker and
Steve Elsworth

with CD-ROM

PEARSON
Longman

Contents

Grammar

Nouns, pronouns and determiners

Nouns and determiners

1 Singular and plural nouns. 4
2 Countable and uncountable nouns 5
3 Counting uncountable nouns 7
4 *a lot of/lots of, many, much, (a) few, (a) little* 8
5 *all, most, some, none* 10
6 *each, every* 12
Check 1 Nouns and determiners 13

Pronouns and possessives

7 Pronouns and possessive adjectives 14
8 Possessive *'s*, possessive *of* 15
9 Reflexive pronouns, *each other* 16
10 *one, ones* 17
11 *somebody, something* etc. 18
Check 2 Pronouns and possessives 20

Articles

12 Definite and indefinite article 21
13 Definite and zero article (1). 22
14 Definite and zero article (2) 23
15 Definite, indefinite and zero article 24
Check 3 Articles 26

Adjectives and adverbs, comparison

Adjectives and adverbs

16 Order of adjectives. 27
17 Comparative and superlative adjectives. 28
18 Adverbs of manner. 30
19 Comparative and superlative adverbs. 31
20 Modifying comparisons: *much faster* etc. 33
21 Adverbs of frequency. 34
22 Adverbs of degree: *very, really* etc. 36
Check 4 Adjectives and adverbs. 37

Comparative structures

23 *as ... as, not as ... as* 38
24 *too, enough, very* 39
25 *so ... that, such (a/an) ... that* 40
Check 5 Comparative structures. 41

Tenses

Present tenses

26 Present simple 42
27 Present continuous 43
28 Present simple or present continuous. 45
29 State verbs 46
Check 6 Present tenses. 47

Past tenses

30 Past simple: regular verbs 48
31 Past simple: irregular verbs 49
32 Past continuous 51
33 Past continuous and past simple 53
34 *used to* 54
Check 7 Past tenses. 56

Perfect tenses

35 Present perfect: form and use 57
36 Present perfect with *just, already, yet* 59
37 Present perfect with *ever, never* 60
38 Present perfect with *for, since* 62
39 Present and past simple, present perfect 63
Check 8 Present perfect 65

40 Past perfect simple 66
41 Past perfect and past simple 67
Check 9 Past and perfect tenses 69

Future forms

42 *be going to* and *will* 70
43 Present continuous or *be going to* 71
44 Present simple and continuous for future 72
Check 10 Future forms 73

Modal verbs

45 Ability and possibility: *can, could, be able to* 74
46 Permission: *can, could, be allowed to* 75
47 Possibility: *may, might, could*. 77
48 Certainty and deduction: *must, can't* 78
49 Requests: *can, could, would*. 79
50 Offers and suggestions: *will, shall, can, could* 80
Check 11 Modal verbs (1) 81

51 Obligation and necessity: *must, have to, need to* 82
52 Prohibition: *mustn't, can't, not be allowed to* 83
53 Lack of necessity: *don't have to, don't need to* 84
54 Advice: *should, ought to, must* 85
Check 12 Modal verbs (2) 87

Sentence and text structure
Statements and questions

55 Word order: direct and indirect objects 88
56 *there is/are* vs. *it is* 89
57 Making questions 91
58 Question words as subject or object 93
59 Prepositions at the end of questions 94
60 Question tags 95
61 Short responses with *so, neither/nor* etc. 96
62 Short responses: *I think so. I hope not.* 97
Check 13 Statements and questions 98

-ing forms and infinitives

63 *-ing* forms as subjects of sentences 99
64 Verbs followed by *-ing* form or *to*-infinitive........ 100
65 Verbs followed by object + *to*-infinitive 101
Check 14 *-ing* forms and infinitives................. 102

The passive

66 The passive: form and use 103
67 The passive + *by* 105
68 The causative: *have something done* 106
Check 15 The passive 107

Reported speech

69 Direct speech: punctuation 108
70 Reported statements 109
71 Reporting verbs: *say* and *tell* 111
72 Reported questions 112
73 Reported commands and requests 114
Check 16 Reported speech 116
74 Indirect questions........................ 117
75 *Wh*- question words + *to*-infinitive............. 118
Check 17 Indirect questions.................... 119

Relative clauses

76 Defining relative clauses 120
77 Other ways of identifying people and things 121
Check 18 Relative clauses 123

Linking words and structures

78 Addition: *and, also, too, as well* 124
79 *both ... and, either ... or, neither ... nor* 125
80 Contrast: *but, although/though, however*.......... 126
81 Reason: *because (of), as, since, so, therefore* 128
82 Purpose: *to, in order to, so that*............... 129
Check 19 Linking words and structures (1) 131
83 Saying when things happen.................. 132
84 Future time clauses 133
85 *before/after + -ing*........................ 134
86 Sequencers 135
Check 20 Linking words and structures (2)......... 136

Conditionals

87 The zero conditional 137
88 The first conditional 138
89 *unless* 140
90 The second conditional 141
Check 21 Conditionals 143

VOCABULARY
Prepositions

91 Prepositions of place...................... 144
92 Prepositions of movement 146
93 Prepositions of time (1) 147
94 Time expressions with no preposition 149
95 Prepositions of time (2) 150
96 *with, by* 151
97 *like* 152
Check 22 Prepositions 153

Prepositional phrases

98 Prepositional phrases: time 154
99 Prepositional phrases: place and activity 155
100 Other prepositional phrases.................... 156
Check 23 Prepositional phrases 157

Words that go together

101 Adjective + preposition 158
102 Verb + preposition 159
103 Phrasal verbs 160
104 *make, do, have, get*....................... 161
Check 24 Words that go together.................. 162

Word formation

105 Adjectives ending in *-ed* and *-ing*................ 163
106 Negative prefixes........................... 164
107 Forming adjectives........................ 165
108 Forming nouns 166
109 Compound nouns 167
110 Compound adjectives 168
Check 25 Word formation 169

Appendices

Appendices 170
Index 175
Answer key 177

Nouns and determiners

1 Singular and plural nouns

- To make a singular noun into a plural noun, add -s or -es. Be careful of spelling changes:
  brother → brother**s**   match → match**es**   baby → bab**ies**   leaf → lea**ves**
- Remember the common irregular plural nouns:
  man → men   woman → women   child → children   person → people
  foot → feet   tooth → teeth   deer → deer   fish → fish   sheep → sheep

▶▶   **See Appendix 1: Spelling rules for plural nouns, page 170.**

P R A C T I C E

1a   Complete the table.

Singular	Plural	Singular	Plural
teacher	*teachers*	person	
potato		bus	
secretary		thief	
beach		box	
half		student	
disco		foot	
dress		place	
sheep		day	

1b   Complete the sentences. Use the plural of the word in brackets.

0 Are there any good ...*restaurants*... near here? (restaurant)

1 I can't find my .... Where are they? (key)

2 I usually have .... for lunch. (sandwich)

3 How many .... do we need for the salad? (tomato)

4 The .... are in the cupboard, next to the .... (glass, dish)

5 The .... are on those .... over there. (dictionary, shelf)

6 The .... are in the living room. (child)

7 You can buy fresh .... at the market. (fish)

8 Are there any .... for me? (message)

2 Countable and uncountable nouns

- Countable nouns are things that can be counted. They have a singular and plural form: *book → books   glass → glasses*
- Uncountable nouns cannot be counted. They do not have a plural form: ~~one milk   two waters   three breads~~
- We use *a/an* with singular countable nouns: *Has he got **a car**? I'd like **an apple**, please.*
- We use *some* with plural countable nouns and uncountable nouns in affirmative sentences: *I'd like **some eggs**, please. There's **some water** in the jug.*
- We use *any* with plural countable nouns and uncountable nouns in negative sentences and questions: *They didn't have **any apples**. Did you buy **any eggs**? They didn't have **any water**. Have we got **any milk**?*
- We usually use *some* in questions when we make offers and requests: *Would you like **some** apples? Can I have **some** more coffee, please?*
- We use *no* to mean 'not one/not any' with singular and plural countable nouns and uncountable nouns. We use *no* with an affirmative verb: *There **are no cars** in the city centre. They **had no water**.*

PRACTICE

2a Write *C* after the countable nouns and *U* after the uncountable nouns.

friend	*C*	music		butter	
bread	*U*	DVD player		furniture	
rice		money		flat	
book		plate		oil	
sugar		cheese		sand	
car		information		banana	
office		bag		shampoo	
soup		vegetable		tea	

2b Marc is going to visit London and his friend is giving him some advice. Complete the sentences. Use *a*, *an* or *some*.

0 Don't forget to change ....*some*.......... money before you go.

1 Have you got .... map of the city?

2 Here are .... addresses of cheap hotels.

3 Take .... umbrella. It often rains in London.

4 It's a good idea to take .... raincoat.

5 Pack .... warm clothes. It's sometimes cold in September.

6 Remember to take .... camera with you – I want to see your photos!

2c   **Circle the correct answer.**

o My sister's married, but she hasn't got *some /* (*any*) children.

1 I eat *some / any* fruit every day, usually apples or bananas.

2 My father works in *a / an* office and my mother's *a / an* hairdresser.

3 Do you have *a / any* homework this evening?

4 Would you like *some / a* tea?

5 I don't put *some / any* salt on my food. I don't like it.

6 Have you got *a / any* brothers or sisters?

7 The room's empty. There's *no / any* furniture in it.

8 There weren't *some / any* people at the bus stop. I was the only person there.

9 What *a / an* terrible smell! Open the window and let in *a / some* fresh air.

10 Gloria hasn't got *no / any* pets, but she'd like a cat.

2d   **Re-write the sentences. Use *any* or *no*.**

o We haven't got any money.   *We've got no money.*

1 There isn't any milk in the fridge.   ....

2 There are no shops open today.   ....

3 He's got no friends at work.   ....

4 There aren't any buses after midnight.   ....

5 I haven't got any free time tomorrow.   ....

6 There's no sugar in my coffee.   ....

2e   **Complete the conversations. Use *a*, *some*, *any* or *no*.**

A: I'd like (o) ....*some*........ information about trains, please. Are there
      (1) .... trains to Oxford on Saturday afternoon?

B: Let's see. There's (2) .... train at 4.35, but there are (3) ....
      trains after that.

A: OK, the 4.35 is fine. Can I have two return tickets, please?

———————————————

A: Can I help you?

B: Yes. I'd like (4) .... oranges, please.
      Two kilos. And (5) .... bananas.

A: I'm sorry. We haven't got (6) ....
      bananas today. Would you like
      (7) .... apples instead? We have
      (8) .... special offer today.

B: Yes, thanks. A kilo, please.

3 Counting uncountable nouns

● We can count some uncountable nouns by using a countable noun + *of*:
  – *a bit of wood*   *a lump of sugar*   *a slice of toast*
  – *a bottle of water*   *a box of chocolates*   *two cups of tea*   *a glass of milk*
  – *250 grams of cheese*   *a litre of milk*   *five kilos of potatoes*
● We can also use *a piece of* with some nouns: *a piece of advice*   *a piece of furniture*
  a piece of information   *a piece of luggage*   *a piece of music*   *a piece of news*
  a piece of paper

PRACTICE

3a **Label the pictures. Use the words in the box.**

| bar | ~~bottle~~ | carton | jar | loaf | slice | tin | tube |

0   1   2   3

4   5   6   7

0 a .... *bottle* .... of water   4 a .... of jam

1 a .... of toast   5 a .... of bread

2 a .... of tuna   6 a .... of orange juice

3 a .... of chocolate   7 a .... of toothpaste

3b **Complete the conversations. Use a word to count the uncountable noun.**

  0 **A:** Go to bed early tonight.
     B: That's a good .... *piece* .... of advice. Thanks.

  1 **A:** Hello. Can I help you?
     B: Yes, I'd like 300 .... of cheese, please.

  2 **A:** I heard an interesting .... of news this morning.
     B: Really? What?

  3 **A:** I want to brush my teeth.
     B: There's a new .... of toothpaste in the cupboard.

  4 **A:** Can you give me a .... of paper, please?
     B: Here you are.

  5 **A:** A typical family uses 160 .... of water every day.
     B: That's incredible!

  6 **A:** You can only take one .... of hand luggage on the plane.
     B: I know!

4 *a lot of/lots of, many, much, (a) few, (a) little*

- We use *a lot of/lots of, many, much, (a) few* and *(a) little* to talk about quantity.
- We use *a lot of/lots of* (= a large number/amount of) with plural countable nouns and uncountable nouns: **Lots of people** have fast Internet connections. There's **a lot of information** for travellers on the Web.
- We use *many* with plural countable nouns and *much* with uncountable nouns in negative sentences and questions: *Have you got **many films** on DVD? I haven't got **much energy** at the moment.*
- We use *a few* (= a small number of) with plural countable nouns and *a little* (= a small amount of) with uncountable nouns: *Can I ask you **a few questions**? I'd like **a little milk** in my coffee, please.*
- We use *few* and *little* to mean 'an extremely small number/amount of': ***Few** people read poetry these days. She had **little** time to study and failed the exam.*
- We use *How much/How many* in questions and *not much, not many, a lot, a few* and *a little* in short answers: ***How many** computer games have you got? **A lot.**/**Not many.**/Just **a few**.*

⚠️ We can use *many, much* and *a lot* without a noun: *He collects stamps, but he hasn't got **many**. Did your mobile cost **much**? They watch TV **a lot**.*

PRACTICE

4a **Complete the sentences. Use *many* or *much*.**

0 I don't have ....*much*........ free time these days, so I don't often cook.

1 There aren't .... good restaurants in this part of town.

2 How .... sugar do you take in your coffee?

3 They don't eat .... eggs. Just one or two a week.

4 How .... red meat do you eat every week?

5 How .... kilos of rice do you want me to buy?

6 I don't drink .... coffee. It stops me from sleeping at night.

7 We don't buy .... takeaways. We don't think they're healthy.

8 Do you eat .... Indian food? We eat it all the time!

4b **Circle the correct answer.**

A: I went to see (0)(*a few*)/ *a little* flats this morning.

B: Did you like any?

A: One flat was nice. There are (1) *a few / a little* shops nearby and it's near the university, but it only gets (2) *a few / a little* sunlight, so it's quite dark. And there's (3) *a few / a little* water coming in through one of the windows. But there's another problem: we can't move in for (4) *a few / a little* weeks.

B: That's not good.

A: Mike, I've invited (5) *a few / a little* friends for dinner tonight. Could you give me (6) *a few / a little* help to get things ready?

B: Sure. What do you want me to do?

A: Well, we've only got (7) *a few / a little* bread left. Could you get some more? And could you wash up (8) *a few / a little* dishes for me?

4c **Complete the sentences. Use *a lot of*, *few* or *little*.**

0 Her diet's not very healthy. She eats ......*a lot of*...... meat but very ......*few*......... vegetables.

1 I love music. I've got .... CDs but very .... space to put them in.

2 He's lazy. He does very .... housework and watches .... TV.

3 It wasn't a good party. We invited .... people but .... came.

4 Come on! We've got very .... time and .... things to do.

5 We're ecological. We recycle .... rubbish and use very .... water.

6 There's .... information on the Internet, but unfortunately, there are .... really good sites.

4d **Circle the correct answer.**

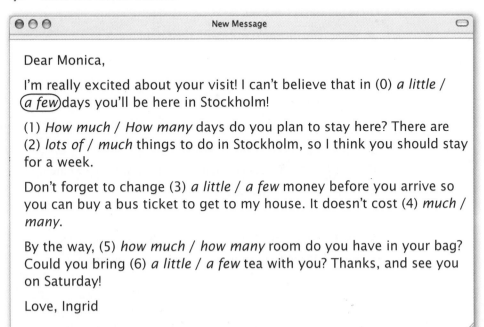

Dear Monica,

I'm really excited about your visit! I can't believe that in (0) *a little /* *a few* days you'll be here in Stockholm!

(1) *How much / How many* days do you plan to stay here? There are (2) *lots of / much* things to do in Stockholm, so I think you should stay for a week.

Don't forget to change (3) *a little / a few* money before you arrive so you can buy a bus ticket to get to my house. It doesn't cost (4) *much /* *many*.

By the way, (5) *how much / how many* room do you have in your bag? Could you bring (6) *a little / a few* tea with you? Thanks, and see you on Saturday!

Love, Ingrid

5 *all, most, some, none*

- *All, most, some* and *none* express the following quantities:

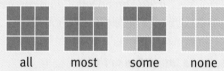

all   most   some   none

- We use *all/most/some* + plural or uncountable noun to talk about people or things in general: ***All plants*** *need water.* ***Most pollution*** *comes from cars.* ***Some people*** *like sport.*

- We use *most/some/none* + *of* + *the/this/my* etc. to talk about specific things: ***Most of the clothes*** *in this shop are expensive.* ***Some of those photos*** *are very old.* ***None of their friends*** *smoke.*

- *All* and *all of* are possible before *the/this/my* etc. to talk about specific things, but *all of* is less common: ***All*** *(**of**) my friends like video games.*

- *None* is negative, so we use it with an affirmative verb: ***None*** *of the questions* ***were*** *easy.*

- We use a singular verb with a singular or uncountable noun: ***None of the cheese is*** *French.*

- We use a singular or plural verb with a plural noun: ***None of my friends is/are*** *rich.*

PRACTICE

5a   Circle the correct answer.

  0 *Some /* (*Most*) people write with their right hand.

  1 Most students here are British, but *most / some* are Italian.

  2 *Some / Most* sports are very dangerous.

  3 *Some / All* fish can swim.

  4 *Most / All* tigers live in Asia, but some live in zoos in other continents.

  5 *Some / Most* people have not walked on the moon.

  6 *Most / All* astronauts are men, but *some / most* are women.

  7 *Some / All* countries have a capital city.

  8 *Some / All* mountains have snow on them all year round.

  9 *Some / Most* web pages on the Internet are in Japanese.

 10 *Some / All* big companies need to have an Internet site.

5b **Complete the sentences. Use *of* or –.**

0 I only know some ......*of*...... the people in this photo.

1 None .... my colleagues smoke.

2 We like all .... types of music, but jazz is our favourite.

3 Some .... these paintings are lovely. How much are they?

4 I'm sorry, but none .... the paintings are for sale.

5 Most .... his friends live in the neighbourhood.

6 Some .... children watch too much television.

7 She still sees most .... her school friends.

8 Most .... people like chocolate.

5c **Complete the questionnaire results. Use the words in the box.**

all	all of	~~most~~	most of	none of	some	some of

I asked the people in the class about computers. (0) ....*Most*..... students (13 out of 15) have a computer at home and (1) .... these students (13 out of 13) have an Internet connection. (2) .... students (4 out of 13) have a slow connection, but (3) .... the people I spoke to (9 out of 13) have a fast connection. (4) .... students (15 out of 15) use the Internet a lot and spend (5) .... their time (30%) looking for information and chatting to friends. (6) .... the people I spoke to (0 out of 15) do shopping on the Internet!

5d **Write sentences. Use *all*, *most*, *some* or *none*. Use *of* where necessary.**

0 0% / this information / is / true
None of this information is true.
....

1 80% / my friends / like going to the cinema
....

2 5% / people / work at night
....

3 0% / these mobiles / have a camera
....

4 Are / 100% / your brothers and sisters / vegetarian?
....

5 My brother / spends / 100% / his free time reading comics
....

6 75% / young people / get / 45% / their music from the Internet
....

6 *each, every*

- We use *every* + singular countable noun + singular verb to talk about the people or things in a group when we are thinking about them all together: ***Every student** in the class **is taking** the exam.* (every student = all the students)

- We use *each* + singular countable noun + singular verb to talk about the people or things in a group when we are thinking about them individually: *The teacher spoke to **each student** in turn. **Each bedroom has** a shower.*

- *Each* and *every* have a similar meaning, but we cannot use *every* to talk about two things: *The waiter carried a plate in **each hand**.* (Not *in every hand*)

- We can use *each* + *of* + *the* + plural countable noun: ***Each of the students** received a prize.*

- We can use *each* on its own: *I'd like one of **each**, please.*

P R A C T I C E

6a **Complete the sentences. Use *each* or *every*.**

   o I walk our dog ......*every*...... morning before breakfast.

   1 The man was holding a baby in .... arm.

   2 They made six cakes for the party and the guests ate .... one.

   3 .... student in the class forgot to do the homework.

   4 She liked the black and the brown tops, so she bought one of ....

   5 I got the same birthday present from .... of my brothers!

   6 .... language has things that are difficult to learn.

   7 She was wearing a different sock on .... foot.

   8 .... of the bedrooms has its own bathroom.

6b **Complete the exam preparation advice. Use *each* or *every*. Sometimes both are possible.**

When you're studying for your final exam, it's important to revise a little (o) ......*every*...... day. Make a study card for (1) .... of the topics you studied and revise for (2) .... topic on the syllabus, not just the ones you're interested in. The exam has two parts and you have one hour to do (3) .... part. The first part has twenty questions that carry five marks (4) .... Don't spend more than three minutes on (5) .... question and answer (6) .... question if you can. In part two, remember that you don't need to understand (7) .... word in the text to answer the comprehension questions. Make sure you read (8) .... of the composition titles carefully before you start writing.

Check 1 Nouns and determiners

1 **Complete the conversation. Use the words in the box.**

each every many no none

A: Did you take (1) .... photos at the wedding?

B: I took lots. Why?

A: Could you send them to me? (2) .... of my photos are very good. They've got white lines on them.

B: But I took hundreds! I can't send you (3) .... photo I took!

A: Well, could you send me the best ones?

B: If you want, I can put a copy of (4) .... of the best ones on a CD.

A: That's a good idea. When can you do that?

B: Is Monday OK? I've got (5) .... time before the weekend.

A: Thanks. Monday will be fine.

/ 5

2 **Match and make questions.**

6 Can I have a loaf of ☐

7 Could you buy a few ☐

8 Could you put a little ☐

9 Did you get a carton of ☐

10 Do we have some of ☐

a that delicious blue cheese?

b fruit in my yoghurt?

c brown bread, please?

d potatoes at the shop?

e milk at the supermarket?

/ 5

3 **Choose the correct answer.**

Fun recipes for kids: Pancakes

This is (11) ...... great recipe for kids. Pancakes take (12) ...... time to make, you don't need to buy (13) ...... special ingredients, and (14) ...... children love them!

To make pancakes for four (15) ...... , you need some flour (110g), 2 eggs, (16) ...... milk (200ml) and water (75ml). Mix the flour and eggs together, and add the milk and water. Then put some of the mixture in a frying pan and cook the pancake on both sides. Serve (17) ...... pancake with (18) ...... lemon and (19) ...... sugar.

If you don't use (20) ...... the mixture, simply put it in the fridge for the next day!

11 A a	B an	C some	D a lot of
12 A some	B much	C many	D little
13 A a few	B no	C any	D a lot
14 A most	B most of	C a	D any of
15 A child	B person	C persons	D people
16 A litre	B some	C any	D none
17 A a	B some	C each	D much
18 A a few	B a little of	C a slice of	D piece of
19 A some	B some of	C any	D any of
20 A much	B many	C none	D all

/ 10

Total: / 20

✓ Self-check

Wrong answers	Look again at	Try CD-ROM
11, 15	Unit 1	Exercise 1
5, 13, 16, 19	Unit 2	Exercise 2
6, 9, 18	Unit 3	Exercise 3
1, 7, 8, 12	Unit 4	Exercise 4
2, 10, 14, 20	Unit 5	Exercise 5
3, 4, 17	Unit 6	Exercise 6

Now do **Check 1**

Pronouns and possessives

7 Pronouns and possessive adjectives

Subject pronouns	I	you	he	she	it	we	you	they
Object pronouns	me	you	him	her	it	us	you	them
Possessive adjectives	my	your	his	her	its	our	your	their
Possessive pronouns	mine	yours	his	hers	–	ours	yours	theirs

PRACTICE

7a **Circle the correct answer.**

0 I saw Sarah yesterday, but (she)/ her didn't see I /(me).

1 My family and I have three cats. *We / Us* really love *they / them*.

2 We're going to the cinema. Would *you / your* like to come with *us / ours*?

3 The Westons are *our / ours* neighbours. *Their / Theirs* flat is above *our / ours*.

4 Alice has a jacket like *my / mine*, but *her / hers* is grey.

5 I have a message for your mother. Can you give *it / its* to *her / hers*?

6 Those aren't *my / mine* keys. They're *your / yours*.

7b **Complete the letter. Use one word in each gap.**

Dear María,

I saw (0) .....*your*..... advertisement for a pen friend on the Internet and
decided to write to (1) .... (2) .... name's Emma and I'm
from Oxford in England. As you know, Oxford is famous for
(3) .... university. There are a lot of students and tourists here.
(4) .... live with (5) .... family. I have a younger brother.
(6) .... name's Tim. (7) .... plays football and sometimes
I play with (8) .... I also have a sister. (9) ....'s a student
in London, so we only see (10) .... at weekends.
I love all kinds of sport, music and travelling. This summer I'm going
to the south of Spain. My parents have some friends there and
(11) ....'ve invited all of (12) .... to stay with them in
(13) .... villa.
Well, I've told you a little about my life. I hope you'll write and tell me
about (14) ....

Jane

8 Possessive *'s*, possessive *of*

- To show that something belongs to someone:
  - we add *'s* to all singular nouns and to plural nouns that do not end in -*s*: This is **Paul's** jacket. She's the **girl's** mother. This is the **children's** room.
  - we add an apostrophe (') to plural nouns that end in -*s*: *My* **parents'** *flat is quite small.*

- When one person or thing belongs to two people, we add *'s* to the end of the second name: *He's* **Tom and Ray's** *father.* (Not ~~Tom's and Ray's father~~)

- To show that something belongs to things and places, we use noun + *of* + noun: *We left before* **the end of the film**. (Not ~~the film's end~~)

- We often use noun + noun for some common combinations of words: *Where are the* **car keys**? (Not ~~the keys of the car~~)

 There can be more than one possessive *'s* in a phrase or sentence: *That's* **John's father's** *car.*

P R A C T I C E

8a **Re-write the sentences. Put the apostrophe in the correct place.**

   0 My fathers study is over there.   *My father's study is over there.*

   1 Sams room is next to my parents room.   ....

   2 The twins playroom is down the hall.   ....

   3 My uncles names are David and Mark.   ....

   4 Davids wifes name is Sheila.   ....

   5 Their childrens names are Pat and Clare.   ....

   6 Pat and Clares room is on the right.   ....

8b **Complete the sentences. Use the words in brackets.**

   0 The ....*cat's bowl*........ is empty. Can you give her some food? (bowl / cat)

   1 I live at the .... – on the sixth floor. (top / the building)

   2 I went to stay at my .... last summer. (house / grandparents)

   3 I've painted the .... blue. (walls / bathroom)

   4 The .... is Canberra. (capital / Australia)

   5 .... lived in France before she came here. (teacher / Lisa)

   6 The .... are over there. (changing rooms / women)

   7 Can you switch off the .... when you leave? (light / kitchen)

   8 There's a bus stop at the .... (end / the street)

9 Reflexive pronouns, *each other*

I → myself	you → yourself	he → himself	she → herself
it → itself	we → ourselves	you → yourselves	they → themselves

- We use reflexive pronouns for actions we do to ourselves, not to someone else. Compare: *I cut **the bread**. I cut **myself**.*

- We can also use reflexive pronouns for emphasis: *I did all the work **myself**.* (Nobody helped me.)

- A few verbs are followed by a reflexive pronoun to form an idiom: *Please **help yourself**. The food's over there. Children! **Behave yourselves**! I **enjoyed myself** at the party.*

- Compare reflexive pronouns and *each other*:

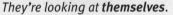

*They're looking at **themselves**.*

*They're looking at **each other**.*

PRACTICE

9a Complete the sentences. Use reflexive pronouns.

- **0** Don't come with us, Mum. We can look after ......*ourselves*...... .

- **1** Enjoy .... in London, you two! I'll see you next week.

- **2** When David cut .... , the nurse gave him three stitches.

- **3** That kettle switches .... off automatically.

- **4** Jo's a really good artist. She painted those posters ....

- **5** Nobody helped me organise the concert. I did it all .... !

- **6** Some film actors do all the dangerous stunts ....

9b Circle the correct answer.

- **0** We met on the Internet. We write to *ourselves* / (*each other*) every day.

- **1** Helen and Annie have known *themselves* / *each other* for years.

- **2** The actors put on their make-up and looked at *themselves* / *each other* carefully in the mirror.

- **3** She's my best friend. We tell *ourselves* / *each other* everything.

- **4** It's a self-service restaurant, so please serve *yourselves* / *each other*.

- **5** We work in groups so that we can help *ourselves* / *each other*.

- **6** Look after the children and make sure they behave *themselves* / *each other*.

10 *one, ones*

We can use *one* instead of repeating a singular countable noun, and *ones* instead of repeating a plural noun: *Which bag do you like? This **one**. These shoes are too big. I prefer the other **ones**.*

 We can use *one/ones* after an adjective: *I've got three cats, a black **one** and two grey **ones**.*

PRACTICE

10a Circle the correct answer.

o A: Do you like this shirt?   **B:** No, I like that (one)/ ones.

1 A: Can I try on those earrings?   **B:** These silver *one / ones*?

2 A: This pen doesn't work.   **B:** I've got another *one / ones* in my bag.

3 A: Excuse me, this fork's dirty.   **B:** I'm sorry. I'll get you a clean *one / ones*.

4 A: Have you seen my shoes?   **B:** Are they the *one / ones* in the bathroom?

5 A: Can I borrow your mobile?   **B:** Sorry, I haven't got *one / ones*.

6 A: Which gloves are yours?   **B:** The blue *one / ones*.

10b Complete the conversations. Use *one, ones, the one* or *the ones*.

o A: Let's go to a Chinese restaurant tonight. Which ......*one*...... is best?
  B: ...*The one*.... in Mill Street's good.

1 A: That painting's my favourite.
  B: Which .... ?
  A: .... of the girl with the white hat.

2 A: I can't decide which trousers to get.
  B: .... white .... are nice.

3 A: Have you seen that film?
  B: Which .... ?
  A: .... about the plane crash.

4 A: I think that's Kevin's house.
  B: Which .... ?
  A: .... with the garden at the front.

5 A: These little cakes look delicious. Which .... shall we buy?
  B: My favourites are .... with cream.

6 A: Are these your DVDs?
  B: Which .... ?
  A: .... on the floor.

11 *somebody, something* etc.

For things	something, anything, nothing, everything
For people	somebody/someone, anybody/anyone, nobody/no one, everybody/everyone
For places	somewhere, anywhere, nowhere, everywhere

● We use *something/somebody/somewhere* in affirmative sentences:
*There's **something** for you in that bag. Someone's **waiting** to see you.*

● We use *something/somebody/somewhere* in offers and requests: *Shall I bring you **something** cool to drink? Could **somebody** help me, please?*

● We use *anything/anybody/anywhere* in negative sentences and questions: *I can't find my glasses **anywhere**. Is **anyone** here a doctor?*

● We use *nothing/nobody/nowhere* with an affirmative verb: ***Nobody can see** us.*

● We can use *something, anybody, nowhere* etc. with:
 – an adjective: *Is there **anything interesting** on TV?*
 – *to* + infinitive: *We had **nowhere to go**.*
 – the word *else*: *Let's do **something else**.*

● If *everything/everyone* is the subject, it is followed by a singular verb: ***Everything is** ready. **Everyone likes** her.*

 somebody = someone, anybody = anyone, nobody = no one, everybody = everyone: *Is **everyone**/**everybody** ready?*

PRACTICE

11a Complete the sentences. Use the words in the box.

> anybody   anything   anywhere   no one   ~~nothing~~
> nowhere   someone   something   somewhere

0 We must go shopping. There's ....*nothing*.... in the fridge.

1 I saw .... on TV about green tea. Apparently, it's good for you.

2 Munich is .... in Germany, but I don't know where exactly.

3 Has .... seen Tracey's keys? She can't find them.

4 I'll be in Paris next Thursday, but I've got .... to stay. Can I stay with you?

5 We don't want .... else to eat, thank you. We're really full.

6 It's terrible! An old man got on the bus, but .... gave him their seat.

7 Did you go .... interesting for your holidays this summer?

8 Could .... open that window, please? I'm not tall enough.

11b **Re-write the sentences. Use *any-* or *no-*.**

0 They didn't say anything to me.　　They ....*said nothing*........ to me.

1 We have nowhere to go.　　We .... to go.

2 I didn't see anyone.　　I ....

3 There isn't anywhere else like Paris.　　There .... else like Paris.

4 She knows nothing about cars.　　She .... about cars.

5 He listens to nobody.　　He ....

6 I can't tell you anything else.　　I .... else.

7 There isn't anybody in the street.　　There .... in the street.

8 They didn't eat anything all day.　　They .... all day.

11c **Complete the answers. Use *some-*, *no-* or *every-* + *-body*, *-thing* or *-where*.**

0 A: What are you doing now?　　B: ....*Nothing*........ . Why?

1 A: Who came to the party?　　B: .... All my friends.

2 A: Where did you go last night?　　B: .... I stayed at home.

3 A: What do you want to do tonight?　　B: .... relaxing. I'm really tired.

4 A: Who are you talking to?　　B: .... It's the answering machine.

5 A: What do we need to study?　　B: .... It'll all be in the exam.

6 A: Where are you going on holiday?　　B: .... hot. It's really cold here.

7 A: Who did you see?　　B: .... I was the only person there.

8 A: What do you want to watch?　　B: .... exciting. I hate boring programmes.

9 A: Where did you go?　　B: .... We saw everything!

10 A: Who did you meet at the party?　　B: .... nice. Her name's Cheryl.

11d **Complete the conversations. Use *something*, *somebody* etc.**

A: Do you want to go (0) .....*anywhere*.... tonight?

B: Let's go (1) .... nice for dinner.

A: Is there (2) .... in particular you want to eat? Indian food? Chinese?

B: How about some Thai food?

A: Wait a minute. It's Saturday. (3) .... will be full.

B: That's true. Let's get (4) .... to eat at home, then.

A: A takeaway. Good idea!

────────────────

A: It's very quiet in here. Where is (5) .... ?

B: They're in the meeting.

A: What meeting? (6) .... told me about a meeting.

B: Oh, Michael, don't you read your e-mails?

Check 2 Pronouns and possessives

1 Complete the sentences. Use the words in the box.

| each other their them they themselves |

1 Leslie's students have only one class a week, so she gives .... a lot of homework.

2 The teachers at Leslie's school prepare their classes ....

3 They also help .... prepare exams for the students.

4 On the last day of the course, the teachers give the students .... exam results.

5 If the students have worked hard, ... normally pass the exam.

/ 5

2 Complete the sentences. Use the words in brackets and 's or of where necessary.

6 Nobody stayed until the
.... (end / the film)

7 I can't find the ....
(keys / car)

8 This is the ....
(bedroom / children)

9 You can sit in the ....
(back / the car)

10 This is my ....
(house / parents)

/ 5

3 Complete the conversations. Use one word in each gap.

A: I can't find my sunglasses.

B: There are some sunglasses on the table. Are they (11) .... ?

A: Those red (12) .... ? No, they aren't. Mine are black.

B: Maybe you left them (13) .... else.

A: Have you seen Valerie's composition?

B: Yes, I have. It's excellent. Do you think she wrote it (14) .... ?

A: Oh, yes. She used a dictionary, but (15) .... helped her.

/ 5

4 Circle the correct answer.

Dear Laura,

We're writing to thank you for inviting (16) us / ourselves to your birthday lunch on Saturday. (17) Anything / Everything was delicious and we loved the little cakes, especially the chocolate (18) one / ones. Did you make all the food (19) you / yourself? It was good to see your new house, too. Now you live in the country we don't see (20) us / each other very often, but please come for lunch at our house next time you're in town.

Love, Jake and Delia

/ 5

Total: / 20

✓ Self-check

Wrong answers	Look again at	Try CD-ROM
1, 4, 5, 11, 16	Unit 7	Exercise 7
6, 7, 8, 9, 10	Unit 8	Exercise 8
2, 3, 14, 19, 20	Unit 9	Exercise 9
12, 18	Unit 10	Exercise 10
13, 15, 17	Unit 11	Exercise 11

Now do **Check 2**

Articles

12 Definite and indefinite article

- We use *a/an* with a singular noun when we talk about something for the first time. We use *the* with a singular or plural noun when we talk about something for the second time: *I bought **a** jacket and **a** scarf yesterday. **The** jacket's blue and **the** scarf's grey. These are my cassettes and CDs. **The** cassettes are old, but **the** CDs are new.*
- We use *a/an* with a singular noun when we talk about a thing, but we do not say which thing we mean: *Susan's reading **a** book.* (We are talking about one book, but we do not say which book.)
- We use *the* if we are talking about a specific thing: *Susan's reading **the** new book by William Bradley.* (We are talking about one specific book.)
- We use *the* when it is clear which thing we mean because there is only one: *John's in **the** kitchen.* (There is only one kitchen in the house.) *We looked up at **the** moon.* (There is only one moon.)

P R A C T I C E

12a Complete the sentences. Use *a*, *an* or *the*.

0 Can I have ......*a*........ cup of coffee, please?

1 .... sun is really hot at this time of year.

2 Jane isn't in her room. I think she's in .... garden.

3 There's .... new film on at the cinema. Would you like to see it?

4 They've got two children, ... boy and .... girl. .... boy's fifteen and .... girl's eleven.

5 I love swimming in .... sea when I go on holiday.

6 Anna and Eric live in .... old house in .... small village.

12b Circle the correct answer.

Last Saturday was (0)@/ *the* beautiful day, so my friends and I had
(1) *a* / *the* picnic in (2) *a* / *the* garden. We made some sandwiches and
(3) *a* / *the* salad, got some plates and forks from (4) *a* / *the* kitchen and lots
of drinks from (5) *a* / *the* fridge. Then we got (6) *a* / *the* big blanket and some
cushions from (7) *a* / *the* living room, and put them on (8) *a* / *the* grass. We
carried (9) *a* / *the* food and drinks outside and put everything on (10) *a* / *the*
blanket. Then we sat on (11) *a* / *the* cushions and had our picnic. (12) *A* / *The* sun
was warm and we had a lovely time!

13 Definite and zero article (1)

- We use *the* with the names of oceans, seas, rivers, deserts, groups of islands and mountain ranges. We also use *the* with the names of countries when these are plural, and the names of countries which include the words *Kingdom*, *Republic* and *States*: **the** *Pacific Ocean*   **the** *Mediterranean*   **the** *Nile*   **the** *Gobi Desert*   **the** *Bahamas*   **the** *Alps*   **the** *Netherlands*   **the** *United Kingdom*

- We do not use *the* with the names of lakes, mountains, continents, countries, cities, towns, villages and streets: *Lake Superior*   *Mount Everest*   *Asia*   *France*   *London*   *Oxford Street*

PRACTICE

13a Write the nouns in the box in the correct group.

Amazon ~~Amazon~~ Andes ~~Asia~~ Canada Caribbean Sea Chile Dominican Republic Europe Istanbul Indian Ocean Park Avenue Philippines Rhine Sahara Desert Lake Como Mount Fuji

the		–	
Amazon		*Asia*	

13b Complete the sentences. Use *the* or – .

0 The largest desert in the world, ...*the*...... Sahara, is 9,000,000 square kilometres.

1 .... Himalayas grow a few centimetres every year.

2 There is only one time zone in .... China.

3 .... Fiji Islands are in .... Pacific Ocean.

4 .... Mediterranean Sea is part of .... Atlantic Ocean. It lies between .... Europe, ... Africa and .... Asia.

5 .... Fifth Avenue in .... New York is one of the most famous shopping streets in the world.

6 The longest river in the world, ... Nile, is about 6,700 kilometres long.

7 .... Russia is nearly twice as big as .... United States of America.

8 .... Netherlands is a very flat country, with no mountains.

9 .... Lake Baikal in .... Siberia is the biggest lake in the world.

10 .... Iceland is a large island in .... Atlantic Ocean.

14 Definite and zero article (2)

- We usually use *the* before the places we visit in a town: *the cinema   the theatre
  the post office   **the** bank   **the** supermarket   **the** chemist's   **the** doctor's
  the hairdresser's*
- We sometimes use *a/an* with these words to mean 'one of many'. Compare:
  *I went to **the cinema** on Saturday. There's **a** new **cinema** in West Street.*
- We do not usually use *the* with *home, school, college, university, work, town,
  hospital* and *prison: I go to **work** at eight o'clock.*

 We use *a/an* or *the* with *school, college, university, hospital, prison* etc. when
we are talking about the building, not the institution. Compare: *My sister's at
university. It's **a** modern **university**. My aunt's in **hospital**. Where's **the hospital**?*

PRACTICE

14a Complete the sentences. Use *the* or – .

0 My mother goes to ......*the*...... baker's every day.

1 I was at .... home all day on Sunday,
   watching television.

2 My brother went to .... college for three
   years. He studied Economics.

3 Jane isn't feeling well, so she's gone to
   .... doctor's.

4 Would you like to go to .... cinema
   tonight?

5 I left .... school when I was sixteen and
   found a job.

6 If you're going to .... chemist's, can you
   get me some aspirins?

14b Circle the correct answer.

0 I've got toothache. I'll have to go to *dentist's /* (*the dentist's*).

1 We go to *supermarket / the supermarket* every Saturday.

2 Excuse me. Is there *a / the* post office near here?

3 She went to *university / the university* in Germany.

4 I usually go to *work / the work* at about half past eleven.

5 There's *a / the* market near my home where I buy fruit and vegetables.

6 Are you going to *disco / the disco* on Saturday night?

14C **Complete the conversations. Use *a*, *the* or – .**

A: There's a new play on at (0) ......*the*...... theatre. Would you like to go?

B: I don't know. I don't want to get (1) .... home late.

A: OK. Let's go to (2) .... cinema instead. That starts a bit earlier.

A: What are you planning to do after you leave (3) .... school?

B: Well, my parents want me to go to (4) .... university, but I don't want to.

A: How about working in (5) .... bank instead?

A: I'm going to (6) .... town this afternoon. Do you need anything?

B: Yes, please. Can you get me some stamps from (7) .... post office?

A: Sure. I'll go there before I go to (8) .... hairdresser's.

A: I feel terrible. I'm not going to (9) .... work today.

B: Shall I make an appointment for you to go to (10) .... doctor's?

A: No, it's just a cold. But can you get me some medicine? There's (11) .... chemist's near your office, opposite (12) .... hospital.

15 Definite, indefinite and zero article

- We use *the* with:
  - the names of cinemas, theatres, museums and hotels: **the** *National Theatre*
  - surnames when we are talking about more than one member of a family: **the** *Simpsons* (the Simpson family)
  - musical instruments: *I'm learning to play* **the** *guitar.*
  - the phrase *listen to the radio*: *I like listening to* **the** *radio.*
- We use *a/an*:
  - to talk about a person's job: *I'm* **a** *journalist.*
  - to describe something or someone with *to be*: *That's* **a** *good book.*
  - to mean 'each' or 'per': *I drink four cups of coffee* **a** *day. He never drives at more than 80 kilometres* **an** *hour.*
- We do not use *a/an* or *the* with:
  - the names of people: *Where's Susan?*
  - street names: *They live in King Street.*
  - school subjects: *I study Mathematics and Economics.*
  - sports and games: *I play tennis. Can you play chess?*
  - meals: *I usually have toast for breakfast.*
  - languages: *Paul speaks French and Spanish.*
  - the phrase *watch television*: *She watches television after work.*
- We do not use *the* with plural nouns and uncountable nouns when we are talking about something in general: *I don't like vegetables.* (Not *the vegetables*)

PRACTICE

15a **Complete the sentences. Use *a, an, the* or –.**

 0 My brother started playing ......*the*...... piano when he was four.

 1 They stayed at .... Palace Hotel in San Francisco.

 2 Do you know .... Sarah? She's a friend of mine.

 3 I'd like to be .... actor, but it's a difficult profession.

 4 My favourite cinema is .... Odeon in .... Morrison Street.

 5 Anne visits her grandparents once .... week.

 6 .... Wilsons live in Brighton now.

 7 The children are playing .... football in the park.

 8 I really want to learn .... Italian and .... Portuguese.

 9 .... diamonds cost a lot of money.

 10 We usually have .... dinner at seven.

 11 These tomatoes cost two euros .... kilo.

 12 My worst subject at school was .... History.

 13 Please be quiet! I'm trying to listen to .... radio.

 14 *Oliver Twist* is .... popular book by Charles Dickens.

 15 I must go to .... library tonight and return my library books.

 16 Do you watch .... television every evening?

15b **Complete the e-mail. Use *a, the* or –.**

```
 ● ● ●                         New Message                              ⬭

  Dear Peter,

  My name is (0) ......–...... Darren and I live in Manchester. I'm
  (1) ............. student. I'm studying (2) ............. Maths and Business
  Studies, but I don't like college much. The only thing I like is
  (3) ............. football. I train four or five times (4) ............. week
  and play for my local team. I'd like to be (5) ............. professional
  footballer and play for Manchester United. Then I could earn millions
  of pounds (6) ............. year and travel all over the world. I don't
  speak any foreign languages, but that's not a problem – everyone
  speaks (7) ............. English nowadays. I like music too.  I want to
  learn to play (8) ............. drums, but my parents won't let me. Oh
  well! What about you? What do you do? Write and tell me.

  Best wishes, Darren
```

Check 3 Articles

1 Complete the sentences. Use *a* or *the*.

1 My sister works in .... shop in west London.

2 I have to go to .... bank this morning. What time does it open?

3 We've got .... cat and .... dog. .... cat always sleeps on my bed.

4 How often do you go to .... cinema?

5 My mother always buys meat at .... butcher's.

/ 5

2 Complete the sentences. Use *the* or –.

6 Cycling is a very popular sport in .... Netherlands.

7 .... Pyrenees are a range of mountains between France and Spain.

8 Students in the UK study .... Maths until they're sixteen.

9 .... Volga River flows across Russia to the Caspian Sea.

10 The Atlantic Ocean is .... world's second largest ocean.

/ 5

3 Complete the e-mail. Use *a*, *the* or – .

```
○ ○ ○                New Message                ▭

Hi, Fred!

Well, here we are in (11) .............
London. We're staying in (12) .............
really nice hotel in Notting Hill. It's quite
cheap – only £60 (13) ............. night.
I'm sitting in (14) ............. hotel at the
moment, waiting for (15) ............. Paul.
He's gone to (16) ............. supermarket
next door to buy some bread and cheese
for (17) ............. lunch – it's incredibly
expensive to eat out all the time!

Tonight we want to go to (18) .............
theatre. We're going to see
(19) ............. play called The Mousetrap
at (20) ............. theatre near Leicester
Square. Hope it's good. I'll write soon.

Pam
```

/ 10

Total: / 20

Self-check

Wrong answers	Look again at	Try CD-ROM
1, 3, 10, 12, 14, 19	Unit 12	Exercise 12
6, 7, 9, 11	Unit 13	Exercise 13
2, 4, 5, 16, 18, 20	Unit 14	Exercise 14
8, 13, 15, 17	Unit 15	Exercise 15

Now do **Check 3**

Adjectives and adverbs

16 Order of adjectives

When there is more than one adjective before a noun, we use this order:

	opinion	size	age	shape	colour	nationality	material	+ noun
an	ugly				red		cotton	shirt
some		big		square		Turkish		carpets
a	pretty		young					girl

P R A C T I C E

16a Write the words in brackets in the correct place.

   0 an old vase (Chinese)   *an old Chinese vase* ....

   1 a cotton scarf (dark blue)   ....

   2 a huge building (stone)   ....

   3 some paper bags (red)   ....

   4 a little plastic dinosaur (horrible)   ....

   5 some black leather boots (new)   ....

   6 some large ceramic plates (Italian)   ....

16b Put the words in the correct order.

HOUSE SALE!

We are moving house and have decided to sell these things:

   0 round / table / plastic / big / a   *a big round plastic table* ....

   1 curtains / long / some / cotton / Indian   ....

   2 black / four / metal / chairs / comfortable   ....

   3 oil / Dutch / beautiful / painting / a   ....

   4 enormous / wardrobe / wooden / a(n)   ....

   5 a / carpet / little / lovely / round   ....

   6 Peruvian / a / square / colourful / bedcover   ....

Interested? Come round any time this weekend!

17 Comparative and superlative adjectives

	Adjective	Comparative (+ *than*)	Superlative
One-syllable and most two-syllable adjectives	tall, thin, pretty, happy, clever, quiet, simple	taller, thinner, prettier, happier, cleverer, quieter, simpler	the tallest, the thinnest, the prettiest, the happiest, the cleverest, the quietest, the simplest
Other two-syllable adjectives	boring, serious, careful, crowded	more boring, more serious, more careful, more crowded	the most boring, the most serious, the most careful, the most crowded
Longer adjectives	exciting, beautiful, comfortable	more exciting, more beautiful, more comfortable	the most exciting, the most beautiful, the most comfortable

● These adjectives are irregular: *good → better → the best   bad → worse → the worst   far → farther/further → the farthest/furthest*

● We can also use *less than, the least* to form comparatives and superlatives: *clean → less clean → the least clean   famous → less famous → the least famous*

● We can use superlatives with the preposition *in*: *He's **the best** student **in** the class. It's **the most expensive** city **in** the world.*

● We can compare nouns using *more/the most*: *I have **more CDs** than you, but you have **more DVDs**. Our team won **the most games** this year.*

▶▶ *See Appendix 2: Spelling rules for comparative and superlative adjectives, page 170.*

PRACTICE

17a Complete the sentences. Use the comparative or superlative.

0 Is London ....*the largest*........ city in the UK? (large)

1 This year it's .... than it was last year. (hot)

2 What's .... way to get to the centre? (good)

3 The library's .... place in the university for studying. (quiet)

4 Books are .... than computer games. (entertaining)

5 What time does .... flight to London leave? (early)

6 A computer is .... than a typewriter. (useful)

7 That's .... excuse I've ever heard! (bad)

8 The first story she told was .... than the second one. (funny)

9 This book is .... than that one. (interesting)

10 It's .... weight I've ever lifted! (heavy)

17b **Complete the second sentence so that it means the same as the first. Use no more than three words.**

0 Is there one way to get around London that's better than the others?
What's ......*the best*.............. way to get around London?

1 London's very busy compared to other cities in the UK.
London's .... city in the UK.

2 The Underground is fast compared to other means of transport.
Other means of transport are .... the Underground.

3 Buses are cheaper than taxis.
Buses .... expensive than taxis.

4 Driving is the most stressful way to get around the city.
Driving is .... relaxing way to get around the city.

5 The Underground is more crowded than buses.
Buses are .... the Underground.

17c **Write sentences about Jim, Helen and Mark. Use the information below.**

	Jim	Helen	Mark
0	2 brothers	1 brother	3 brothers
1	3 pairs of trainers	5 pairs of trainers	1 pair of trainers
2	2 gold medals	4 gold medals	3 gold medals
3	6 MP3s	2 MP3s	8 MP3s

0 Jim has ......*more brothers*............ than Helen. Mark has ......*the most brothers*............ .

1 Jim has .... than Mark. Helen has ....

2 Mark has .... than Jim. Helen has ....

3 Yesterday Jim downloaded .... than Helen. Mark downloaded
....

17d **Complete the article. Use the comparative or superlative of the words in the box.**

| easy   good   ~~interesting~~   popular   populated   quiet   welcoming |

With its castles, historic towns and beautiful scenery, Northumberland is one
of (0) ......*the most interesting*......... places in the north of England. However,
it doesn't get many visitors and is (1) .... with tourists than
the nearby Lake District. This is perhaps (2) .... thing about it.
Northumberland is (3) .... county in England, so you can
walk or drive for hours and not see anyone else. Its towns are
(4) .... and more relaxing than those in the Lake District
and it's (5) .... to find a place to stay. Some people say that
the people in Northumberland are also (6) .... to visitors.

18   Adverbs of manner

- We use adjectives to describe people or things: *She's a **brilliant** scientist.*
- We use adverbs of manner to describe how someone or something does something: *He speaks **quietly**.*
- To make an adverb, we usually add *-ly* to the end of an adjective: *He's a **slow** worker. He works **slowly**.*
- This adverb is irregular: *good → well*
- These words can be both adjectives and adverbs. They do not change: *fast → fast   hard → hard   early → early   late → late*
- We do not put adverbs between the verb and the object: *She does her homework quickly.* (Not *~~She does quickly her homework.~~*)

▶▶   **See Appendix 3: Spelling rules for adverbs, page 170.**

P R A C T I C E

18a Complete the sentences. Use adverbs.

o   Jon has violin lessons, but he still plays
     ....*terribly*........ . (terrible)

1   Bye, Nick. Drive .... ! (safe)

2   You should study journalism. You write
     .... (beautiful)

3   We waited .... for the exam to start.
     (nervous)

4   They worked very .... to finish the job on time. (hard)

5   The lights will come on .... when it gets dark. (automatic)

6   Look outside! It's snowing .... (heavy)

7   Three people can sit .... in the back seat of the car. (comfortable)

8   I can carry those suitcases .... I don't need any help. (easy)

18b Circle the correct answer.

o   Could you finish your coffees *quick /* (*quickly*)? The café's closing now.

1   Her new job is very *stressful / stressfully*.

2   Chris opened the door *quiet / quietly*.

3   Your Italian's very *good / well*. Have you lived in Italy?

4   Tim thanked her *polite / politely* when she offered to help him.

5   The child smiled *happy / happily* when she saw her presents.

6   Most Hollywood films have *happy / happily* endings!

7   I didn't sleep *good / well* last night.

8   You're very talented, but to succeed you also need to be *lucky / luckily*.

18c Re-write the sentences. Use adverbs.

0 She's a brilliant dancer.   *She dances brilliantly.*
....

1 He's a quick thinker.   ....

2 I'm a good singer.   ....

3 She's a noisy eater.   ....

4 You're hard workers.   ....

5 He's a careful driver.   ....

6 They're fast runners.   ....

18d Complete the e-mail. Use adjectives or adverbs.

○ ○ ○   New Message   ⬭

Hi, Maxi!

How are you? Things are going really (0) ......*well*...... (good) here in
Strasbourg. I arrived a month ago and because my French is quite
(1) .... (fluent), I found a job (2) .... (immediate). I'm
working in a hotel. The job's (3) .... (tiring) because I have to
get up early, but the hotel's part of an (4) .... (international)
company, so if I make a (5) .... (good) impression, I'm sure I'll
find work (6) .... (easy) in another country. The only problem
is my German. It's really (7) .... (bad). There are a lot of
German tourists at the hotel and I can only understand them if they
speak (8) .... (slow)!

What about you? Write and tell me what you're doing.

Ruben

---

19 Comparative and superlative adverbs

- To form the comparative and superlative of adverbs:
  - we add *more* (*than*) or *the most* before adverbs ending in *-ly*: *Could you drive* **more slowly**? *Martha writes* **the most imaginatively**.
  - we add *-er* (*than*) or *the -est* to one-syllable adverbs: *Tom works* **harder than** *Nick. Sam works* **the hardest**.
- Some adverbs are irregular: *well → better → the best   badly → worse → the worst*
- We can also use *less* + adverb (+ *than*) and *the least* + adverb to form comparatives and superlatives: *This manager works* **less efficiently** *than the last one. She speaks three languages, but she speaks French* **the least fluently**.

PRACTICE

19a Complete the sentences. Use the comparative.

0   We're late. Could you walk ....*more quickly*........ ? (quickly)

1   Please drive .... You're making me nervous! (carefully)

2   You speak English .... now than you did last year. (well)

3   She studies .... than her brother. (hard)

4   I can't understand you. Can you speak .... ? (slowly)

5   Young children behave .... when they're tired. (badly)

6   We need to work .... or we'll lose our jobs! (efficiently)

7   Always put your things in the right place. Then you can find them
    .... (easily)

8   Let me write the letter. I type .... than you. (fast)

19b Complete the sentences. Use the superlative.

0   They all sing beautifully, but Zoe sings *the most beautifully* .

1   Everybody writes imaginatively, but Raymond writes ....

2   You all think creatively, but Derek thinks ....

3   We all trained hard, but Robyn trained ....

4   It rains heavily here all year, but in July it rains ....

5   All her books sell well, but this one sells ....

6   They all speak loudly, but Lynn speaks ....

7   We all played badly, but I played ....

8   The kids all eat fast, but Marcel eats ....

**19c Complete the conversation. Use the comparative or superlative and *than* where
necessary.**

Toni: Hi, Rob. I'm Toni. I'm teaching your class next week while you're on holiday.
Can you tell me about it?

Rob: There are just three students, so they work (0) ..*more quickly than*.. (quickly)
a lot of bigger classes. Of the three, Marta speaks (1) ....
(fluently), but she must learn to speak (2) .... (carefully).
She makes a lot of mistakes. Jonas works (3) .... (slowly)
the other two, but he also works (4) .... (hard) of all and
he's very accurate. As for Dominic, he expresses himself
(5) .... (simply) the other two, but of the three, his English
is improving (6) .... (fast).

Toni: Thanks for that. They sound like a nice group!

20 Modifying comparisons: *much faster* etc.

- To say that there is a big difference between two people or things, we can use *far/a lot/much* + comparative adjective/adverb: *I work **a lot harder** than Piet, but his results are **much better** than mine.*

- To say that there is a small difference, we can use *a little/a (little) bit/slightly* + comparative adjective/adverb: *This phone's **slightly more expensive**, but the battery lasts **a little longer**.*

 If there is a noun after the comparative adjective, we can only use *much, far* or *slightly: a/an + much/far/slightly* + comparative adjective + singular noun: *We need **a much bigger car**.* (Not *We need a lot bigger car.*)

PRACTICE

20a Put the words in the correct order.

0 Brazil is *a lot bigger than Colombia* . (bigger / than / a lot / Colombia)

1 Gold is .... (a little / silver / than / heavier)

2 Girls grow up .... (than / faster / slightly / boys)

3 Fishing is .... (golf / more popular / a bit / than)

4 Computer games sell .... (CDs / better / than / far)

5 Women drive .... (safely / a bit / more / men / than)

6 Dogs are .... (than / far / cats / friendlier)

7 Yoga is .... (easier / a lot / than / karate)

8 DVDs are .... (much / videos / than / better)

20b Complete the sentences. Use the correct form of the words in brackets.

0 Tom's ....*far taller*........ than the other boys in his class. (far / tall)

1 My new computer's .... than the old one. (a lot / powerful)

2 Roger hits the ball .... than Derek. (a bit / hard)

3 This jacket's too small. Have you got a .... one? (slightly / large)

4 My English is .... than it was a year ago. (much / bad)

5 If we walk .... , we'll get to the cinema in five minutes. (a little / fast)

6 This sofa costs more, but it's .... (far / comfortable)

7 Our new house is .... than our old one. (a lot / big)

8 Could you speak .... , please? (a bit / quietly)

21 Adverbs of frequency

0%					100%
never	hardly ever rarely seldom almost never	occasionally sometimes	often usually	almost always nearly always	always

- We use adverbs of frequency to say how often somebody does something or how often something happens.
- Adverbs of frequency come after the verb *be*, but before other verbs: *I'm **usually** energetic in the mornings. We **never drink** coffee.*
- In negative sentences and questions, they come before the main verb: *I **don't often** see my brother. **Do** you **always walk** to work?*
- We can put *occasionally*, *often*, *sometimes* and *usually* at the beginning or the end of a sentence: ***Sometimes** he works on Saturdays. We go out for dinner **occasionally**.*

 We can use these expressions to talk about frequency: *every day/week/month/year, once/twice/three times a week/month/year* etc. They usually come at the end of a sentence: *We go out **every day**. He goes swimming **twice a week**.*

 We can use *a lot* and *much* to talk about frequency: *They go out **a lot**. They don't go out **a lot/much**.*

PRACTICE

21a Re-write the sentences. Put the adverbs in the correct place.

o I have fruit for breakfast. (sometimes)
I sometimes have fruit for breakfast.

1 We are tired in the evening. (always)

....

2 He goes to the cinema. (almost never)

....

3 They watch TV. (rarely)

....

4 She writes letters. (seldom)

....

5 I stay up late. (hardly ever)

....

6 The trains are on time. (almost always)

....

7 We don't eat fish. (often)

....

8 She cooks for herself. (never)

....

21b Put the words in the correct order.

0   have / I / always / pasta for lunch
   I always have pasta for lunch.
   ....

1   he / does / always / early / get up / ?
   ....

2   never / she / sees / her brother
   ....

3   don't / phone / my parents / often / me
   ....

4   make / you / the same mistakes / always
   ....

5   they / are / at home / hardly ever
   ....

6   usually / to work / don't / we / drive
   ....

7   play / you / often / tennis / do / ?
   ....

8   late for class / is / rarely / she
   ....

21c Complete the exam essay. Use the words in the box.

~~almost always~~   always   every   hardly ever   never
once a year   sometimes   twice a week   usually

My grandmother's 78, but she's a lot more active than many young people I know. She (0) .....*almost always*..... goes for a walk before breakfast, she goes swimming (1) .... , on Mondays and Wednesdays, and (2) .... Friday she goes to a ballroom dancing class. She only missed one class last year! (3) .... she gets the bus to go shopping, but only when it's raining. She (4) .... cycles into town. She (5) .... drinks alcohol, just a glass of champagne (6) .... , on her birthday. She has an active mind too. She (7) .... watches television because she says the programmes are boring and she (8) .... reads for an hour or two a day.

22 Adverbs of degree: *very, really* etc.

- We use adverbs of degree to make adjectives and adverbs stronger or weaker.
- We can use *very* and *really* before an adjective or adverb to make it stronger, and *extremely* to make it very strong: *This cake is **really nice**. They work **extremely hard**.*
- We can use *quite*, *fairly* and *a bit* before an adjective or adverb to make it weaker. We usually use *a bit* with a negative adjective or adverb: *Sheila sings **fairly well**. The film is **quite interesting**, but I don't want to watch it again. I feel **a bit tired**.*
- *Quite* comes before *a/an*, but *very, really, extremely* and *fairly* come after *a/an*: *We live in **quite a** small house, but it's got **an extremely** big garden.*

⚠ We do not use *a bit* + adjective + noun: ~~It's a bit long film.~~

PRACTICE

22a Put the words in the correct order.

0 our / speaks / teacher / fast / really *Our teacher speaks really fast.*

1 cheap / these chairs / quite / are ....

2 fairly / Sonia / slowly / walks ....

3 drives / very / he / dangerously ....

4 in / live / we / a / flat / big / quite ....

5 tired / a bit / feeling / I'm ....

6 was / the / extremely / long / film ....

7 computer / it's / an / quite / old ....

8 really / you / unhealthily / eat ....

22b Circle the correct answer.

0 Hair grows *a bit* / (*really*) slowly – just half a millimetre a day.

1 Canada is *quite* / *a very* big country. Only Russia is bigger.

2 I'll be home *a bit* / *really* late tonight – about half an hour later than usual.

3 My great-grandmother's *fairly* / *really* old. She'll be 103 this year!

4 Jan studies *quite* / *a bit* hard, but never more than an hour a day.

5 Cheetahs can run *fairly* / *very* fast. They're the fastest animals on land.

6 I've got *quite a* / *an extremely* big bedroom, but there's no space for a table.

7 He speaks Hindi *fairly* / *extremely* well. He can have a simple conversation in it.

8 Antarctica is *a bit* / *extremely* cold. In winter temperatures can fall to –80°C.

Check 4 Adjectives and adverbs

1 Put the words in the correct order.

1 bought / he / a / hat / Mexican / big

....

2 we / tired / usually / are / in the evening

....

3 comfortable / that one / more / is / much / than / this chair

....

4 glass / building / horrible / square / in the city centre / there's / a

....

5 I / chocolate / eat / often / don't

....

6 quite / restaurant / that's / good / a

....

7 in / student / is / best / the class / he / the / ?

....

/ 7

2 Circle the correct answer.

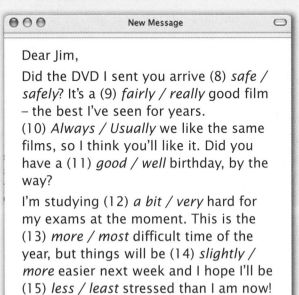

Dear Jim,

Did the DVD I sent you arrive (8) *safe / safely*? It's a (9) *fairly / really* good film – the best I've seen for years.
(10) *Always / Usually* we like the same films, so I think you'll like it. Did you have a (11) *good / well* birthday, by the way?

I'm studying (12) *a bit / very* hard for my exams at the moment. This is the (13) *more / most* difficult time of the year, but things will be (14) *slightly / more* easier next week and I hope I'll be (15) *less / least* stressed than I am now!

Liam

/ 8

3 Complete the second sentence so that it means the same as the first. Use no more than three words.

16 The actor gave a good performance and impressed everyone.
The actor performed .... and impressed everyone.

17 She sings more expressively than he does.
He sings .... she does.

18 We play that piece of music less brilliantly than they do.
They play that piece of music
.... we do.

19 The critic reviewed the play enthusiastically.
The critic wrote an .... review of the play.

20 Last night's audience was less warm than tonight's audience.
Tonight's audience was ....
last night's audience.

/ 5

Total: / 20

✓ **Self-check**

Wrong answers	Look again at	Try CD-ROM
1, 4	Unit 16	Exercise 16
7, 13, 15, 20	Unit 17	Exercise 17
8, 11, 16, 19	Unit 18	Exercise 18
17, 18	Unit 19	Exercise 19
3, 14	Unit 20	Exercise 20
2, 5, 10	Unit 21	Exercise 21
6, 9, 12	Unit 22	Exercise 22

Now do **Check 4**

Comparative structures

23 as ... as, not as ... as

- We use *as* + adjective/adverb + *as* to say that two people or things are the same or equal: *I'm **as tall as** you now. He can run **as fast as** his friend.*
- We use *not as* + adjective/adverb + *as* to say that two people or things are not the same: *This basketball court is**n't as good as** the one at school. Alex does**n't** play the guitar **as well as** Jamie.*

▶▶ **For comparative and superlative adjectives and adverbs, see Units 17 and 19.**

PRACTICE

23a **Complete the sentences. Use *as ... as* and the words in the box.**

| badly carefully ~~fast~~ good tired well well |

0 Mike is a fast runner, but he can't run ....*as fast as*........ Rob.

1 I only met him last week. I don't know him .... you do.

2 Alain doesn't sing very well, but he doesn't sing .... Joe.

3 That was a long day. Are you .... me?

4 That drawing is fantastic – you draw .... a professional artist.

5 These pizzas aren't .... the ones I ate in Italy.

6 Boys don't always write .... girls.

23b **Complete the second sentence so that it means the same as the first. Use no more than three words.**

0 Your computer is newer than my computer.
My computer isn't ....*as new as*.......... your computer.

1 Anne and Sarah are equally sensitive.
Anne is .... Sarah.

2 Our new neighbourhood is noisier than our old one.
Our old neighbourhood wasn't .... our new one.

3 Mick works harder than Peter.
Peter doesn't work .... Mick.

4 Wayne played worse than Donna.
Donna didn't play .... Wayne.

5 I thought the film was more exciting than the book.
I thought the book wasn't .... the film.

6 The Maths exam was easy and the English exam was equally easy.
The Maths exam was .... the English exam.

24 *too, enough, very*

We use *too* and *enough* with adjectives and adverbs. *Too* means 'more than you need'. *Not ... enough* means 'less than you need'. We use them in these patterns:

● *too* + adjective/adverb: *The man's voice was **too soft**. He spoke **too softly**.*

● *not* + adjective/adverb + *enough*: *My bag is**n't big enough**. They do**n't** speak English **well enough**.*

● *too* + adjective/adverb + *to* + infinitive OR (*not*) adjective/adverb + *enough* + *to* + infinitive: *He's **too young to vote**. He is**n't old enough to vote**.* (He can't vote.)

● *too* + adjective/adverb + *for somebody* + *to* + infinitive OR (*not*)+ adjective/adverb + *enough* + *for somebody* + *to* + infinitive: *It's **too cold for us to swim** today. It is**n't warm enough for us to swim** today.* (We can't swim. It's too cold.)

● *Very* means 'a lot'. Compare: *This game is **very expensive**.* (But maybe I'll buy it.) *This game is **too expensive**.* (It costs more than I can pay.)

PRACTICE

24a **Complete the sentences. Use *too* or *not ... enough* and the words in brackets.**

0 We wanted to go cycling, but it was ......*too windy*...... . (windy)

1 I'm going to bed. I'm .... to eat any supper. (tired)

2 These jeans are .... to wear to the party. (clean)

3 Helen needs new shoes. These ones are .... for her now. (small)

4 We need two pizzas. This one is .... for four people. (big)

5 It's .... to see the film now. It started twenty minutes ago. (late)

6 Gina had a bad cold yesterday. She was .... to play tennis. (well)

24b **Join the sentences. Use the words in brackets.**

0 She doesn't work hard. She won't pass her exams. (enough)
   She doesn't work hard enough to pass her exams.

1 He's short. He can't reach that shelf. (too)
   ....

2 We aren't in Rome very long. We can't see the whole city. (enough)
   ....

3 The man was very angry. He couldn't speak. (too)
   ....

4 They're sixteen years old. They can't drive yet. (enough)
   ....

5 The music at the disco was very loud. We couldn't have a conversation. (too)
   ....

6 Dan doesn't play the guitar well. He can't become a musician. (enough)
   ....

25 *so ... that, such (a/an) ... that*

- We use *so ... that* and *such (a/an) ... that* to talk about the result of something.
- We use *so* + adjective/adverb + *that* without a noun: *The painting was **so beautiful that** I wanted to buy it. We drove **so fast that** we got there in an hour.*
- We use *such* + adjective + uncountable/plural noun: *It was **such horrible weather** that we stayed at home. They're **such large trees** that they hide the view*
- We use *such a/an* + adjective + singular noun: *It was **such a big pizza** that I couldn't finish it.*

PRACTICE

25a Complete the sentences. Use *so*, *such* or *such a*.

0 She danced ....*so*.......... well that she won the competition.

1 There you are! It's .... dark that I didn't see you at first.

2 My dad has .... big feet that he can never find shoes to fit.

3 Anna has .... small bedroom that she can't get a computer in it.

4 These instructions are .... confusing that I can't understand them.

5 The food was cooked .... badly that we complained to the manager.

6 We had .... bad weather on holiday that we came home two days early.

7 It was .... boring film that we left before the end.

8 She ate .... slowly that she was the last person to finish her lunch.

25b Circle the correct answer.

⚪⚪⚪   New Message   ⬭

Dear Helen,

Hello from Malta! I'm having (0) *so* /(*such*) a good time that I don't want to leave. The weather's great. It's (1) *so / such* hot that I go to the beach every afternoon. I'm staying with a host family, Mr and Mrs Campbell. They're (2) *so / such* friendly people that I really feel at home here. But their children are (3) *so / such* noisy that sometimes it's difficult to do my homework. The college is nice too, with students from all over the world. Some of them speak with (4) *so / such* strong accents that they're a bit hard to understand, but my teacher speaks (5) *so / such* clearly that I understand everything he says. When I come home, my English will be (6) *so / such* good that you won't believe it!

See you soon,

Jasmine

Check 5 Comparative structures

1 Circle the correct answer.

1 Those trainers are *too / so* expensive for me to buy.

2 The university is *so / such* big that I always get lost!

3 Mike's got *such / such a* terrible cold that he's not coming with us.

4 Ellie's sister's really nice, but she isn't as *pretty / prettier* as Ellie.

5 These clothes aren't as *smart / smart enough* for a job interview.

/ 5

2 Complete the second sentence so that it means the same as the first. Use no more than three words.

6 Mary's birthday party was better than mine.
My birthday party wasn't
.... Mary's.

7 My living room was crowded and we couldn't dance.
My living room was .... that we couldn't dance.

8 The music at Mary's party was louder than the music at my party.
The music at my party wasn't
.... the music at Mary's party.

9 Mary's birthday cake was very big and we had two pieces each!
Mary's birthday cake was big
.... for us to have two pieces each!

10 We had a very good time and nobody wanted to leave.
We had .... good time that nobody wanted to leave.

/ 5

3 Choose the correct answer.

Last week I went for a walk in the mountains with my friends. It was (11) ...... a beautiful day that we walked a long way, talking and laughing. A few hours later, we were (12) ...... tired to walk any more, so we had lunch by a lake. It was (13) ...... hot that we went for a swim, but the water was (14) ...... cold as ice. We sat on some rocks until we were dry (15) ...... to put our clothes on. On the way back, we walked so slowly (16) ...... it started to get dark and soon it wasn't light (17) ...... to see the path. Suddenly, we saw a fox, but it was (18) ...... frightened as we were and it ran away. That night I was (19) ...... tired, so I went to bed early, but I was (20) ...... exhausted to sleep.

11	A so	B such	C too	D enough
12	A very	B enough	C too	D as
13	A so	B too	C enough	D as
14	A too	B so	C as	D enough
15	A enough	B so	C very	D as
16	A than	B as	C enough	D that
17	A as	B such	C very	D enough
18	A such	B as	C enough	D such
19	A very	B enough	C such	D as
20	A very	B too	C so	D such

/ 10

Total: / 20

✓ Self-check

Wrong answers	Look again at	Try CD-ROM
4, 6, 8, 14, 18	Unit 23	Exercise 23
1, 5, 9, 12, 15, 17, 19, 20	Unit 24	Exercise 24
2, 3, 7, 10, 11, 13, 16	Unit 25	Exercise 25

Now do **Check 5**

Present tenses

26 Present simple

We use the present simple to talk about:

- situations or states that are always or usually true: *We **live** in a flat.*
- habits and events or actions that happen regularly, often with adverbs of frequency (e.g. *always, often, usually*) and other time expressions (e.g. *on Mondays, every day, in the morning*): *We **usually get up** at six o'clock. He **goes** to the gym **every week**.*

▶▶ *For adverbs of frequency, see Unit 21.*

▶▶ *See Appendix 4: Spelling rules for present simple verbs, page 171.*

Affirmative	I/you/we/they **eat**	he/she/it **eats**
Negative	I/you/we/they **don't eat**	he/she/it **doesn't eat**
Question	**Do** I/you/we/they **eat**?	**Does** he/she/it **eat**?
Short answers	Yes, I/you/we/they **do**. No, I/you/we/they **don't**.	Yes, he/she/it **does**. No, he/she/it **doesn't**.

PRACTICE

26a Complete the sentences. Use the present simple of the verbs in brackets.

0   Lorna .....*often watches*..... TV in the evening, but Alice .....*usually reads*..... . (often / watch, usually read)

1   I'm often tired. I .... hard and I .... very much. (work, not relax)

2   My mother .... to the gym every day, but my father .... any exercise. (go, not do)

3   Sophia .... in London, but she .... the weekend in the country with her parents. (live, often / spend)

4   Jane and Richard .... to concerts often, but they .... to music a lot at home. (not go, listen)

5   Angus .... from Glasgow, but he .... with a strong Scottish accent. (come, not speak)

6   We .... to town. We .... the train – it's quicker. (not drive, usually / catch)

26b Complete the questions and short answers. Use the present simple of the verbs in brackets.

0 A: *Do you usually get up* early? (you / usually / get up)   B: No, ...*I don't*.... .

1 A: .... to university? (Tim / go)   B: Yes, ...

2 A: .... out every Sunday? (they / go)   B: No, ...

3 A: .... black? (Sue / always / wear)   B: Yes, ...

4 A: .... tennis every day? (you / play)   B: No, ...

5 A: .... near you? (they / live)   B: Yes, ...

6 A: .... from the USA? (she / come)   B: No, ...

26c Complete the interview. Use the present simple of the verbs in the box.

borrow   catch   drive   not use   put   recycle   travel   walk   ~~work~~

A: Excuse me. I (0) ....*work*.......... for the local council. Can I ask you about our services? First, (1) .... you .... by public transport often?

B: No. My husband and I (2) .... public transport at all. We (3) .... everywhere. My daughter usually (4) .... to school, but she sometimes (5) .... the bus if the weather's bad.

A: I see. Next, (6) .... you .... paper, plastic and glass?

B: Yes, I (7) .... everything in the containers at the supermarket.

A: Good. Finally, (8) .... you .... books from the public library?

B: No, never. We don't have time to read very much.

27 Present continuous

- We use the present continuous to talk about:
  - something that is happening now: *Wait a minute. I'm texting my friend.*
  - temporary situations: *She's from Peru, but she's studying in Spain this year.*
- We often use the present continuous with the following time words and phrases: *now, right now, at the moment, today: We're getting ready to go out now.*

▶▶ *See Appendix 5: Spelling rules for verbs + -ing, page 171.*

Affirmative	Negative	Question
I'm eat**ing**	I'm **not** eat**ing**	**Am** I eat**ing**?
you/we/they**'re** eat**ing**	you/we/they **aren't** eat**ing**	**Are** you/we/they eat**ing**?
he/she/it**'s** eat**ing**	he/she/it **isn't** eat**ing**	**Is** he/she/it eat**ing**?

Short answers		
Yes, I **am**.	Yes, he/she/it **is**.	Yes, we/you/they **are**.
No, I'm **not**.	No, he/she/it **isn't**.	No, we/you/they **aren't**.

PRACTICE

27a Complete the sentences. Use the present continuous.

0   My dad watches a lot of sport. This month he ...._'s watching_........ the Olympics.

1   You don't usually play well, but today you .... brilliantly!

2   I usually read novels, but at the moment I .... anything.

3   We usually have lunch at twelve, but today we .... lunch at two.

4   He often works on Saturdays, but he .... today. He's at home.

5   They don't often save money, but at the moment they .... to buy a car.

6   She usually runs a marathon every year, but this year she .... any.

27b Complete the conversations. Use the present continuous of the verbs in brackets.

0   A: ...._Is Donna speaking_........... Italian to that man? (Donna / speak)

    B: Yes, she ....*is*....... . She ...._'s learning_............. it at night school. (learn)

1   A: .... the party? (you / enjoy)

    B: Yes, we .... We .... a great time. (have)

2   A: What .... here? (you / do)

    B: I .... for some friends. (wait)

3   A: .... her computer? (Holly / use)

    B: No, she .... She .... any work today. (not do)

4   A: .... the news at the moment? (they / watch)

    B: No, they .... They .... dinner. (prepare)

27c Complete the phone conversation. Use the present continuous of the verbs in brackets.

A: How (0) ...._'s the holiday going_..... (the holiday / go)?

B: We (1) .... (have) a great time! I
   (2) .... (learn) to windsurf.

A: Wow! (3) .... (Gary / take) lessons too?

B: No, he (4) .... He (5) .... (not do) anything except relaxing on the beach and sleeping.

A: (6) .... (you / get) very brown?

B: Yes, we (7) .... And you? (8) .... (you / enjoy) your holiday?

A: No, I (9) .... It's cloudy and cold, but at least it
   (10) .... (not rain) today.

B: Oh dear! Listen, I must go now. I'll see you next week. Bye!

28 Present simple or present continuous

Compare the present simple and present continuous:
*He **usually goes** to the cinema on Saturdays, but **today** he's **staying** in.*

P R A C T I C E

28a Circle the correct answer.

0   Why *do you wear* / (*are you wearing*) a coat? It's hot today.

1   *Do tigers live* / *Are tigers living* in Africa?

2   We *have* / *'re having* a big party in the garden every
summer.

3   I *don't eat* / *'m not eating* a lot of chocolate because
it's bad for you.

4   Listen, I think someone *calls* / *'s calling* us.

5   This month they *make* / *'re making* a new film starring
Johnny Depp.

6   She usually *goes* / *is going* to see her cousins once a
month.

7   Martha *cooks* / *'s cooking* lunch at the moment.

8   Film stars *usually buy* / *are usually buying* their clothes
at expensive shops.

**28b Complete the conversation. Use the present simple or present continuous of the
verbs in brackets.**

Lisa: Polly! What a surprise! What (0) ......*are you doing*.... (you / do) here in York?

Polly: Hi, Lisa! I (1) .... (buy) a new guitar. Do you remember the
band I'm in? Well, we (2) .... (play) at the Sports Club in
Hathern every Saturday night.

Lisa: Great! That's fantastic!

Polly: Yes. What about you? What (3) .... (you / do) these days?

Lisa: I (4) .... (still / study) architecture – this is my final year.
At the moment I (5) .... (work) in an architect's office to
get some work experience. Listen, I sometimes (6) .... (go)
home to Hathern at the weekend. Can I come and listen to you and your
group?

Polly: Of course! There's a great atmosphere at the club! Everyone knows the
songs and people (7) .... (dance) too. We usually
(8) .... (start) playing at eight o'clock.

Lisa: I'll definitely see you soon, then, Polly!

29 State verbs

State verbs describe states, not actions. We usually use them in the present simple, not the present continuous. Here are some common state verbs:

- attitude verbs: *like, love, hate, want, prefer, need, wish: I **like** this soup. I **need** some coffee right now.*
- mental/thinking verbs: *believe, think, know, remember, understand: He **thinks** I'm French. I'm sorry, I **don't understand**.*
- sense/perception verbs: *hear, see, smell, taste: **Do** you **see** that man over there?*
- others: *be, have (= 'possess'), belong, own, cost, mean: That book **belongs** to Jim.*

P R A C T I C E

29a Circle the correct answer.

```
 ● ● ●                          New Message                          ⬭

 Dear Anne,

 We (0) have /'re having a fantastic holiday. We (1) stay / 're staying in
 a villa in Tuscany. It (2) belongs / 's belonging to Giuseppe, a friend of
 my father's, and it (3) has / 's having a big swimming pool. Giuseppe
 (4) makes / 's making dinner at the moment and it (5) smells /
 's smelling really good. I (6) love / 'm loving Italian food!

 I (7) don't know / 'm not knowing how long we can stay here, but we
 (8) don't want / aren't wanting to leave, that's for sure!

 Tessa
```

29b Complete the conversations. Use the present simple or present continuous of the verbs in brackets.

0   A: I ....*like*........ that ring. Is it new? (like)

   B: It's not mine. It ....*belongs*........ to my grandmother. (belong)

1   A: What's up? You .... (not dance)

   B: It's this music. I .... salsa. (hate)

2   A: I met Paolo today. He says you .... him. (know)

   B: Paolo? I .... anyone called Paolo. (not remember)

3   A: What .... in my room? (you / do)

   B: You .... my dictionary and I .... it. (have, need)

4   A: I .... that's Jack over there. (think)

   B: Where? I .... him. (not see)

5   A: .... an e-mail to Jenny? (he / write)

   B: Yes. He .... to invite her to his party. (want)

Check 6 Present tenses

1 Circle the correct answer.

1 He *doesn't understand / isn't understanding* when people speak quickly.

2 Can you be quiet? We *try / 're trying* to do some work.

3 They *have / 're having* a meeting every Tuesday.

4 *Does Ellie want / Is Ellie wanting* to come with us tonight?

5 *Do you read / Are you reading* anything at the moment?

/ 5

2 Write sentences. Use the present simple or present continuous.

6 Excuse me. what time / the museum / close / on Sundays?

....

....

7 Listen! someone / sing / a song

....

....

8 people / not eat / late at night in Britain

....

....

9 she / carry / a briefcase / to work every day

....

....

10 I can't find my glasses. you / sit / on them?

....

....

/ 5

3 Complete the article. Use the present simple or present continuous of the verbs in the box.

> go not have try want work

Life's very busy for Belinda Lee these days. At the moment she (11) .... on a new film with Oscar winner Tom McCall. She (12) .... much time to relax, but she (13) .... to the gym every day and she always (14) .... to see her friends at the weekend.

She and her husband (15) .... to sell their house because they're going to move to Hollywood next year. We wish them lots of luck!

/ 5

4 Complete the questions. Use the present simple or present continuous of the verbs in brackets.

16 .... to watch a DVD? (you / want)

17 Listen. Why .... a funny noise? (my computer / make)

18 .... dinner? I'm hungry. (mum / cook)

19 Is that Paul's car? Or .... to his dad? (it / belong)

20 Why .... up posters everywhere? (those people / put)

/ 5

Total: / 20

✓ Self-check

Wrong answers	Look again at	Try CD-ROM
6, 8, 9, 13, 14	Unit 26	Exercise 26
7, 10, 11, 17, 18, 20	Unit 27	Exercise 27
2, 3, 5	Unit 28	Exercise 28
1, 4, 12, 15, 16, 19	Unit 29	Exercise 29

Now do **Check 6**

Past tenses

30 Past simple: regular verbs

- We use the past simple to talk about:
  - single actions that started and finished in the past, often with definite time expressions like *yesterday, last week, a year ago*: *I **finished** college **a year ago**.*
  - actions that happened regularly in the past, often with expressions of frequency (e.g. *often, always, every week* etc.) or duration (e.g. *for a year, when I was a child*): *I **played** football every week **when I was a child**.*
  - states and situations that were true in the past but are not true now: *I **lived** in London when I was young, but now I live in Liverpool.*
- To form the past simple of regular verbs, we add *-ed* to the verb: *walk → walked*
  play → played   like → liked
- We use *did/didn't* + infinitive in negative sentences and questions: *I **didn't like** the film. **Did** you **play** tennis last Saturday?*

▶▶ **See Appendix 6: Spelling rules for verbs + -ed, page 171.**

Affirmative		Ann	visit**ed**	her friend.
Negative		Ann	**didn't visit**	her friend.
Question	Did	Ann	visit	her friend?

P R A C T I C E

30a Complete the sentences. Use the past simple of the verbs in brackets.

0 I ...... *watched* ...... a really good film on TV last night. (watch)

1 The bus .... fifteen minutes late yesterday. (arrive)

2 My parents .... much when they were young. (not travel)

3 I .... to my friend for an hour on the phone yesterday. (chat)

4 We .... basketball at primary school. (not play)

5 My sister .... French at university. (study)

6 He .... at a fantastic hotel on holiday last summer. (stay)

7 My friends .... to go out last Saturday night. (not want)

8 I .... the summer holidays when I was a child. (love)

9 The rain .... after fifteen minutes. (stop)

10 I .... my car last week, so now it's really dirty. (not clean)

11 They .... jazz when they were young, but now they love it. (not like)

12 We .... the heavy boxes up the stairs to the sixth floor. (carry)

30b Complete the story. Use the past simple of the verbs in brackets.

"This (0) ..*happened*.. (happen) a year ago. I usually drive to the town centre to meet my friend for lunch on Saturdays, but that day I (1) .... (decide) to take the bus. I (2) .... (wait) at the bus stop for ten minutes, but the bus (3) .... (not arrive), so I (4) .... (try) to call my friend from a nearby phone box. Unfortunately, she (5) .... (not answer) and while I was there, I (6) .... (miss) the bus! So I (7) .... (start) to walk. When I finally (8) .... (arrive) at the restaurant an hour later, my friend (9) .... (not believe) my story and (10) .... (shout) at me for being late!"

30c Complete the conversations. Use the past simple of the verbs in the boxes.

| dance   ~~enjoy~~   finish   talk   walk |

A: (0) ...*Did*.... you ....*enjoy*....... the party on Saturday night?
B: Yes. The music was great, so I (1) .... a lot. And I (2) .... to some interesting people.
A: What time (3) .... the party .... ?
B: At about two. Then I (4) .... home.

| hate   live   move   start   travel   work |

A: (5) .... you .... in London when you were a child?
B: No. My father (6) .... as a diplomat and we (7) .... all over the world.
A: When (8) .... you .... to London?
B: Five years ago, when I (9) .... work. I (10) .... it at first, but now I love it.

31 Past simple: irregular verbs

Some verbs do not form the past simple with *-ed*. They are irregular: *eat → ate*
drink → drank   *find → found*   *go → went*   *see → saw*

▶▶ **See Appendix 11: Irregular verbs, pages 172–173.**

Affirmative		They	**won**	the prize.
Negative		They	**didn't win**	the prize.
Question	**Did**	they	**win**	the prize?

⚠ The past simple of *be* is *was/were*: *I **was** busy. They **weren't** at home. **Was** Mark with you?*

P R A C T I C E

31a Complete the sentences. Use the past simple.

Every year	Last year
0 We go to a different country on holiday.	We ......*went*...... to Greece.
1 We see the famous monuments.	We .... the Parthenon.
2 We take a lot of photos.	We .... more than 100 photos.
3 We sleep late every morning.	We .... until ten o'clock.
4 We eat the local food.	We .... some Greek salad.
5 We meet some interesting people.	We .... a Greek family.
6 We buy souvenirs to take home.	We .... a beautiful vase.

31b Complete the story. Use the past simple of the verbs in brackets.

"Last week my mother (0) ......*lent*...... (lend) me her car and I (1) ....
(drive) to a nearby town. I parked the car in a side street and I (2) ....
(do) some shopping. When it (3) .... (be) time to go home, I realised
that I (4) .... (not remember) where the car (5) .... (be). I
(6) .... (spend) about an hour looking for it, but I (7) .... (not
find) it. I (8) .... (feel) really stupid. Finally, I (9) .... (ring) my
mother. Fortunately, she (10) .... (not get) angry. She (11) ....
(tell) me to leave the car and come home. So I (12) .... (catch) a bus and
the next day we (13) .... (go) back together and (14) .... (find)
the car."

31c Complete the conversations. Use the past simple of the verbs in brackets.

0 **A:** Where ......*did you put*...... your keys? (you / put)
   B: I think I ......*left*...... them on the table. (leave)

1 **A:** What time .... ? (the concert / begin)
   B: It .... at nine, but some people .... late.
   (begin, come)

2 **A:** What .... you for your birthday? (your parents / give)
   B: A sweater. But my sister .... me anything! (not give)

3 **A:** Where .... yesterday when I called? (you / be)
   B: I .... at home, but I .... the phone. (be,
   not hear)

4 **A:** How .... your leg? (you / break)
   B: I .... off my bike. (fall)

5 **A:** What .... to the wedding? (your brother / wear)
   B: He .... a new suit. It .... 500 euros! (wear,
   cost)

32 Past continuous

We use the past continuous to talk about:

- an action that was in progress at a particular time in the past, often with time expressions like *at one o'clock, last night*. The action started before that time and continued after that time: *At one o'clock yesterday we were having lunch*.

- an action or state that continued for a long time, often with expressions like *all day, all morning: I was working all day yesterday*.

- two actions that were in progress at the same time in the past, often with the word *while*. Notice when we use a comma (,): *Yuri was washing the car while Katya was watching TV. While Katya was watching TV, Yuri was washing the car*.

⚠️ We use the past simple, not the past continuous, with state verbs: *I heard a noise outside*. (Not ~~I was hearing a noise outside.~~)

Affirmative	I/he/she/it **was walking**	we/you/they **were walking**
Negative	I/he/she/it **wasn't walking**	we/you/they **weren't walking**
Question	**Was** I/he/she/it **walking**?	**Were** we/you/they **walking**?
Short answers	Yes, I/he/she/it **was**.	Yes, we/you/they **were**.
	No, I/he/she/it **wasn't**.	No, we/you/they **weren't**.

▶▶ **See Appendix 5: Spelling rules for verbs + -ing, page 171.**

PRACTICE

32a Complete the sentences. Use the past continuous of the verbs in brackets.

0 I ......*was sitting*...... at home one day, feeling miserable. (sit)

1 It .... and I .... about my summer holidays. (rain, think)

2 Later that day, I .... the Internet. (surf)

3 I .... for anything in particular. (not look)

4 Then I found an interesting site. A new airline .... cheap flights to India. (advertise)

5 Some of my friends .... round India. (travel)

6 They were in Delhi and they .... a wonderful time. (have)

7 Suddenly, it seemed like a good idea to join them and two days later I .... at home in cold, miserable England; I .... to Delhi! (not sit, fly)

8 When I got off the plane, my friends .... to meet me. (wait)

32b **Complete the conversations. Use the past continuous of the verbs in brackets.**

0 **A:** What ....*were you doing*.......... yesterday evening? I knocked on the door,
but no one answered. (you / do)

B: I ....*was listening*.......... to loud music. I didn't hear you knock. (listen)

1 **A:** Where .... at eight o'clock this morning? (Karl / go)

B: To a job interview. That's why he .... a suit and tie. (wear)

2 **A:** .... the computer all morning? (you / use)

B: Yes, I .... I .... to some friends online. (chat)

3 **A:** The neighbours .... a lot of noise last night! (make)

B: Yes, I know. They .... their wedding anniversary while the
rest of us .... to get some sleep! (celebrate, try)

4 **A:** I didn't see Eve or George in August. What .... ? (they / do)

B: Well, Eve .... across the US with some friends and George
.... in his dad's shop. (drive, work)

5 **A:** Who .... to outside the cinema last night? (you / talk)

B: Some friends. We .... the film. (discuss)

6 **A:** I'm so tired! Brian and I .... in the garden all day yesterday! (dig)

B: Really? Why .... ? (you / dig)

32c **Complete the news story. Use the past continuous of the verbs in the box.**

| do | have | plant | ~~rob~~ | sleep | talk | work |

Noisy neighbours help burglars

There was a burglary at the home of local man
Mike Knight yesterday afternoon. It seems that the
thieves (0) ....*were robbing*.......... Mr Knight's house
while he (1) .... some work in his
garden. 'I (2) .... vegetables in the
garden all afternoon,' Mr Knight told reporters,
'and I didn't hear a thing.'

While Mr Knight (3) .... in the
garden, his neighbours (4) .... a
barbecue to celebrate their son's birthday. 'They (5) .... really
loudly,' Mr Knight said.

When Mr Knight went into his house, his dog Goldie (6) ....
peacefully in the living room, but the TV and hi-fi were missing. 'I don't
understand why Goldie didn't bark,' said Mr Knight. 'Maybe the thieves gave
him some sleeping pills!'

33 Past continuous and past simple

- We can use the past simple and past continuous together, to talk about an action that happened while another action was in progress. We use the past continuous for the longer action that was in progress. We use the past simple for the shorter action: *I **was working** when he **arrived**.*

- We often use *when* before the action in the past simple and *while* before the action in the past continuous. Notice when we use a comma (,):
  *I was sleeping **when** the phone **rang**. **When** the phone **rang**, I was sleeping.*
  *The phone rang **while** I **was sleeping**. **While** I **was sleeping**, the phone rang.*

 We use past simple + *when* + past simple to say that one action happened after another action: *We **had** dinner **when** Kim **arrived**. **When** Kim **arrived**, we **had** dinner.* (First Kim arrived. Then we had dinner.)

PRACTICE

33a Complete the sentences. Use *when* or *while*.

o Was it snowing ......*when*........ you went to bed last night?

1 They had lunch .... they were waiting for the plane.

2 .... she put new batteries in the toy, it started working again.

3 .... I was walking home, I fell over and cut my knee.

4 Helen didn't say hello .... I saw her this morning.

5 .... you were out jogging, Frank brought your book back.

6 Did everybody go home .... the concert finished?

33b Write sentences. Use the past simple and past continuous.

o while / I / do / the washing up / I / break / a glass
   While I was doing the washing up, I broke a glass.

1 your mother / ring / while / you / have / a bath
   ....

2 when / we / see / them / they / buy / food / for the party
   ....

3 while / she / shop / she / meet / on old friend
   ....

4 we / park / our car / when / we / have / the accident
   ....

5 what / you / read / when / I / come / into the room?
   ....

6 while / I / chop / the onions / I / cut / my finger
   ....

33c **Complete the article. Use the past simple or past continuous of the verbs in brackets.**

A funny thing (0) ....*happened*.......... (happen) while I
(1) .... (fly) to London last summer. When I
(2) .... (get) on the plane, I (3) ....
(take off) my jacket and put it in the overhead locker. When the passenger next
to me (4) .... (sit) down, I was surprised to see that she
(5) .... (wear) the same jacket as me.

Anyway, the plane (6) .... (land) and we went to
pick up our bags at the luggage carousel. While I (7) ....
(wait) for my bags, I (8) .... (decide) to listen to some music.
But when I (9) .... (look) for my MP3 player in my jacket
pocket, it (10) .... (not be) there. Then I realised I had
the woman's jacket – and she had mine!

34 *used to*

We use *used to* to talk about:

● actions that happened regularly in the past, but do not happen now: *He **used to do**
a lot of sport when he was young. We **didn't use to go** to the cinema very often.*

● something that was true in the past, but is not true now: *She **used to be** very shy,
but now she's quite confident.*

 We can use *used to* and the past simple in the same way, to talk about actions or
events that happened regularly, or about things that were true in the past: *When
I was at college, I **used to go/went** swimming every week. She **used to love/loved**
dancing when she was young.*

 We cannot use *used to* for actions or events that happened only once in the past:
*I **went** to the cinema last week.* (Not *I used to go to the cinema last week.*)

Affirmative	I/you/he/she/it/we/they **used to live** here.
Negative	I/you/he/she/it/we/they **didn't use to live** here.
Question	**Did** I/you/he/she/it/we/they **use to live** here?
Short answers	Yes, I/you/he/she/it/we/they **did**.
	No, I/you/he/she/it/we/they **didn't**.

PRACTICE

34a **Complete the sentences. Use *used to* and the verbs in brackets.**

0 He ......*used to play*...... football every week when he was young. (play)

1 She .... a vegetarian, but now she eats meat. (be)

2 They .... in a flat, but now they live in a house. (live)

3 I .... about money, but now I do. (not worry)

4 We .... to school by bus when we were children. (go)

5 She .... long hair when she was a child. (not have)

34b **Write questions. Use *used to*.**

0 where / you / live? ....*Where did you use to live?*............................

1 he / go / swimming every week? ....

2 they / have / a smaller car? ....

3 what / she / do / for a living? ....

4 you / do / sports at school? ....

5 it / be / more expensive to fly? ....

34c **Complete the conversation. Use *used to* and the verbs in brackets.**

A: What was your childhood like?

B: Quiet. I (0) ......*used to live*...... (live) in a very small village.

A: What (1) .... (you / do) in your free time?

B: Well, I (2) .... (like) listening to music in my room. I wasn't very sociable. I (3) .... (not have) many friends.

A: (4) .... (you / go) to concerts to hear other violinists play?

B: No, I didn't. My parents (5) .... (not give) me much pocket money, so I couldn't afford to go.

A: And (6) .... (your parents / come) to see you when you started playing in concerts yourself?

B: Yes, they (7) .... (come) often, but now they're too old.

34d **Complete the sentences. Use *used to* or the past simple of the verbs in brackets. Use *used to* whenever possible.**

0 We ......*went*...... to Turkey for our holiday last year. (go)

1 We .... in a band when we were kids. (play)

2 I .... any housework yesterday. (not do)

3 She .... as a waitress before she .... famous. (work, become)

4 They .... a lot of sweets when they were children. (not eat)

5 He .... a lot to do yesterday. (not have)

6 It .... a lot last week. (rain)

Check 7 Past tenses

1 Complete the conversation. Use the words in the box.

did did didn't wasn't were

A: (1) .... you going to the cinema when I saw you last night?

B: No, I (2) .... , actually. I was on my way to a concert.

A: What group (3) .... you see?

B: It was an orchestra.

A: Classical music?

B: Yes. I (4) .... use to like it, but I love it now.

A: So what (5) .... you hear?

B: Beethoven's seventh symphony and *Leonora 1* and *3*.

A: Right. I'm not sure I know those.

/ 5

2 Circle the correct answer.

6 I didn't hear the doorbell because I *listened* / *was listening* to music.

7 Did you have a big party *while* / *when* school finished for the summer?

8 My father *didn't go* / *wasn't going* to university. He left school at fourteen.

9 They *went* / *used to go* travelling for a year before they started university.

10 *While* / *When* she had the idea for her first novel, she was teaching in Turkey.

/ 5

3 Complete the sentences. Use the past simple or past continuous of the verbs in brackets.

11 I .... French for five years, but I don't remember it now. (study)

12 I .... while I was talking to you on the phone earlier! (drive)

13 He .... his leg last year in a skiing accident. (break)

14 I .... your e-mail because it arrived very late. (not read)

15 Where .... at about five o'clock? I thought I saw you at the station. (you / go)

/ 5

4 Circle the correct answer.

Some of my best childhood memories come from when I lived in the north of England. It was very cold in winter and it often (16) *use to* / *used to* snow. I remember one day it (17) *used to snow* / *was snowing* very hard when my brother and I got up. We (18) *went* / *were going* to the bus stop, but there weren't any buses, so we couldn't go to school. Later on, one of my classmates (19) *phoned* / *used to phone* me and we spent the morning playing outside. Suddenly, a man came skiing down the hill and almost (20) *knocked* / *was knocking* me over. That was the funniest moment of the day.

/ 5

Total: / 20

✓ Self-check

Wrong answers	Look again at	Try CD-ROM
11, 20	Unit 30	Exercise 30
3, 5, 8, 13, 14, 18	Unit 31	Exercise 31
12, 15	Unit 32	Exercise 32
1, 2, 6, 7, 10, 17	Unit 33	Exercise 33
4, 9, 16, 19	Unit 34	Exercise 34

Now do **Check 7**

Perfect tenses

35 Present perfect: form and use

- We use the present perfect to talk about an action that happened in the past and has a result in the present: *I've forgotten* her name. (I can't remember it now.) *He hasn't washed* the car. (It isn't clean now.) *I've lost* my phone. (I can't find it now.) *They haven't finished* lunch. (They're eating now.) *Has Linda tidied* her room? (Is her room tidy now?)

- To form the present perfect, we use *has/have* + past participle:

Affirmative	I/you/we/they**'ve eaten**	he/she/it**'s eaten**
Negative	I/you/we/they **haven't eaten**	he/she/it **hasn't eaten**
Question	**Have** I/you/we/they **eaten?**	**Has** he/she/it **eaten?**
Short answers	Yes, I/you/we/they **have.**	Yes, he/she/it **has.**
	No, I/you/we/they **haven't.**	No, he/she/it **hasn't.**

- To form the past participle of regular verbs, we add *-ed* to the verb: *play → played* *live → lived*

▶▶ **See Appendix 6: Spelling rules for verbs + -ed, page 171.**

▶▶ **See Appendix 11: Irregular verbs, pages 172–173.**

PRACTICE

35a Complete the sentences. Use the present perfect of the verbs in brackets.

0 I'm sorry we can't change these shoes. You ......**'ve worn**...... them. (wear)

1 Peter .... to take his wallet with him. It's on the table. (forget)

2 They .... all their exams. They have two more tomorrow. (not do)

3 Sarah's feeling a bit lonely. Her best friend .... to France. (move)

4 I don't know if Rob's coming. He .... to my invitation. (not reply)

5 The neighbours .... our ladder. I hope they return it soon. (borrow)

6 I think I .... my umbrella at work. I can't find it anywhere. (leave)

7 You can't go to the bank. It .... raining. (not stop)

8 Dinner's ready. I .... some lasagne. (make)

35b Complete the questions. Use the present perfect of the verbs in the box.

arrive	buy	~~drink~~	hurt	plan	start	try

0 ....*Have*.......... we ....*drunk*.......... all the milk? This bottle's empty.

1 .... you .... a present for Ken? It's his birthday next week.

2 Why can't your brother write? .... he .... his hand?

3 .... your parents .... their holiday?

4 .... you .... the new vegetarian restaurant?

5 .... your sister .... her new job?

6 .... Kate .... at your house?

35c Complete the short answers. Match them with the questions in 35b.

a Yes, she .... She's in the kitchen. ☐

b No, I .... I don't know what he wants. ☐

c Yes, they .... They're going to Hawaii. ☐

d No, we ....*haven't*........ . There's some in the fridge. ☐ 0

e Yes, he .... He was playing basketball when he fell. ☐

f No, we .... , but we want to go next weekend. ☐

g No, she .... Tomorrow's her first day. ☐

35d Complete the conversation. Use the present perfect of the verbs in brackets.

A: How's your new flat? Is it ready for you to move in?

B: No, but it's nearly finished. We (0) ....*'ve managed*.......... (manage) to do the most important things.

A: What (1) .... (you / do)?

B: Well, we (2) .... (clean) everything and Steve (3) .... (paint) the living room. He (4) .... (not finish) the bedroom, but I (5) .... (make) some new curtains for it.

A: (6) .... (Steve / repair) the shower?

B: Yes, he says it's OK now. But I (7) .... (not have) the chance to try it.

A: (8) .... (you / buy) any furniture?

B: No, but our parents (9) .... (give) us a table, some chairs and a sofa. And Steve (10) .... (put up) some shelves.

A: It sounds really nice!

36 Present perfect with *just, already, yet*

- We often use *just, already* and *yet* with the present perfect.
- *Just* means 'a very short time ago': *It's just stopped* raining. (It stopped raining a short time ago.)
- *Already* means 'before now' or 'before we expected': *I don't need to wash the car. I've already done it.* (I did it before now.) *Tom's already gone* to bed. (He went to bed before I expected.)
- *Yet* means 'up to now'.
  - We use *yet* with a negative verb to say that something has not happened, but we think it will: *The train hasn't arrived yet.*
  - We also use *yet* in questions: *Have you done your homework yet?*

⚠ *Already* and *just* come after *have/has*. *Yet* comes at the end of a sentence or question.

P R A C T I C E

36a Complete the answers. Use *just* and the present perfect of the verbs in brackets.

0 A: You look happy. What's up?   B: I .....*'ve just passed*..... my driving test. (pass)

1 A: I like your sunglasses.   B: Thanks. I .... them. (buy)

2 A: Jon looks upset. Why?   B: He .... some bad news. (hear)

3 A: Where are Ann and Sam?   B: They .... (leave)

4 A: What's the matter?   B: Someone .... my mobile. (steal)

5 A: Would you like a coffee?   B: No, thanks. I .... one. (have)

6 A: Have they painted the house?   B: No, they .... (start)

36b Write sentences. Use *already* or *yet* and the present perfect.

0 I / wash / the kitchen floor
   I've already washed the kitchen floor.
   ....

1 Sarah and Jane / not do / the washing up
   ....

2 Mark / take out / the rubbish?
   ....

3 Paul / tidy / the living room
   ....

4 Martin and Bill / put / the furniture back?
   ....

5 Sue / not throw away / the old magazines
   ....

6 you / tidy / the CDs?
   ....

36c Complete the e-mail. Use the words in brackets and the present perfect.

○○○   New Message   ▭

Hi, Sam!

How are you? We (0) ......*'ve just arrived*...... (just / arrive) in Venice and everything's perfect. We (1) .... (not unpack / our suitcases / yet), but Pat (2) .... (already / meet) some people and is having a coffee with them. I saw this Internet café, so I decided to write to you. I (3) .... (just / send) a message to mum and dad too.

We (4) .... (not visit / St Mark's Square / yet), but we (5) .... (already / see) a lot of gondolas. Anyway, I hope everything's OK with you. (6) .... (you / book / your holiday / yet)?

Speak soon, Tina

37   Present perfect with *ever, never*

- We can use the present perfect to talk about experiences in our lives up to now: *I've flown in a helicopter. She hasn't eaten Chinese food.*
- We often use *ever* and *never* when we talk about experiences.
  - We use *never* in statements: *We've never been to New York.*
  - We use *ever* in questions to mean 'at any time': *Have you ever ridden a horse?*

 Ever and *never* come between *has/have* and the past participle.

- We use *This is/It's the first time* with the present perfect: ***This is the first time** I've been late for class.*

- We can also use *before*: *I **haven't been** late for class **before**.*

 The verb *go* has two past participles: ***gone*** and ***been***. Compare:

*He's **gone** to Paris.*
(He's in Paris now.)

*He's **been** to Paris.*
(He went to Paris and returned.)

PRACTICE

37a **Write sentences and questions. Use *ever* or *never* and the present perfect.**

0 she / win / a competition?   *Has she ever won a competition?* ....

1 he / write / a poem   ....

2 they / hear / a podcast?   ....

3 she / break / a bone   ....

4 you / find / money / in the street?   ....

5 I / speak / in public   ....

6 they / stay / in a five-star hotel   ....

7 he / eat / octopus?   ....

8 we / see / the sea   ....

9 she / visit / an Asian country?   ....

10 you / meet / anyone famous?   ....

37b **Complete the answers. Use *been* or *gone*.**

0 **A:** You're really brown.   **B:** Yes, I've ......*been*...... on holiday.

1 **A:** Where's Karen?   **B:** She's .... to the supermarket.

2 **A:** Are your parents on holiday?   **B:** Yes, they've .... to Portugal.

3 **A:** Why are you so late?   **B:** I've .... to the bank.

4 **A:** Let's go to Spain this year!   **B:** OK. We haven't .... there before.

5 **A:** Does Steve know France well?   **B:** Yes, he's .... there six times.

6 **A:** Where are Sue and Tom?   **B:** They were here earlier, but they've ....

37c **Complete the conversation. Use the present perfect of the verbs in brackets.**

A: Hi. Are you going to the Paul Wells concert on Saturday night?

B: I don't know. I (0) ....*'ve never heard*.......... (never / hear) of him.

A: He's great.

B: (1) .... (you / see) him in concert before?

A: No, I (2) .... This is the first time that he (3) ....
(play) here. He (4) .... (not tour) much, but my sister
(5) .... (see) him and she says he's really good.

B: Where's he playing?

A: At the Dome. (6) .... (you / ever / go) to a concert there?

B: No, why?

A: Well, it's quite small, so you get a really good view of the stage. Look, I
(7) .... (buy) his new CD. I (8) ....
(not hear) it yet. Would you like to go to my place to listen to it?

B: OK. Great.

38 Present perfect with *for, since*

- We use the present perfect + *for/since* to talk about an action or state that started in the past and continues in the present: *I've lived* here for six years. We **haven't seen** Paul since Friday.
- We use *for* + period of time to say how long something has continued: **for** an hour   **for** two days   **for** a year
- We use *since* + point in time to say when something began: **since** nine o'clock **since** Monday   **since** 2003   **since** I saw her
- We often use *How long* in questions: **How long** have you lived here?

⚠ If the action is finished, we use the past simple. Compare: *I've lived* here for six years. (I live here now.) *I lived* here for six years. (I don't live here now.)

P R A C T I C E

38a Write sentences. Use *for* or *since* and the present perfect.

0 we / have / our new car / last April
We've had our new car since last April.

1 they / not watch / television / two weeks

....

2 Chris / live / here / he was a child

....

3 I / not read / a newspaper / Monday

....

4 it / not rain / months

....

5 I / know / Sam / three years

....

6 Sarah / be married / ten months

....

38b Write questions. Use the present perfect.

0 how long / you / have / that watch?   *How long have you had that watch?*

1 how long / Chris / know / Nora?   ....

2 how long / you / like / football?   ....

3 how long / they / own / a shop?   ....

4 how long / she / live / in her flat?   ....

5 how long / the children / be / asleep?   ....

6 how long / Tom / have / his guitar?   ....

**38c Complete the second sentence so that it means the same as the first.
Use no more than three words.**

0 He became interested in learning the guitar last year.
He's wanted to learn the guitar ....*since*.............. last year.

1 I bought my watch two months ago.
I've had my watch .... two months.

2 She met her best friend when she was six.
She's known her best friend .... six.

3 I liked football when I was young and I still like it.
I .... football since I was young.

4 They bought their cottage in 2003.
They've owned their cottage .... 2003.

5 He started living in his flat three years ago.
He .... in his flat for three years.

6 The children went to sleep an hour ago.
The children have been asleep .... an hour.

7 I first met Beth and Gary ten years ago.
I've known Beth and Gary .... years.

8 We started working here when we left college.
We .... here since we left college.

39 Present and past simple, present perfect

- We use the present perfect, not the present simple, to talk about actions or states that started in the past and continue to the present: *I've known her for three years.* (Not *I know her for three years.*)

- We use the present perfect, not the past simple, to talk about:
  - actions or events that happened or started in the past and have a result in the present: *He's done the washing up. They've cut the grass.*
  - actions or events that happened at an indefinite time in the past, especially if we are not interested in when they happened: *I've been to China. She's read a lot of books.*

- We use the past simple, not the present perfect:
  - to talk about actions that finished in the past. Compare: *She lived in London.* (She doesn't live in London now.) *She's lived in London for five years.* (She lives in London now.)
  - if we say or know when an action or event happened in the past. Compare: *He bought a new bike last weekend. He's bought a new bike, so he's very excited.*

PRACTICE

39a Complete the article. Use the present simple or the present perfect of the verbs in brackets.

One of the people I admire most (0) ....*is*.......... (be) my grandfather. He was born in a small village and he (1) .... (live) there all his life. He (2) .... (never / travel) to another country, but he (3) .... (know) a lot about the world because he (4) .... (read) the newspaper every day. He (5) .... (be) a farmer since he was fourteen and he still (6) .... (get up) early and (7) .... (go) to work in the fields. He's 75 now, but he (8) .... (not want) to retire. I (9) .... (visit) my grandfather every summer since I was a child and I always (10) .... (look forward) to seeing him. He (11) .... (tell) incredible stories. He's the most interesting person I (12) .... (ever / meet).

39b Circle the correct answer.

A: (0) (*Have you ever been*) / *Did you ever go* to France?

B: Yes, we (1) *have / did*. We (2) *'ve been / went* there four times. The last time (3) *has been / was* two years ago.

A: How many times (4) *have you visited / did you visit* Paris?

B: Only once. We (5) *'ve been / went* there in 2004.

A: And (6) *have you travelled / did you travel* much outside Europe?

B: Well, no, we (7) *haven't / didn't*, but we (8) *'ve had / had* holidays in Australia.

A: When (9) *have you been / did you go* to Australia?

B: We (10) *'ve been / were* there for the Olympic Games in 2000.

39c Complete the article. Use the present simple, past simple or present perfect of the verbs in brackets.

What (0) ....*is*.......... (be) a blog? A blog (1) .... (be) a personal webpage and sometimes a journal. Blogging (2) .... (begin) in 1994 when a student, Justin Hall, (3) .... (start) a personal blog on the Internet. He (4) .... (keep) his blog for eleven years. The word 'blog' (5) .... (appear) for the first time in 1999 and the Oxford English Dictionary (6) .... (include) the word in its pages in 2003.

Blogging (7) .... (change) since the early days. Between 2000 and 2004, it (8) .... (become) a favourite activity for teenagers. Since 2004, more and more adults (9) .... (start) blogs too. And now, people (10) .... (write) about all sorts of things, including politics and television.

Check 8 Present perfect

1 Complete the sentences. Use the words in the box. You do not need them all.

already ever for just never since yet

1 Have you heard the good news? They've .... won first prize.

2 Kate's .... eaten Indian food, but she wants to try it.

3 My brother's got a new car, but he hasn't passed his driving test ....

4 We don't need to go to the market again. We've .... been there today.

5 I can't remember his name because I haven't seen him .... years.

/ 5

2 Write questions. Use the present perfect.

6 how long / he / live / in France?

....

7 Your hair's wet. where / you / be?

....

8 they / arrive / yet?

....

9 you / ever / write / a short story?

....

10 Alison / tidy / her room?

....

/ 5

3 Complete the second sentence so that it means the same as the first. Use no more than three words.

11 This is the first time I've been to another country.

I .... to another country before.

12 We bought our tickets six months ago.

We've had our tickets .... six months.

13 My friends visited Italy in 2001, 2004 and 2006.

My friends .... to Italy three times.

14 Jane hasn't flown before.

It's .... Jane has flown.

15 We're waiting for the taxi to arrive.

The taxi .... yet.

/ 5

4 Circle the correct answer.

The London Eye is one of London's most famous sights. It (16) *opens / has opened / opened* to the public in December 1999 and (17) *for / since / yet* then, millions of people have enjoyed a ride on the wheel. The ride lasts about 30 minutes. The wheel (18) *doesn't stop / hasn't stopped / didn't stop*; it moves so slowly that passengers can get on and off while it is in motion.

The London Eye isn't the first big wheel in the city's history. There (19) *is / has been / was* a smaller wheel in London in the nineteenth century. But the London Eye is now a symbol of the city and it (20) *appear / has appeared / appeared* in many films and television programmes.

/ 5

Total: / 20

Self-check

Wrong answers	Look again at	Try CD-ROM
7, 10	Unit 35	Exercise 35
1, 3, 4, 8, 15	Unit 36	Exercise 36
2, 9, 11, 13, 14	Unit 37	Exercise 37
5, 6, 12, 17	Unit 38	Exercise 38
16, 18, 19, 20	Unit 39	Exercise 39

Now do **Check 8**

40 Past perfect simple

- We use the past perfect simple to talk about an action that happened before a particular time in the past: *By ten o'clock this morning, I'd had three cups of coffee.*

```
                                    10.00                      Now
-----------------------------------|---------------------------------|
      ⇧         ⇧         ⇧
```
I had three cups of coffee.

- We often use the past perfect:
  - with *before*, *earlier* and *by* + time reference: *I **had met** him **before**. The guests **had left by eleven o'clock**.*
  - with *because*: *He was tired **because** he **hadn't slept** well.*
  - with *just*, *already*, *yet*, *ever* and *never*. *Just*, *already*, *ever* and *never* come after *had*. *Yet* usually comes at the end of the sentence: *The kids **had already seen** the film. I wanted to go home, but I **hadn't finished** my work **yet**.*

- To form the past perfect simple, we use *had* (*'d*)/*hadn't* + past participle:

Affirmative	I/you/he/she/it/we/they **had finished**
Negative	I/you/he/she/it/we/they **hadn't finished**
Question	**Had** I/you/he/she/it/we/they **finished**?
Short answers	Yes, I/you/he/she/it/we/they **had.**
	No, I/you/he/she/it/we/they **hadn't.**

▶▶ *See Appendix 11: Irregular verbs, pages 172–173.*

PRACTICE

40a Complete the sentences. Use the past perfect of the verbs in brackets.

0 We decided to stay at home because it ....*had started*........ to rain. (start)

1 Your interview went badly because you .... for it. (not prepare)

2 She didn't buy a new dress because she .... all her money. (spend)

3 I couldn't get on the flight because I .... a ticket. (not book)

4 We weren't hungry because we .... a big lunch. (have)

5 He was excited because he .... a horse before. (not ride)

6 All the plates were dirty because nobody .... (wash up)

7 I went to see the film because a friend .... me about it. (tell)

8 She didn't know his name because she .... him before. (not meet)

40b Complete the article. Use the past perfect of the verbs in brackets.

The Swedish tennis star Björn Borg was one of the greatest tennis players of all time. He started playing at the age of nine, when his father gave him his first racket.

Before that, Björn (0) ....*had played*........ (play) hockey and football. By the age of fourteen, he (1) .... (leave) school to dedicate all his time to tennis.

Sweden (2) .... (never / have) a tennis champion before, but by his twentieth birthday, Borg (3) .... (already / won) two French Open Championships and he (4) .... (beat) tennis legends Manuel Orantes and Guillermo Vilas to win them. When he first won Wimbledon in 1976, people were surprised because he (5) .... (not do) well on grass before, but he went on to win another four times. By the age of 26, he (6) .... (also / collect) six French Open titles.

40c Complete the conversations. Use the past perfect of the verbs in brackets.

A: We had a wonderful time in Tunisia.
B: That's great! (0) ...*Had the kids been*... (the kids / be) abroad before?
B: Yes, they (1) .... But they (2) .... (never / be) on a plane.
A: Did you go there because someone (3) .... (recommend) it?
B: No, but we (4) .... (read) a lot of good things about it.

A: Ray loved the computer game we gave him for his birthday.
B: That's good. (5) .... (he / ever / play) it before?
B: No, he (6) .... He (7) .... (never / hear) of it.
A: And did David go to the party in the end?
B: Yes. He and Ray (8) .... (not see) each other for five years!

41 Past perfect and past simple

- We use the past perfect to show that one action or event happened before another action or event in the past. We use the past perfect for the action that happened first and the past simple for the action that happened later: *When we **arrived**, the film **had** already **started**.*

```
--------------------------|------------|
       ⇧                       ⇧          Now
  The film started.        We arrived.
```

- We often use *when* and *by the time* with the past simple to talk about the second of two actions or events in the past. Notice when we use a comma (,): ***When** we got to the airport, the plane **had** already **taken off**. The plane **had** already **taken off when** we **got** to the airport.*

PRACTICE

41a **Which action happened first? Write a sentence. Use the past simple.**

0 When I left home, it had already started to rain.   *First it started to rain.*

1 The train had left by the time he got to the station.   ....

2 When we put on the TV, the film had finished.   ....

3 I'd just turned off my phone when you called me.   ....

4 By the time they got to the restaurant, it had closed.   ....

5 They had sold all the tickets by the time we arrived.   ....

41b **Write sentences. Use the past perfect and the past simple.**

0 when / you / arrive / Peter / just / go / home
   When you arrived, Peter had just gone home.

1 when / we / see / them / they / not finish / decorating their house
   ....

2 Lou / already / try on / ten suits / when / he / buy / the white one
   ....

3 when / I / go / to Argentina / I / never / fly / before
   ....

4 he / already / write / his first novel / by the time / he / be / twenty-two
   ....

5 when / Kelly / join / the army / she / not have / a job / before
   ....

6 they / already / find / work / by the time / they / finish / university
   ....

41c **Complete the story. Use the past perfect or past simple of the verbs in brackets.**

I (0) .... *was* .... (be) at a friend's party on Saturday when something really funny (1) .... (happen). When I (2) .... (arrive), the party (3) .... (not start) yet and my friend was in the kitchen preparing the food. He (4) .... (introduce) me to a woman I (5) .... (not know). But when we (6) .... (start) talking, we realised that we (7) .... (meet) before. We (8) .... (compare) things we (9) .... (do) in the past, but couldn't find a connection. Then I (10) .... (remember). She (11) .... (be) my sister's pen friend and she (12) .... (come) to stay with us for a week one summer.

Check 9 Past and perfect tenses

1 Write sentences. Use the past perfect and past simple.

1 I / never / be / to a wedding / before

....

2 we / arrive / late / because / we / not bring / the address / with us

....

3 the ceremony / already / begin / by the time / we / get / there

....

4 the groom / look / nervous / because / he / forgot / the ring

....

5 by the time / the wedding / be over / it / start / to rain

....

/ 5

2 Complete the conversation. Use the past perfect of the verbs in brackets.

A: Harry failed his driving test last week.

B: That's a pity! (6) .... (he / take) it before?

A: Oh, yes! He (7) .... (already / fail) it twice.

B: Is that because he (8) .... (not practise) enough?

A: No! By the time he took the test this time, he (9) .... (have) about forty lessons.

B: So why did he fail?

A: He says he (10) .... (just / break up) with his girlfriend and couldn't concentrate.

/ 5

3 Circle the correct answer.

"My parents bought our first television when I was ten, but we still (11) *spent / had spent* more time listening to the radio, playing games and talking.

At that time we (12) *never saw / 'd never seen* a colour TV and they certainly (13) *didn' t invent / hadn' t invented* the video recorder yet. By the time I (14) *was / had been* eighteen, my parents (15) *bought / had bought* a big colour TV. It was on all day and we'd practically stopped talking to each other!"

/ 5

4 Re-write the sentences. Use the past perfect.

16 Pele won three World Cups before he retired.
By the time Pele retired, he ....
....

17 First we spoke on the phone and then I read your e-mail.
When we spoke on the phone, I ....
....

18 She did all her homework between six and eight.
By eight, she ....
....

19 They got married just after Kim left university.
When they got married, ...
....

20 The book sold a million copies in 2006.
By the end of 2006, the book ....
....

/ 5

Total: / 20

Future forms

42 *be going to* and *will*

- We use *be going to* and *will* to make predictions.
  - We use *be going to* to talk about something we expect to happen because of evidence we have now: *Look at that blue sky. It's going to be hot today.*
  - We use *will* to talk about something that we think, believe or know will happen in the future: *I think computers will do everything for us in the future.*
- We use *be going to* and *will* to talk about future actions.
  - We use *be going to* if we are talking about things that we have already decided or planned to do: *'What are you going to do tonight?' 'I'm going to stay at home.'*
  - We use *will* to talk about decisions that we make at the moment of speaking: *'Tea or coffee?' 'I'll have tea, please.'*
- The form of *be going to* is: *am/are/is + (not) going to* + infinitive.
- The form of *will* is: *will/won't* + infinitive without *to*.

PRACTICE

42a Circle the correct answer.

0 Look at those black clouds. It *'ll* / *('s going to)* rain.

1 I'm tired now, but I'm sure I *'ll* / *'m going to* feel better in the morning.

2 The plane's moving. It *'ll* / *'s going to* take off very soon.

3 Have you seen Mrs Green? She *'ll* / *'s going to* have a baby.

4 Do you think we *'ll* / *'re going to* have a woman president one day?

5 Liverpool *will* / *are going to* win. The score's 3–0 and there are only two minutes left.

6 In my opinion, people *won't* / *aren't going to* work at all in the future.

42b Complete the conversations. Use *be going to* or *will* and the verbs in brackets.

0 A: What would you like to eat?
B: I can't decide. I think I ....'ll have........ (have) a pasta dish.

1 A: I .... (take) the dog for a walk in a few minutes.
B: We .... (come) with you. We need some fresh air.

2 A: .... (Felix / look for) a job?
B: Yes, but I don't think he .... (find) one easily.

3 A: David .... (make) some tea. Does anyone else want a cup?
B: No, I .... (not have) anything to drink, thanks.

4 A: Hi, Jean. We're stuck in traffic, so we .... (arrive) a bit late.
B: Don't worry. We .... (not start) dinner until you get here.

5 A: I spoke to Paul earlier. He .... (not go) to the party.
B: Really? In that case, I .... (not go) either.

43 Present continuous or *be going to*

- We use the present continuous with a time expression like *tonight*, *this weekend* and *at eight o'clock* to talk about things that we have planned and arranged to do in the future: *I'm meeting Frank at eight o'clock on Thursday.* (We have already arranged our meeting.)

- We use *be going to* to talk about things that we plan to do in the future, but have not yet arranged to do: *We're going to buy a new car soon.* (We don't know when yet.)

▶▶ *For the form of the present continuous, see Unit 27.*

P R A C T I C E

43a **Circle the correct answer.**

A: I'm (0) *stopping* / *going to stop* smoking. And this time I'm not (1) *starting* / *going to start* again.

B: That's good news. Are you (2) *getting* / *going to get* some help?

A: Oh yes. In fact, I'm (3) *seeing* / *going to see* Dr Stevens at four o'clock today and I'm (4) *doing* / *going to do* exactly what he tells me.

———————————————

A: Helen's (5) *coming* / *going to come* round at seven to have dinner with us.

B: I'm not (6) *being* / *going to be* here. I'm (7) *going* / *going to go* to the theatre tonight, remember?

A: Oh no. I totally forgot. What time are you (8) *coming* / *going to come* home?

43b **Re-write the sentences. Use the present continuous or *be going to* form of the verbs in brackets.**

0 I've arranged to have dinner with Toni tonight.
   I ....*'m having*........ dinner with Toni tonight. (have)

1 We've decided to travel around the world before university. (travel)
   We .... around the world before university.

2 What have you arranged to do this weekend? (do)
   What .... this weekend?

3 He's decided to study Russian next year. (study)
   He .... Russian next year.

4 My driving test is on Monday morning. (take)
   I .... my driving test on Monday morning.

5 My parents have decided to live in Spain when they retire. (live)
   My parents .... in Spain when they retire.

6 She's arranged to drive Lucy to the station at five o'clock. (drive)
   She .... Lucy to the station at five o'clock.

44 Present simple and continuous for future

- We can use the present simple to talk about future events that are part of a timetable or programme: *Our flight **leaves** at 7.45. What time **does** the concert **start**?*
- We use the present continuous, not the present simple, to talk about fixed arrangements in the future: *We're **having** dinner with Toni tonight.* (Not *We have dinner with Toni tonight.*)

▶▶ *For the form of the present simple, see Unit 26.*

PRACTICE

44a Circle the correct answer.

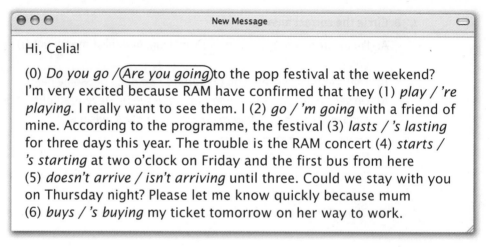

Hi, Celia!

(0) *Do you go /* (*Are you going*) to the pop festival at the weekend? I'm very excited because RAM have confirmed that they (1) *play / 're playing*. I really want to see them. I (2) *go / 'm going* with a friend of mine. According to the programme, the festival (3) *lasts / 's lasting* for three days this year. The trouble is the RAM concert (4) *starts / 's starting* at two o'clock on Friday and the first bus from here (5) *doesn't arrive / isn't arriving* until three. Could we stay with you on Thursday night? Please let me know quickly because mum (6) *buys / 's buying* my ticket tomorrow on her way to work.

44b Complete the conversation. Use the present simple or present continuous of the verbs in the box.

> be   do   film   finish   fly   leave   meet   not do   start

A: Hi, Jo. This is David. Do you want to meet for lunch today?

B: I can't. I have an audition this afternoon. They (0) ....*'re filming*............ a scene for a TV series in town next week and they need extras.

A: Wow! And what time (1) .... the audition?

B: It (2) .... at twelve o'clock, but I don't know exactly when it (3) ....

A: Well, (4) .... you .... anything tonight?

B: I (5) .... some friends tonight, actually.

A: What about tomorrow?

B: I (6) .... to Munich tomorrow. Don't you remember?

A: Of course. What time (7) .... your flight .... ?

B: At two. But I (8) .... anything in the morning. You could help me pack my bags!

Check 10 Future forms

1 Circle the correct answer.

```
 ● ● ●              New Message              ⬭

 Hi, there!

 Just a quick e-mail to say that we're OK
 and that our trip round France has gone
 really well. Tomorrow we (1) 'll take /
 're taking / take the train to Paris. I've
 decided that I (2) 'll visit / 'm going to
 visit / 'm visiting the Louvre when we're
 there, but Jane isn't interested in art,
 so I suppose she (3) 'll do / 's doing /
 does something different. Our train back
 home (4) will leave / is going to leave /
 leaves early on Sunday morning and
 (5) will get / is getting / gets to
 Portsmouth at 14.50. What (6) will
 you do / are you doing / do you do on
 Sunday afternoon? The weather forecast
 on the Internet says it (7) 's raining / 's
 going to rain / rains on Sunday, so
 could you come and meet us? If not,
 don't worry. We (8) 'll walk / 're walking /
 walk home or get a taxi.
```

/ 8

2 Complete the second sentence so that it means the same as the first. Use no more than three words.

9 Gerry has decided to buy a computer on Friday.
Gerry is .... buy a computer on Friday.

10 He has arranged to meet his friend Duncan in front of the shop at five.
He is .... his friend Duncan in front of the shop at five.

11 Duncan thinks it is impossible to find a good computer for less than £400.
Duncan thinks they .... a good computer for less than £400.

12 The boys have arranged to go to the cinema later on.
The boys .... to the cinema later on.

13 They have decided to get tickets for the new comedy.
They .... get tickets for the new comedy.

/ 5

3 Complete the questions. Use the words in brackets.

14 .... their trip to India? What do you think? (they / enjoy)

15 What time .... this afternoon? (the shop / open)

16 What .... at six on Sunday? Please come to our barbecue. (you / do)

17 A: What .... her baby? (Georgina / call)
B: She hasn't decided yet.

18 In your opinion, ... holidays in space one day? (ordinary people / have)

19 What .... at university? Have you decided? (you / study)

20 .... anywhere this weekend? We'd like to see them. (Moira's group / play)

/ 7

Total: / 20

✔ Self-check

Wrong answers	Look again at	Try CD-ROM
2, 3, 7, 8, 9, 11, 13, 14, 17, 18, 19	Unit 42	Exercise 42
6, 10, 12, 16, 20	Unit 43	Exercise 43
1, 4, 5, 15	Unit 44	Exercise 44

Now do **Check 10**

Modal verbs

REMEMBER!

- The modal verbs are: *can, could, may, might, will, would, shall, should, must.*
- We use a modal verb with a main verb to express ability, obligation etc.
- We use the infinitive without *to* after modal verbs: *I **can speak** English.* (Not *I can to speak English.*)
- Modal verbs do not add *-s* after *he/she/it*: *He **can** drive.* (Not *He cans drive.*)
- In negative sentences and questions, the auxiliary *do/does* is not necessary: ***Could** you **open** the window?* (Not *Do you could open the window?*) *You **mustn't be** so careless.* (Not *You don't must be so careless.*)
- Modal verbs do not have tense forms. We use other verbs instead: *I **wasn't able to go** to the party. We **had to get up** early.*
- These verbs and expressions have similar meanings to modal verbs: *be able to, have to, need to, be allowed to, ought to.*

45 Ability and possibility: *can, could, be able to*

- We use *can* to talk about ability and possibility in the present: *I **can** swim. He **can't** drive. **Can** we **buy** stamps here?*
- *Be able to* has a similar meaning to *can*, but it is not as common: *I'm sorry, I'm **not able to** take your call right now.*
- We use *could* or *was/were able to* to talk about general ability and possibility in the past: *She **could/was able to** read by the age of four.*
- For a single action that was completed successfully, we use *was/were able to*, not *could*: ***Were** you **able to** buy a ticket for the concert?* (Not *Could you buy a ticket for the concert?*)
- We use *couldn't* and *wasn't/weren't able to* for both general situations and single actions: *We **couldn't/weren't able to** phone you yesterday.*

PRACTICE

45a **Re-write the sentences. Use *be able to.***

0	Tara can make paper birds.	*Tara is able to make paper birds.*
1	Bob couldn't read until he was six.	....
2	We can see the sea from our window.	....
3	Not many people can drive a bus.	....
4	We could speak to them in English.	....
5	They couldn't dance or sing.	....
6	I couldn't understand the film.	....

45b **Cross out one of the answers if it is incorrect.**

o United ~~could~~ / *were able to* win the match in extra time. The score was 3–2.

1 The shop *could* / *was able to* repair my computer, but it was expensive.

2 After several years in Spain, Gary *could* / *was able to* speak Spanish fluently.

3 *Could you* / *Were you able to* create web pages after the computer course?

4 I failed my first driving test, but I *could* / *was able to* pass the second time.

5 Jessie *couldn't* / *wasn't able to* cook until she was an adult.

6 We *couldn't* / *weren't able to* ski yesterday because it was snowing heavily.

45c **Re-write the sentences. Use the words in brackets.**

o I didn't know how to dance, so I decided to take lessons. (could)
I decided to take lessons because I .... *couldn't dance* ....

1 Luckily, I managed to find classes near my house. (able)
Luckily, I .... classes near my house.

2 At first, I was nervous and it was impossible for me to do what the teacher said. (could)
At first, I was nervous, so I .... what the teacher said.

3 Now, I'm still not a fantastic dancer, but I enjoy it. (can't)
Now, I still .... very well, but I enjoy it.

4 And I know how to dance lots of different styles. (able)
And I .... lots of different styles.

46 Permission: *can, could, be allowed to*

- We use *can* or *am/is/are allowed to* to talk about things we have permission to do: *All students **can/are allowed to** use the computers. **Can I smoke**? No, you **can't**. **Are** candidates **allowed to** use dictionaries? Yes, they are.*

- We use *could* or *was/were allowed to* to talk about permission in the past: *We **could**/ **were allowed to** wear jeans at school.* (We had permission.)

- We use *Can I ... ?* or *Could I ... ?* to ask someone for their permission. *Could* is more formal or polite: ***Can** I use your phone, Kate? **Could** I use the phone, please, Mrs Wilson?*

- To give permission, we can say: *Yes, all right/of course. Certainly.*

- To refuse permission, we can say: *No, sorry, you can't./I'm afraid not.*

- We often give a reason for refusing permission: *Can I borrow your car? No, you can't. It's at the garage.*

 We cannot use *Am I allowed to ... ?* to ask someone for their permission: ***Can we borrow** your ladder, please?* (Not ~~Are we allowed to borrow your ladder, please?~~)

P R A C T I C E

46a Complete the sentences. Use one or two words in each gap.

0   Jenny ......*couldn't*...... leave work early yesterday.

1   **A:** Are we .... to borrow three DVDs from the library?
    B: No, you .... , I'm afraid. The limit is two per person.

2   **A:** Excuse me, sir. .... we use your phone, please?
    B: I'm afraid .... It's out of order.

3   I wasn't allowed .... go to the music festival last month.

4   Dave .... borrow my bicycle if he likes, but he must return it soon.

5   .... you allowed to wear make-up when you were a child?

6   **A:** .... I open the window please? It's very hot in here.
    B: Yes, of .... You .... also open the door if you like.

7   She .... wear trousers to work at the bank, but she isn't allowed to wear jeans.

8   **A:** Excuse me, ... we book a tennis court at two o'clock, please?
    B: Sorry, you can't . They're all booked today, but you .... play tomorrow.

46b Re-write the sentences. Use the words in brackets.

0   In the past boys were allowed to do a lot more than girls. (could)
    In the past boys ....*could do*.......... a lot more than girls.

1   Are we allowed to swim in this part of the river? (can)
    .... in this part of the river?

2   The children can stay up late on Saturdays. (are)
    The children .... late on Saturdays.

3   When we were ten, we were allowed to go to the park on our own. (could)
    When we were ten, we .... to the park on our own.

4   We could take our dog on the beach in France. (to)
    We .... our dog on the beach in France.

5   Jamie is allowed to come on holiday with us this summer. (can)
    Jamie .... on holiday with us this summer.

6   Could you take photos inside the museum? (allowed)
    Were .... photos inside the museum?

7   Visitors were allowed to feed the animals at the safari park. (could)
    Visitors .... the animals at the safari park.

8   You're allowed to play on the computer if no one else needs it. (can)
    You .... on the computer if no one else needs it.

47 Possibility: *may, might, could*

- We use *may, might* or *could* to talk about actions or events that are possible now or in the future: *Pete* **may** *be in Paris now. Jill* **might** *phone me later. It* **could** *rain this afternoon.*

- We use *may not* or *might not*, but not *could not*, to say it is possible that an action or event will not happen now or in the future: *They* **may not** *come tomorrow.* (Not ~~They couldn't come tomorrow.~~) *Pete* **might not** *be there now.* (Not ~~Pete couldn't be there now.~~)

 The short form of *might not* is *mightn't. May not* does not have a short form.

PRACTICE

47a Re-write the sentences. Use the words in brackets.

0	It's possible I'll go to France. (may)	I ....*may go*.... to France.
1	Maybe they're brothers. (might)	They .... brothers.
2	Maybe you'll see Ann in town. (could)	You .... Ann in town.
3	Perhaps she doesn't have a computer. (may)	She .... a computer.
4	It's possible we won't go out tonight. (might)	We .... out tonight.
5	It's possible she doesn't want to play. (may)	She .... to play.
6	Perhaps he's at the cinema. (could)	He .... at the cinema.

47b Complete the e-mail. Use the words in the box.

~~could go~~	could meet	may not be	may work
	might ask	might do	might not have

Hi, Kathy!

Thanks for your e-mail. You asked us what our plans are for the summer. Well, Connie (0) ....*could go*........ to England to work, like she did last year. Jon says he (1) .... something different this summer. He wants to go to India, so he (2) .... for a few weeks or he (3) .... enough money. I don't want to work in the family hotel again. I'd like a change. I (4) .... my parents for the money to come to Florida, so it (5) .... long before I see you again. I (6) .... your family. What do you think? Write soon!

Esther

48 Certainty and deduction: *must, can't*

- We use *must* to say we are sure that something is true now because of what we know: *They own three cars. They **must have** a lot of money.*
- We use *can't* when we think something is impossible now because of what we know: *She **can't be** at home. There are no lights on.*

 Can't is the opposite of *must* here.

PRACTICE

48a Circle the correct answer.

o A: I thought Meena was coming.   B: She is. She *must* / *can't* be outside.

1 A: Is that Britney Spears?   B: No, it *must* / *can't* be! She's in America.

2 A: Zack has five hundred CDs.   B: Wow! He *must* / *can't* love music.

3 A: Rachel lives in France.   B: She *must* / *can't* speak French, then.

4 A: Davy isn't here today.   B: He *must* / *can't* be ill again. Poor Davy!

5 A: I've just eaten a big pizza.   B: Well, you *must* / *can't* be hungry, then.

6 A: Hurry up, it's time to go!   B: It *must* / *can't* be nine o'clock already!

48b Complete the sentences. Use *must* or *can't* and the verbs in brackets.

o A furniture van has arrived next door. Our new neighbours ....*must be*......... here. (be)

1 There's a lot of beautiful old furniture. They .... antiques. (collect)

2 There are toys in those boxes. They .... children. (have)

3 The neighbours have just arrived in a taxi. They .... a car. (own)

4 They're both over sixty, so the toys .... to their children. (belong)

5 I suppose they .... for their grandchildren. (be)

6 I don't see any animals. They .... any pets. (have)

7 I've just seen a snake! The snake .... theirs, surely? (be)

49 Requests: *can, could, would*

- We use *Can you … ? Could you … ?* and *Would you … ?* to ask somebody to do something: *Can you lend me a pen? Could you open the door, please? Would you open your books, please?*
- We use *can* in neutral or informal situations: *Can you move your chair, please?*
- We use *could* to be more polite, or when we want people to do something difficult: *Mike, could you lend me some money?*
- We often use *would* to be polite, especially when we are giving a polite order: *Would you be quiet, please?*
- We also use *would* if we are speaking from a position of authority: *Would you get on with your work, please? Would you get my lawyer on the phone for me?*

PRACTICE

49a Complete the requests. Use the verbs in the box and the words in brackets.

| bring | help | lend | pass | pay | phone | ~~sign~~ |

0 ....*Would you sign*............ your name on the dotted line, please? (would)

1 Dad, ... me the newspaper on the table? (can)

2 Alba, ... for a taxi, please? I'm very late. (would)

3 Waiter, ... us some more bread, please? (could)

4 Danny, ... me find my coat? I've lost it! (can)

5 .... me five pounds until the weekend, Helen? (could)

6 .... attention when I'm speaking? (would)

49b Write requests. Use *can* or *could*.

0 You need change for the ticket machine. You only have a five-pound note.
You ask: *Could you change this five-pound note for me?*..................

1 You want your friend to lend you his DVD of *Lord of the Rings* tonight.
You ask: ....

2 You want your English teacher to translate a song for you.
You ask: ....

3 You want a friend to lend you his camera for a week.
You ask: ....

4 Your neighbours are playing loud music. You want them to turn it down.
You ask: ....

5 Your computer isn't working properly. You want your brother to look at it.
You ask: ....

6 You have asked a stranger for directions, but you want him to speak more slowly.
You ask: ....

50 Offers and suggestions: *will, shall, can, could*

- We use *I/We will ...* and *Shall I/we ... ?* to offer to do something for somebody.
  - *I/We will ...* is quite informal: *We'll drive you to the station if you like.*
  - *Shall I/we ... ?* is more polite. **Shall** *I help you carry your bags?*
- We can use *shall, can* and *could* to suggest something: **Shall** *we go out? We* **can** *go and see a film. We* **could** *go to a restaurant.* (*could* = less sure)
- We can also use expressions like these to make suggestions: **Let's** *go skating.* **Why don't we** *try that new Chinese restaurant?* **How/What about** *having a picnic at the weekend if the weather's fine?* (*How/What about* = informal)

PRACTICE

50 **Re-write the sentences. Use the words in brackets.**

0 I suggest we go for a walk in the country tomorrow. (let's)
Let's go for a walk in the country tomorrow.

1 I think it's a good idea to take sandwiches with us. (can)
....

2 Do you want me to lend you a good pair of walking shoes? (shall)
....

3 I'd like to go to the Lake District. (how about)
....

4 A good way to get there is by bus. (could)
....

5 I can find out the bus times, if you like. (I'll)
....

6 I suggest we stay the weekend. (why don't we)
....

7 Do you think it's a good idea to take a tent and camp? (shall)
....

8 I'd like us to stay in a youth hostel. (what about)
....

9 Yes, I think it's a good idea to stay in the youth hostel. (let's)
....

Check 11 Modal verbs (1)

1 Complete the conversations. Use the words in the box.

can't could could I'll how shall

A: Nicky, (1) .... you look at my computer? The Internet isn't working.

B: Maybe there's a loose connection.

A: No, everything's fine. It (2) .... be that.

B: (3) .... have a look at it after supper.

_____

A: (4) .... about organising a birthday party for Tania?

B: Good idea! We (5) .... have it at my place. (6) .... I ask my flatmates?

A: Yes, that would be fantastic!

/ 6

2 Circle the correct answer.

7 I'm sorry I *'m not able to / couldn't* meet you yesterday. I was busy all day.

8 I'm looking for my address book. It *must / couldn't* be here somewhere.

9 When Steven pushed the door, he *was able to / could* open it.

10 Club members *are allowed to / would* bring a friend once a month.

11 *Could / Shall* you open the door for me, please?

12 Before she got her own car, Kali *could / can* borrow her mother's car.

/ 6

3 Re-write the sentences. Use the words in brackets.

13 Jonas could run faster than anyone else at school. (able)
Jonas .... run faster than anyone else at school.

14 When he was eleven, his parents gave him permission to join an athletics club. (allowed)
When he was eleven, he .... join an athletics club.

15 I'm certain he has a good chance of getting into the national team. (must)
He .... a good chance of getting into the national team.

16 It's possible that he'll win an Olympic medal one day. (may)
He .... an Olympic medal one day.

/ 4

4 Circle the correct answer.

With the **MX3007** digital camera you (17) *can't / will / might* go wrong! You (18) *can / are able / would* look at each photo after you've taken it. If you don't like it, just delete it. Taking the perfect photo is easy! And with a credit card you (19) *can / couldn't / shall* buy online today. The MX3007 (20) *is allowed to / could / must* be yours at the click of a mouse. Don't wait, click NOW!

/ 4

Total: / 20

Self-check

Wrong answers	Look again at	Try CD-ROM
7, 9, 13, 17, 18, 19	Unit 45	Exercise 45
10, 12, 14	Unit 46	Exercise 46
5, 16, 20	Unit 47	Exercise 47
2, 8, 15	Unit 48	Exercise 48
1, 11	Unit 49	Exercise 49
3, 4, 6	Unit 50	Exercise 50

Now do **Check 11**

51 Obligation and necessity: *must, have to, need to*

- We use *must* and *have to* to express obligation or necessity, but there is a difference in meaning.
  - We use *must* when the speaker thinks that it is necessary to do something: *I **must** go – it's late. You **must** have a haircut soon. You **must** be home by midnight.*
  - We use *have to* when an action is necessary because another person says so, or there is a rule: *You **have to** be seventeen to drive a car.* (It's the law.)
- We can also use *need to* to say that something is necessary: *I'm bad at tennis. I **need to** practise.*
- *Must* has no past form; we use *had to*: *We **had to** study philosophy at school.*
- The past of *need to* is *needed to*: *They **needed to** win the match to stay in the league.*
- To ask if something is necessary, we usually use *have to* or *need to*, not *must*. We form questions with *do/does/did*: ***Do** you **have to** help at home? **Do** we **need to** buy any food? **Did** she **need to** take a taxi?*

PRACTICE

51a Circle the correct answer.

  0   I haven't got any stamps. I (*need to*)/ *had to* go to the post office.

  1   Does Marlon *have to* / *must* wear a tie at work?

  2   Maggie *has to* / *had to* look after her baby niece yesterday.

  3   Did you *must* / *need to* buy more food, or was there enough?

  4   When you arrive at a hotel, you *have to* / *has to* register at reception.

  5   Excuse me, do new students *must* / *need to* go to the registration office?

  6   Jason *must* / *have to* stop arriving late, or he'll be in trouble!

51b Complete the sentences. Use the correct form of the words in brackets.

  0   My hair is too long. I ....*need to get*.......... a haircut. (need to / get)

  1   Her watch is broken. She .... a new one. (have to / buy)

  2   I couldn't stay in my old flat. I .... another one. (have to / find)

  3   We haven't got any food! We .... to the supermarket. (must / go)

  4   It's only six o'clock. .... we .... now? (need to / leave)

  5   Your room is dirty. You really .... it! (must / clean)

  6   Was the concert free, or .... you .... ? (have to / pay)

51c Circle the correct answer.

A: What was the hardest thing about working on breakfast TV?

B: Definitely the worst thing was that I (0) *must /(had to)/ have to* get up at four o'clock in the morning, so I (1) *must / has to / needed to* be in bed by eight at night, when all my friends were enjoying themselves.

A: Did you ever sleep late?

B: Oh, yes! Several times! The producer (2) *must / had to / need to* phone me to wake me up.

A: In your new job do you (3) *must / have to / needs to* spend a lot on clothes?

B: Yes, I (4) *must / have to / need* wear different clothes every day. It's in my contract!

A: (5) *Must / Has / Does* a TV presenter need to have any special qualifications?

B: No, not really, but in my opinion, you (6) *must / has to / need* understand how the studio works, or you'll never be really good.

52 Prohibition: *mustn't, can't, not be allowed to*

- We use *mustn't, can't* and *not allowed to* to say that something is forbidden: *You **mustn't** tell anyone; it's a secret. Sorry, you **can't** eat or drink in here. They **aren't allowed to** have visitors in the hostel.*

- We use *couldn't* and *wasn't/weren't allowed to*, not *mustn't*, to say that something was forbidden in the past: *We **couldn't** play football in the street. I **wasn't allowed to** walk to school on my own.*

PRACTICE

52a Look at the signs. Then complete the sentences. Use the words in brackets.

0 You ....*aren't allowed to sit*........ on the grass in the park. (allowed)

1 People .... here. It's dangerous. (mustn't)

2 You .... in the library. (allowed)

3 Visitors .... the exhibits in the museum. (mustn't)

4 They .... the building without permission. (couldn't)

5 Students .... the computers without permission. (can't)

6 We .... in the restaurant last night. (allowed)

52b Complete the article. Use the words in the box.

> can't / leave   ~~can't / sit~~   couldn't / have   mustn't / talk
> not allowed / do   not allowed / drink   not allowed / listen

Mick hates his new job. He and his colleagues have to work long hours, but they
(0) ......**can't sit**...... down and they (1) .... to the radio. They
(2) .... to each other either. They (3) .... anything
except work! Yesterday Mick felt ill, but he (4) .... a rest because he
was so busy. He (5) .... even .... a glass of water. The problem
is that the job's well-paid and he needs the money, so he (6) ....

53 Lack of necessity: *don't have to, don't need to*

- We use *don't have to, didn't have to, don't need to* and *didn't need to* to say that
  something is not or was not necessary: You **don't have to** wait for me. I'll come later.
  I **didn't need to** take a jacket – it was quite hot.

⚠ *Must* and *have to* are similar, but *mustn't* and *don't have to* are different.
  Compare: I **mustn't** go. (It's forbidden to go.) I **don't have to** go. (It isn't necessary
  for me to go. I can decide.)

▶▶ **For mustn't, see Unit 52.**

P R A C T I C E

53a Match the sentence halves.

> ## Work in our Adventure Park
> ### Do you want to do something different every day?
> No experience necessary. • 3-day training course. • Choose mornings or evenings – or both!
> We provide: a uniform, free accommodation in a hostel, transport to the Park. • Work with us!
> Apply now to: jmorrison@BAP.co.uk

o	You don't have to do	*b*	a	in the morning if you don't want to.
1	You don't have to train	☐	b	the same thing every day.
2	You don't have to work	☐	c	your own uniform.
3	You don't have to pay	☐	d	a car to work.
4	You don't need to drive	☐	e	for your accommodation.
5	You don't need to buy	☐	f	for a long time.
6	You don't need to have	☐	g	any experience.

53b Circle the correct answer.

o You (*mustn't*) / *don't have to* say things like that. It's cruel.

1 Oh, it's only Monday. I *mustn't* / *don't need to* return my library books today.

2 When we were children, my brother *mustn't* / *didn't have to* do the washing up.

3 Office workers *mustn't usually* / *don't usually have to* work at weekends.

4 Emma *didn't have to* / *doesn't need to* wait very long at the doctor's yesterday.

5 You *mustn't* / *don't have to* be late for the coach. It leaves at six.

6 We *mustn't* / *didn't need to* spend a lot on holiday. Everything was very cheap.

53c Complete the sentences. Use the correct form of the words in brackets.

o I ate a big lunch before I went, so I ....*didn't need to eat*.......... there. (need to / eat)

1 We .... any food. The fridge was already full. (need to / get)

2 Now he's retired from football, he .... every day. (have to / train)

3 The flowers were lovely, but you .... me anything! (need to / give)

4 You .... smart clothes to the party. Jeans are fine. (have to / wear)

5 Lucie .... to town. Her sister took her in the car. (have to / walk)

6 Why is Mary buying shoes again? She .... any more! (need to / buy)

7 The house is in perfect condition. They .... it. (need to / paint)

8 I .... last night. We went out to eat. (have to / cook)

54 Advice: *should, ought to, must*

- We use *should* and *ought to* to give advice: *You **should** stay at college. You **ought to** help her.* (It's a good thing to do.) *You **shouldn't** leave. You **ought not to** spend so much money.* (It's not a good thing to do.)
- We often use *should* to ask for advice: *What **should** we do?*

  ⚠ We often use *think* in negative sentences and questions: *I **don't think** you **should** worry.* (You shouldn't worry.) *Do you think I **should** buy a new shirt?*

- We also use *must/mustn't* to give strong advice: *You **must** go and see his new film! You **mustn't** forget to visit the castle on the hill.*

P R A C T I C E

54a Write sentences.

0 you / should / take / more exercise
You should take more exercise.
....

1 you / must / try / the new kebab restaurant
....

2 I / should / eat / more vegetables?
....

3 she / should / not / go out / every night
....

4 I / think / they / ought / join / a gym
....

5 you/ think / I / should / get / a haircut?
....

6 you / ought / not / watch / so much TV
....

54b Complete the letters. Use the words in the box.

| mustn't   ought to drink   ought to talk   should also try |
| should I   ~~should take~~   shouldn't do |

Dear Abby,

I've got a problem. I can't sleep these days and I'm always tired. My sister thinks that I (0) .....*should take*........... sleeping pills. My mum says I (1) .... hot milk before bed. And my best friend says I (2) .... anything because it's normal. Who (3) .... listen to? Please help!

Dear Donna,

This is a difficult problem. First of all, I think you (4) .... to your doctor. Pills may not be the answer. You (5) .... to relax before you go to bed. And lastly, your friend is right. You (6) .... worry about it. Sleep problems don't usually last for very long.

Good luck!

Check 12 Modal verbs (2)

1 Circle the correct answer.

1 I *mustn't* / *'m not allowed* to wear jeans at work.

2 You *mustn't* / *ought* give up football. The team needs you.

3 You *don't have to* / *mustn't* pay to get into the museum – it's free.

4 She *didn't need to* / *mustn't* get a taxi because there was a free bus.

5 It's not a very popular restaurant, so we *mustn't* / *don't have to* book a table.

/ 5

2 Complete the interview. Use the words in the box.

> didn't have to   had   have to
> needed to   wasn't allowed to

A: Was your childhood very strict?

B: No, I had a lot of freedom, but I
(6) .... go home late at night on my own.

A: Did you (7) .... help in the house?

B: Yes, I was the eldest of four, so I
(8) .... to look after the others, but I (9) .... do a lot of housework. School was different! I
(10) .... do a lot of extra work to pass my exams.

/ 5

3 Complete the sentences. Use the correct form of *have to, be allowed to* and *can*.

11 It's necessary for her to check in two hours before her flight.
She .... check in two hours before her flight.

12 Passengers are forbidden to have more than 20 kilos of luggage.
Passengers .... have more than 20 kilos of luggage.

13 You can't reserve a seat before the flight.
You .... to reserve a seat before the flight.

14 It's necessary for passengers to show a boarding pass before they get on the plane.
Passengers .... show a boarding pass before they get on the plane.

15 It's forbidden to use a mobile phone during the flight.
You aren't .... use a mobile phone during the flight.

/ 5

4 Complete the sentences. Use the words in brackets.

16 Amir and Bimal eat a lot of sweets. (shouldn't)
'You .... so many sweets.'

17 Tony doesn't get enough sleep. (must)
'You .... some more sleep.'

18 You think Amy should see the film. (must)
'You .... the film.'

19 Jan doesn't eat any fruit. (ought)
'You .... some fruit.'

20 Joy tells people my secrets. (mustn't)
'You .... people my secrets.'

/ 5

Total: / 20

Self-check

Wrong answers	Look again at	Try CD-ROM
7, 8, 10, 11, 14	**Unit 51**	Exercise 51
1, 6, 12, 13, 15, 20	**Unit 52**	Exercise 52
3, 4, 5, 9	**Unit 53**	Exercise 53
2, 16, 17, 18, 19	**Unit 54**	Exercise 54

Now do **Check 12**

Statements and questions

55 Word order: direct and indirect objects

Some verbs can have two objects. Some of these verbs are: *bring, buy, cook, fetch, get, give, lend, make, offer, pass, send, show, take, teach, tell, write*. We can use two different structures with these verbs:

Subject	Verb	Object (person)	Object (thing)	
I	gave	Dan	my phone number.	
He	made	Amy	dinner.	

Subject	Verb	Object (thing)	to/for	Object (person)
I	gave	my phone number	to	Dan.
He	made	dinner	for	Amy.

- We use *to* + object after *bring, give, lend, offer, pass, send, show, take, teach, tell* and *write*.
- We use *for* + object after *buy, cook, fetch, get* and *make*.

PRACTICE

55a Put the words in the correct order.

0 they / their new house / us / showed
They showed us their new house.
....

1 any money / them / the bank / won't lend
....

2 didn't tell / her name / me / she
....

3 the deposit / have / you / paid / them / ?
....

4 gave / a watch / Sue / we / for her birthday
....

5 I / all the family / made / lunch
....

6 me / some milk / could / you / fetch / ?
....

7 I / an expensive toy / the child / bought
....

8 have / him / offered / they / the job / ?
....

55b Re-write the sentences. Use *to* or *for*.

  0 We sent all our friends postcards.   *We sent postcards to all our friends.*

  1 Did Matt get you a drink?   ....

  2 Will you show me your photos?   ....

  3 Can you pass Bill the salt?   ....

  4 I've made Laura a cake.   ....

  5 The waiter brought us our food.   ....

  6 They haven't given me the bill.   ....

  7 She didn't buy me a ticket.   ....

  8 I often take my grandmother flowers.   ....

  9 He taught the class the words of the song.   ....

  10 Please could you send me a photo?   ....

55c Re-write the sentences.

  0 She made some coffee for her mother.   *She made her mother some coffee.*

  1 She fetched her father a newspaper.   ....

  2 She took some library books to her aunt.   ....

  3 She cooked her brother some lunch.   ....

  4 She sent a birthday card to her grandmother.   ....

  5 She bought a present for her friend.   ....

  6 She made a cup of tea for her neighbour.   ....

  7 She brought a hot drink to her uncle.   ....

  8 She got her sister some fruit.   ....

  9 She taught her dog a new trick.   ....

  10 She told her brother a bedtime story.   ....

56   *there is/are* vs. *it is*

- We use *there is/are* to say that something or somebody exists: ***There's** a university in my town.* ***There isn't** a castle.* ***Are there** any parks?*
- We use *there is/are* when we talk about something for the first time. We use *it's/ they're* when we refer to something for the second time: ***There's** a university.* ***It's** new.* ***There are** two parks.* ***They're** near the centre.*
- We also use *it* to talk about the weather, the time, days and distance: ***It** rains a lot in winter.* ***It's** five o' clock.* ***It's** Tuesday today.* ***It's** three kilometres to the beach.*

PRACTICE

56a **Complete the conversation. Use the correct form of *there is* or *there are*.**

A: Would you like to come and visit? (0) ....*There are*.......... lots of things to do in Bath.

B: I'd love to, but (1) .... any cheap hotels?

A: You can stay with me if you like. I live very near the centre.

B: Thanks. And what (2) .... to do and see in Bath?

A: Well, (3) .... lots of museums, including the Roman Baths Museum. (4) .... a famous cathedral and of course, (5) .... some nice shops too.

B: Is it busy at this time of year?

A: No, (6) .... much tourism in winter, so (7) .... many tourists at the moment.

56b **Circle the correct answer.**

Australia Flat Swap

We'd like to swap our flat in January or February next year. We live in a modern flat near the beach. (0)(*There are*)/ *They're* two bedrooms. (1) *There are / They're* both quite big and each of them has a view of the sea. (2) *There's / It's* a communal garden with an area for a barbecue. (3) *There isn't / It isn't* a garage, but (4) *there's / it's* a parking space. (5) *There's / It's* right next to the flat. (6) *There's / It's* a road in front of the flat, but (7) *there isn't / it isn't* busy, so (8) *there isn't / it isn't* much noise. (9) *There are / They're* some shops about five minutes away. (10) *There aren't / They aren't* expensive and you can find everything you need there.

Please contact us if you're interested

56c **Re-write the sentences. Use *it*.**

0 The weather is warm and sunny today.   *It's warm and sunny today.*

1 Paul's birthday was yesterday.   ....

2 The distance to the airport is six kilometres.   ....

3 The time is half past eleven.   ....

4 The weather was cloudy yesterday.   ....

5 From London to Edinburgh is a long way.   ....

6 Yesterday was Tuesday.   ....

57 Making questions

● *Yes/No* questions are questions that we can answer with 'yes' or 'no'. They begin with an auxiliary verb (*be, have, do*) or a modal verb (e.g. *can, should, will*). We put the subject after the auxiliary/modal verb:

I	am	late.
Am	I	late?

They	are	listening to music.
Are	they	listening to music?

He	has	finished.
Has	he	finished?

	She	likes	cats.
Does	she	like	cats?

● *Wh*-questions begin with a question word (e.g. *when, where, why*). After the question word, we use the same word order as in *Yes/No* questions.

	He	is	going to the bank.
Where	is	he	going?

		We	play	tennis once a week.
How often	do	you	play	tennis?

PRACTICE

57a Write *Yes/No* questions.

0 It rains a lot in Scotland.
  Does it rain a lot in Scotland?

1 We're going for a picnic tomorrow.

  ....

2 Pat's a good cook.

  ....

3 Mary can type fast.

  ....

4 You saw the football match yesterday.

  ....

5 She has a lot of work to do.

  ....

6 They'll be here soon.   ....

7 Andy's gone to the post office.   ....

8 He should speak to the director.   ....

9 They watch TV most evenings.   ....

10 It's snowing heavily.   ....

57b **Write the questions. Use the question words in the box.**

| what time | ~~when~~ | where | which | who | whose | why |

o A: *When is he going to move house?* .... B: He's going to move house <u>next year</u>.

1 A: .... B: I borrowed <u>Anita's</u> dictionary.

2 A: .... B: He was crying <u>because he was sad</u>.

3 A: .... B: They've gone <u>to the park</u>.

4 A: .... B: She's arriving <u>at half past eight</u>.

5 A: .... B: I prefer <u>the blue one</u>.

6 A: .... B: We're meeting <u>Paul</u> tonight.

57c **Write questions. Then match the questions and answers.**

o how old / your brother / be?   *How old is your brother?* .... [f]

1 how often / they / go / to the gym? .... ☐

2 how much / a room / cost? .... ☐

3 how big / your flat / be? .... ☐

4 how / you / usually / get / to work? .... ☐

5 how long / you / study / last night? .... ☐

6 how tall / you / be? .... ☐

7 how many cousins / you / have? .... ☐

8 how far / it / be / to the bus stop? .... ☐

a Three hours. **b** By bus. **c** £80 a night. **d** 70 square metres. **e** Twice a week.
f He's 23. **g** About 50 metres. **h** I only have two. **i** 1.75m

57d **Write the questions.**

A: Hi, Mark. I haven't seen you for ages. (o) *Where are you living now?* ....

B: I'm living in Manchester.

A: Really? (1) ....

B: Oh, I've lived there for about a year.

A: (2) ....

B: Yes, I do. I like it a lot.

A: (3) ....

B: I went there to study. I'm doing a course in journalism.

A: That's great! (4) ....

B: Yes, it is. It's very interesting.

A: (5) .... when you finish?

B: Good question. I don't know what I'm going to do yet. I'd like to travel a bit.

A: (6) ....

B: I'd like to go to Australia. But I'm not sure yet.

58 Question words as subject or object

- *Who* and *what* can be the subject or object of a question. Compare:

Subject	Object
Who saw you? **Alice** saw me.	**Who** did you see? I saw **Alice**.
What happened? **Nothing** happened.	**What** did you do? I didn't do **anything**.

- When *who* or *what* is the subject, the word order is like a statement: subject + verb + object.
- When *who* or *what* is the object, we put an auxiliary or modal verb (*be, do, have, can, will* etc.) before the subject.

PRACTICE

58a Write questions.

0　A: Somebody's playing music upstairs.　B: *Who's playing music upstairs?*

1　A: Dee does something every Friday.　B: ....

2　A: Something might happen tonight.　B: ....

3　A: I met somebody for lunch yesterday.　B: ....

4　A: We can see something over there.　B: ....

5　A: Somebody's left a message.　B: ....

6　A: They're going to visit somebody.　B: ....

58b Complete the questions.

A: Now, for €1,000, who (0) ....*played*............ Rick Blane in the film *Casablanca*?

B: Let me see. Yes. I think Humphrey Bogart played Rick Blane.

A: That's right. And for €2,000, what (1) .... ?

B: I think Dr Baird invented the television.

A: Correct. Now, Italy won the 2006 World Cup. Who (2) .... ?

B: That's easy. They beat France.

A: Correct. And for €8,000, what (3) .... on 14th April 1912?

B: The Titanic sank. I think that's what happened on 14th April 1912.

A: Right again. Now, who (4) .... *All you need is love*?

B: The Beatles wrote it. Am I right?

A: You are. And for €32,000, what (5) .... in 1993?

B: The Nobel Peace Prize. Nelson Mandela won the Nobel Peace Prize in 1993.

A: Correct. And so, for €64,000. Who (6) .... the novel *Oliver Twist*?

B: *Oliver Twist*? Let me see. I don't know that one.

A: I'm sorry. Time's up. The answer is Charles Dickens. Charles Dickens wrote *Oliver Twist*.

59 Prepositions at the end of questions

If a question begins with *who, what, where, which* etc. and has a preposition in it, the preposition usually comes at the end of the question: **Who** are you talking **to**? **Who** is the letter **from**? **What** are you looking **at**? **What** did she write **about**?

PRACTICE

59a Put the words in the correct order.

0 is / for / what job / applying / he / ? *What job is he applying for?*

1 who / to / were / speaking / you / ? ....

2 they / did / at / which hotel / stay / ? ....

3 Peter / is / what / good / at / ? ....

4 about / what / Lisa / was / angry / ? ....

5 Paula / is / who / to / married / ? ....

6 did / for / you / which pizza / ask / ? ....

7 at / what / they / were / looking / ? ....

8 what / about / are / you / thinking / ? ....

59b Write the questions.

0 A: What *'s she looking for* .... ?
  B: She's looking for her keys again.

1 A: What .... ?
  B: I'm afraid of the dark.

2 A: Who .... ?
  B: He went on holiday with his friends.

3 A: What .... ?
  B: They were talking about computers.

4 A: What .... ?
  B: We're interested in adventure sports.

5 A: Who .... ?
  B: This dog? Oh, it belongs to Jerry.

6 A: Who .... ?
  B: She gave the money to me.

7 A: What .... ?
  B: I'm listening to some jazz.

8 A: Who .... ?
  B: She's probably waiting for her dad.

60 Question tags

- Question tags are short questions we add to the end of statements. We use them:
  - when we are sure about something and want the other person to agree: *'It's cold outside, **isn't it?**' 'Yes, it is.'*
  - when we are not sure about something and want to make sure that our information is correct: *'They live in Manchester, **don't they?**' 'Yes, they do./No, they don't.'*
- We form question tags with the auxiliary/modal verb from the statement + pronoun. If there is no auxiliary or modal verb, we use a form of *do* with the present and past simple.

Positive statement + negative tag	Negative statement + positive tag
You **play** tennis, **don't you?**	They **didn't understand, did they?**
I've **failed, haven't I?**	He **couldn't sing, could he?**

 Notice the negative question tag from *I am*: *I'm right, **aren't I?***

P R A C T I C E

60a Circle the correct answer.

0 It wasn't very warm at the weekend, (was) / wasn't it?

1 Chloe's invited you to the party, *isn't / hasn't* she?

2 I didn't pass the exam, *did / didn't* I?

3 You weren't listening to me, *were / did* you?

4 We can't get into the club with jeans on, *do / can* we?

5 The last bus goes at ten o'clock, *isn't / doesn't* it?

6 He isn't very happy, *is / isn't* he?

7 You'll see Lewis tomorrow, *don't / won't* you?

8 They hadn't been to America before, *had / hadn't* they?

60b Complete the questions. Use question tags.

0 You're Edith, ...*aren't you*........ ?

1 You don't recognise me, ... ?

2 We haven't seen each other for years, ... ?

3 Your mother was a teacher, ... ?

4 Our brothers went to the same school, ... ?

5 When we last met, you'd just sold your house, ... ?

6 Your brother isn't working at the moment, ... ?

7 We could meet for coffee one day, ... ?

8 You won't forget to phone me, ... ?

61 Short responses with *so, neither/nor* etc.

- To agree with someone or add similar information, we can use:
  - *so* + auxiliary verb + subject OR subject + auxiliary verb + *too*: *'Ken **loves** jazz.'* *'**So does Brian.**/**Brian does too.**'*
  - *neither/nor* + auxiliary verb + subject OR subject + negative auxiliary verb + *either*: *'My coffee **wasn't** hot.'* *'**Neither was mine.**/**Mine wasn't either.**'*
- We use *so/too* after a positive statement and *neither/nor/either* after a negative one: *'They**'ve finished.**' '**So has Jenny.**/**Jenny has too.**' 'We **can't speak** French.'* *'**Nor can I.**/**I can't either.**'*
- The auxiliary verb depends on the verb in the statement. If there is no auxiliary or modal verb in the statement, we use a form of *do* with the present and past simple: *'I **saw** the film.' '**So did we.**'*

⚠ To agree with someone, we can also use *Me too*: *'I hate loud noise.' '**Me too!**'*

PRACTICE

61a Match the sentences and short responses.

o	I love rainy days.	☑ *d*	a	Neither were you.
1	We aren't going to Jon's party.	☐	b	Mine don't either.
2	He's never eaten caviar.	☐	c	I did too.
3	You were late yesterday.	☐	d	Me too.
4	My parents don't smoke.	☐	e	Nor are we.
5	We had pasta for dinner last night.	☐	f	So were the others.
6	You weren't trying very hard.	☐	g	Neither can I.
7	I can't come to class today.	☐	h	So had we.
8	He'd finished the exam in an hour.	☐	i	I haven't either.

61b Complete the short responses.

o A: I'm a big fan of country music.   B: So ....*am*........ I.

1 A: Gerard didn't like the film.   B: .... Joe.

2 A: Your pizza isn't very big.   B: Yours ....

3 A: Maria wasn't studying last night.   B: .... Lynn.

4 A: We could see everything.   B: They ....

5 A: My DVDs have arrived!   B: .... mine.

6 A: I'm reading a good book at the moment. B: I ....

7 A: You hadn't done the washing up.   B: Neither .... you.

8 A: I'll phone Helen tonight.   B: So .... I.

62 Short responses: *I think so. I hope not.*

- We use *I think so* and *I hope so* to give a positive answer to a question or to agree with someone without repeating what the other person said: *'Is John here?' 'I think so.'* (I think John's here.) *'Are we leaving soon?' 'I hope so.'* (I hope we're leaving soon.)

- The negative forms of *I think so* and *I hope so* are *I don't think so* and *I hope not*: *'Has the film started?' 'I don't think so.'* (Not *'I think not.'*) *'Have they lost your book?' 'I hope not.'*

PRACTICE

62a Write short responses.

0 A: Are you coming to the cinema tonight?
    B: .....*I think so.*.......................... (I think I'm coming to the cinema.)

1 A: Did Lynn pass the exam?
    B: .... (I hope she passed it.)

2 A: Is Dan unhappy about losing the match?
    B: .... (I don't think he's unhappy about losing it.)

3 A: Do you think it'll be cold tonight?
    B: .... (I hope it won't be cold.)

4 A: Was that the last bus?
    B: .... (I think it was the last bus.)

5 A: Has someone stolen your bicycle?
    B: .... (I hope someone hasn't stolen it.)

6 A: Can I wear jeans to the wedding?
    B: .... (I don't think you can wear jeans.)

62b Complete the short responses. Use *think* or *hope*.

0 A: Is it the 16th today?   B: I ....*don't think so*.... . I think it's the 15th.

1 A: Did Vic read your diary?   B: I .... It's private!

2 A: Are we going to be late?   B: I .... Mum hates it if we're late!

3 A: Is dinner ready?   B: I .... I'm really hungry!

4 A: Was Picasso French?   B: I .... I think he was Spanish.

5 A: Did you lock the front door?   B: I .... But I'll just check.

6 A: Did Jules get the job?   B: I .... She needs the money!

7 A: Is Frank going to the party?   B: I .... I don't like him.

8 A: Had you met Sue before?   B: I .... Her face wasn't familiar.

Check 13 Statements and questions

1 Circle the correct answer.

A: What (1) *happen / happened / did happen* to your bicycle?

B: I crashed into the back of a car.

A: Are you all right?

B: Yes, but I'm worried. You see, a friend lent (2) *to me the bicycle / the bicycle to me / me to the bicycle*. It's not mine.

A: Can you repair it?

B: I (3) *think not / hope not / don't think so*. I think I'll have to buy her a new one.

A: I hate to say this, but (4) *so do I / neither do I / I am too*. How much (5) *bicycles cost / do bicycles cost / cost bicycles?*

B: I've got no idea, but they aren't cheap!

/ 5

2 Complete the sentences. Use one word in each gap.

6 A: Excuse me. Is there a post office near here?

B: Yes, there is. ....'s opposite the cinema.

7 A: Can you help me? I need to change some money.

B: .... are two banks in the High Street.

8 A: Excuse me. Is there a youth hostel in the town centre?

B: I think .... , but you should ask at the tourist office.

9 A: Are there any museums here?

B: Yes, but ....'re closed on Mondays.

10 A: I don't really want to see the sights.

B: I don't ....

/ 5

3 Put the words in the correct order.

11 dinner / us / for / Julie / last night / made

....

12 Sarah / he / the address / told

....

13 did / where / come / those flowers / from / ?

....

14 listening / me / you / to / are / ?

....

15 to / you / give / did / the letter / who / ?

....

/ 5

4 Complete the questions and question tags.

16 A: You went to Majorca in the summer, ... you?

B: Yes, I did.

17 A: Who .... ?

B: I went with my friends.

18 A: It's hot in Majorca, ... it?

B: Yes. Sometimes it gets very hot!

19 A: Who .... ?

B: My parents paid for it.

20 A: How long .... ?

B: I stayed there for two weeks.

/ 5

Total: / 20

-ing forms and infinitives

63   *-ing* forms as subjects of sentences

We often use the *-ing* form like a noun, as the subject of a verb: **Smoking** *is bad for you.*

▶▶   ***See Appendix 5: Spelling rules for verbs + -ing, page 171.***

P R A C T I C E

63a **Complete the sentences. Use the correct form of the verbs in brackets.**

  0 ....*Watching*........ too much TV is bad for you. (watch)

  1 .... public transport can help reduce pollution in cities. (use)

  2 .... on an uncomfortable chair all day is bad for your back. (sit)

  3 .... in front of a computer for hours can hurt your eyes. (work)

  4 .... rubbish is one way to help protect the environment. (recycle)

  5 .... in the sun is dangerous if you don't wear sun cream. (lie)

  6 .... is a great way to meet people from other countries. (travel)

63b **Complete the article. Use the correct form of the verbs in the box.**

do   drink   eat   ~~learn~~   relax   sleep   study   take   walk

Avoiding STRESS

In today's world we have to do more and more things in less and less time. That's why (0) ......*learning*...... to avoid stress is so important. And stress doesn't just affect people at work. (1) .... hard for exams is stressful for students too.

So what can we do to avoid stress? (2) .... a short break every hour is important. You aren't wasting time when you relax. On the contrary, (3) .... is essential.

(4) .... plenty of water is important too and so is (5) .... a balanced diet. (6) .... exercise three or four times a week also helps you to relax. (7) .... to school or work is a good option if you don't have time to go to the gym. And last but not least, (8) .... seven or eight hours a night is essential.

64 Verbs followed by *-ing* form or *to*-infinitive

● We use the *-ing* form of a verb after certain verbs: *I **enjoy playing** video games. Have you **finished eating**?*

▶▶ **See Appendix 8: Verbs followed by *-ing* form, page 172.**

● We use the infinitive with *to* after certain verbs: *She **wants to go** home. **We've arranged to have** lunch together tomorrow.*

▶▶ **See Appendix 9: Verbs followed by *to*-infinitive, page 172.**

⚠ To make an *-ing* form or infinitive negative, we put *not* in front of it: *I hate **not having** enough free time. She prefers **not to lend** people things.*

PRACTICE

64a Circle the correct answer.

  0 We expect *seeing* / (*to see*) them at the party tonight.

  1 I keep *getting* / *to get* e-mails from people I don't know.

  2 They're planning *building* / *to build* a new leisure centre in town.

  3 We can't afford *travelling* / *to travel* abroad on holiday this year.

  4 Have you ever considered *becoming* / *to become* a vegetarian?

  5 I'm very tired and I want *staying* / *to stay* at home tonight.

  6 I'll tell you what Andy said if you agree *not telling* / *not to tell* anyone else.

  7 You should avoid *going* / *to go* swimming for a couple of hours after eating.

  8 I've decided *not doing* / *not to do* a Saturday job next year.

64b Complete the e-mail. Use the correct form of the verbs in brackets.

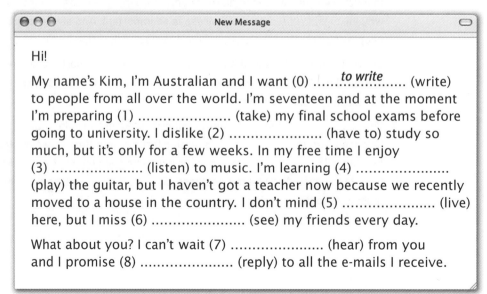

⊖ ⊖ ⊖	New Message	⬭

Hi!

My name's Kim, I'm Australian and I want (0) ......*to write*...... (write) to people from all over the world. I'm seventeen and at the moment I'm preparing (1) .... (take) my final school exams before going to university. I dislike (2) .... (have to) study so much, but it's only for a few weeks. In my free time I enjoy (3) .... (listen) to music. I'm learning (4) .... (play) the guitar, but I haven't got a teacher now because we recently moved to a house in the country. I don't mind (5) .... (live) here, but I miss (6) .... (see) my friends every day.

What about you? I can't wait (7) .... (hear) from you and I promise (8) .... (reply) to all the e-mails I receive.

65 Verbs followed by object + *to*-infinitive

- Some verbs can be followed by an object + *to*-infinitive: *My friend **wants me to help** him. Their parents **allow her to buy** her own clothes.*
- Some verbs always need an object: *Ron**'s teaching Sergio to play** the guitar.* (Not ~~*Ron's teaching to play the guitar.*~~)
- Other verbs are sometimes followed by an object, depending on the meaning we want to express: *We **expect to arrive** soon.* (We think that we will arrive soon.) *We **expect the bus to arrive** soon.* (We think that the bus will arrive soon.)

 We can use the infinitive with *to* or the infinitive without *to* after *help*: *She **helped me to water** the garden. She **helped me water** the garden.*

▶▶ **See Appendix 10: Verbs followed by object + to-infinitive, page 172.**

▶▶ **For ask and tell, see Unit 71.**

PRACTICE

65a Complete the sentences. Use an object if necessary.

0   I'm going to the shops now. Do you want ....*me*........ to get you anything?

1   His parents are strict. They don't allow .... to go out during the week.

2   Where are my car keys? I need .... to leave now and I can't find them.

3   Your friends are nice. Why don't you invite .... to have dinner with us?

4   Don't expect .... to see that CD again! Lee never returns the things he borrows.

5   We're going to the cinema tonight. Would you like .... to come too?

6   Sophie has a great voice. Who taught .... to sing so well?

65b Complete the second sentence so that it means the same as the first. Use no more than three words.

0   This table's heavy, so please lift the other end.
    This table's heavy, so I need ....*you to lift*............ the other end.

1   Laura came on holiday with us because Holly invited her.
    Holly invited .... on holiday with us.

2   When do you think Harry will get here?
    When do you expect .... here?

3   Raymond left a message, so please call him.
    Raymond wants .... him.

4   We don't stay up late because our parents don't allow it.
    Our parents don't allow .... up late.

5   They're moving house on Sunday and some friends are helping them.
    Some friends are helping .... house on Sunday.

Check 14 -ing forms and infinitives

1 Complete the sentences. Use the correct form of the verbs in the box.

be come not understand see speak take

1 Last year we decided .... and live in Italy.

2 .... far away from home isn't a problem.

3 But sometimes we miss .... our friends in Britain.

4 .... Italian made life difficult at first.

5 We taught ourselves .... a little Italian using a phrasebook.

6 And now we're planning .... classes in a language school.

/ 6

2 Circle the correct answer.

○○○   New Message   ⬭

Hi, everyone!

As you know, we're hoping (7) *moving / to move* into our new flat soon, but we need (8) *doing / to do* a lot of work first. You've all offered (9) *helping / to help* us and (10) *painting / to paint* is the biggest job left to do. Now, we know that (11) *decorating / to decorate* is hard work, so we'd like (12) *to come / you to come* to a painting party on Saturday. That will allow (13) *to finish / us to finish* decorating the flat in a day. In return, we'll buy food and drink for everyone. How does that sound?

PS If your friends are free that day, invite (14) *to come / them to come* too!

/ 8

3 Complete the article. Use the correct form of the verbs in brackets.

THE WEEKEND WEATHER

From our weather woman
Claire Mills

After a dry but cold week, the weather is expected (15) .... (get) worse this weekend, with heavy snow in the south of the country. (16) .... (drive) in these conditions is dangerous, so avoid (17) .... (make) journeys that are not absolutely essential. If you need (18) .... (travel), the following advice will help you (19) .... (arrive) safely. Phone the people at your destination before you leave so that they know when to expect you. Don't forget (20) .... (take) your mobile phone with you and phone for help if conditions get worse.

/ 6

Total: / 20

✓ **Self-check**

Wrong answers	Look again at	Try CD-ROM
2, 4, 10, 11, 16	Unit 63	Exercise 63
1, 3, 6, 7, 8, 9, 15, 17, 18, 20	Unit 64	Exercise 64
5, 12, 13, 14, 19	Unit 65	Exercise 65

Now do **Check 14**

The passive

66 The passive: form and use

- In an active sentence, the subject is the 'doer' who performs the action of the verb. In a passive sentence, the object of the active verb becomes the subject. Compare:

	subject	action	object
Active	A thief	stole	my bag.
Passive	My bag	was stolen.	

- We use the passive:
  - when the doer is not known or not important: *My wallet **has been stolen**!* (I do not know who stole my wallet.) *The castle **was built** in 1150.* (It is not important who built the castle.)
  - when the doer is obvious or 'people in general': *The thief **was arrested**.* (It is the job of the police to arrest people.) *Cars **are made** in many countries.*

- We form the passive with an appropriate form of *be* + past participle:

Present simple	Champagne **is made** in France.
Past simple	The dog **was found** safe and well.
Present perfect	Your room **has been painted**.
will	A new road **will be built** next year.

▶▶   *See Appendix 11: Irregular verbs, pages 172–173.*

- To form negative sentences, we put *not* after *be*: *My bag **wasn't stolen**.*
- To make questions, we put *be* before the subject: ***Was** my bag **stolen**?*

P R A C T I C E

66a Write sentences. Use the passive.

0   kimonos / wear / in Japan   *Kimonos are worn in Japan.*

1   the new bridge / finish / next year   ....

2   the new drug / not test / yet   ....

3   spaghetti / make / from wheat   ....

4   paper / invent / in China   ....

5   500 student flats / build / last year   ....

6   the winner / announce / tomorrow ....

7   the invitations / already / send ....

8   pineapples / grow / in hot countries   ....

66b Complete the sentences. Use the passive form of the verbs in brackets.

o I got this jacket in a charity shop. It *'s never been worn* . (never / wear)

1 .... the house next door .... yet? (sell)

2 Our plane left sixteen hours late, but we .... anything to eat. (not give)

3 .... these grapes .... locally? They're delicious. (grow)

4 The missing boy .... yet. They're still looking for him. (not find)

5 When .... the Internet .... ? (create)

6 The results .... to us next week. (send)

66c Complete the article. Use the passive form of the verbs in brackets.

The first modern **OLYMPIC GAMES** (0) .... *were held* .... (hold) in Athens in 1896. Fourteen countries (1) .... (invite) to take part. Nowadays, over 200 countries send athletes to the Games and in Athens in 2004 over 300 gold medals (2) .... (award) in 28 different sports. Both the Winter and Summer Olympics (3) .... (hold) every four years. The 2012 Games (4) .... (stage) in London. The new Olympic stadium (5) .... (already / start) and the organisers say that it (6) .... (finish) a year before the Games.

66d Re-write the sentences. Use the passive.

o For a long time, they recorded music on vinyl records.
For a long time, ... *music was recorded on vinyl records* ....

1 Nowadays, they release albums on CDs.
Nowadays, albums ....

2 They developed the CD in the 1980s.
The CD ....

3 People use CDs to store music or computer software.
CDs ....

4 They make CDs from plastic and aluminium.
CDs ....

5 They have sold billions of CDs in the last twenty years.
Billions of CDs ....

6 Maybe one day people will download all music from the Internet.
Maybe one day all music ....

7 But probably people will buy CDs for a few years to come.
But probably CDs ....

67 The passive + *by*

● If we want to mention the doer of the action in a passive sentence, we use *by* + agent (= the person/thing that does the action):

	subject	action	object	agent
Active	A fire	destroyed	the theatre.	
Passive	The theatre	was destroyed		**by a fire.**

● When we ask who or what does the action, *by* comes at the end of the question: Who **was 'The Scream' painted by**?

P R A C T I C E

67a Re-write the sentences. Use the passive and *by* + agent if necessary.

o George Lucas made *Star Wars*.   *Star Wars was made by George Lucas.*

1 They speak three languages in Switzerland. ....

2 Thieves once stole the FIFA World Cup. ....

3 Alexander Fleming discovered penicillin. ....

4 About 1,500 people have climbed Everest. ....

5 They award the Nobel Peace Prize every year. ....

6 They have discovered water on Mars. ....

67b Complete the questions about the sentences in 67a. Use the passive.

o A: When .... *was Star Wars made* .... ?
B: There are six *Star Wars* films! Which one are you talking about?

1 A: What languages .... ?
B: French, German and Italian.

2 A: Who .... ?
B: No one knows. A dog found it.

3 A: How .... ?
B: By accident, I think.

4 A: When .... for the first time?
B: In 1953.

5 A: In which city .... ?
B: In Oslo.

6 A: How .... ?
B: A spacecraft took samples.

68 The causative: *have something done*

- We use the causative form (*have something done*) when we do not do something ourselves but arrange for someone else to do it for us. Compare: *Sarah cut her hair yesterday.* (She cut her hair herself.) *Sarah **had her hair cut**.* (She arranged for someone else to her cut hair for her.)

- We can use *get something done* in a similar way. *Get* is less formal than *have*, and we often use it when we are speaking: *I **get my car serviced** at the local garage.*

- The form is: subject + *have* + object + past participle:

| Present simple | I **have all my clothes made** for me. |
| Past simple | We **had our bathroom modernised** last year. |

P R A C T I C E

68a Re-write the sentences. Use the causative form.

0	Someone tested his eyes.	He	*had his eyes tested* .
1	Someone repaired her CD player.	She	....
2	Someone takes their photo once a year.	They	....
3	Someone shaved my head.	I	....
4	Someone makes Leah's clothes.	Leah	....
5	Someone cleans our house.	We	....
6	Someone painted my living room.	I	....
7	Someone polished their shoes.	They	....
8	Someone delivers my newspaper every day.	I	....

68b Complete the conversations. Use the words in brackets.

1 A: (0) .... *Did you get your TV repaired* .... all right? (you / get / your TV / repair)

B: Yes. In fact, we (1) .... last week. (have / it / fix)

2 A: Kay, where (2) .... these days?
(have / your hair / cut)

B: At Guy's. I (3) .... there too.
(get / my nails / manicure)

3 A: When (4) .... ?
(she / get / her passport photo / take)

B: Yesterday, at P&P. She (5) .... while she waited.
(have / it / develop)

4 A: Bruno (6) .... in a magazine last month.
(have / a short story / publish)

B: That's fantastic! I didn't know he wrote short stories.

Check 15 The passive

1 Circle the correct answer.

This week the film *Monsoon Destiny* opens in the USA. The film (1) *made / was made* in India and it (2) *directs / was directed* by Bob Heinz. Mona Sethi and Bruce Smith (3) *star / are starred* in this romantic comedy.

A follow-up film called *After the Monsoon*, (4) *will film / will be filmed* next year. An unknown actor (5) *has chosen / has been chosen* to star in it, but nobody knows his name yet.

/ 5

2 Circle the correct answer.

The film stars ANGELA ROSS and KEVIN MASON (6) *are married / will be married* in the garden of Angela's home in Beverley Hills tomorrow. Angela (7) *had / was* a rose garden created specially for the ceremony and a thousand people (8) *have invited / have been invited* to the wedding. Angela's wedding clothes have been designed (9) *by / from* her sister Gina, the famous fashion designer.

After their honeymoon, the couple will live in Kevin's home in Santa Barbara. They (10) *have the house redecorated / had the house redecorated* a few weeks ago. Angela's mansion is now for sale. It (11) *hasn't been sold / hasn't sold* yet, but lots of people will be interested.

/ 6

3 Complete the second sentence so that it means the same as the first. Use no more than three words

12 Gustave Eiffel built the Eiffel Tower for the Paris Exhibition of 1889.
The Eiffel Tower was built for the Paris Exhibition of 1889 .... Gustave Eiffel.

13 They used 18,038 pieces of iron to build the tower.
18,038 pieces of iron .... to build the tower.

14 The Prince of Wales opened the tower.
The tower .... by the Prince of Wales.

15 Over six million people a year visit the Eiffel Tower.
The Eiffel Tower .... over six million people a year.

16 People know the Eiffel Tower all over the world as the symbol of Paris.
The Eiffel Tower .... all over the world as the symbol of Paris.

/ 5

4 Write sentences. Use the passive or causative form.

17 the Eiffel Tower / use / as a radio transmitter
....

18 no one / kill / during its construction
....

19 the Eiffel Tower / paint / every seven years
....

20 every year millions of people / their photo / take / in front of the Eiffel Tower
....

/ 4

Total: / 20

Self-check

Wrong answers	Look again at	Try CD-ROM
1, 2, 3, 4, 5, 6, 8, 11, 13, 14, 16, 17, 18, 19	Unit 66	Exercise 66
9, 12, 15	Unit 67	Exercise 67
7, 10, 20	Unit 68	Exercise 68

Now do **Check 15**

Reported speech

69 Direct speech: punctuation

- We use direct speech to report the exact words a person says: **'She comes from Germany,'** *he said.*
- *I/she/he/we/they said* can come before or after the speaker's words: **They said,** *'We're going home now.' 'We're going home now,'* **they said.**
- Punctuation is important when we write direct speech:

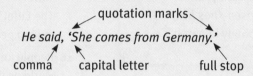

quotation marks

He said, 'She comes from Germany.'

comma   capital letter   full stop

⚠ There is no comma after a full stop or a question mark: *'How are you?' he asked.*

PRACTICE

69a Re-write the sentences. Change the order of the reporting verb and the speaker's words.

0 Max said, 'The bus is late.'   *'The bus is late,' Max said.*

00 'It's already ten to nine,' Peter said.   *Peter said, 'It's already ten to nine.'*

1 'We won't get to work on time,' Max said. ....

2 Peter asked, 'What shall we do?' ....

3 Max said, 'Here's the bus now.' ....

4 'There are lots of people on it,' Max said. ....

5 'It isn't going to stop,' Peter said. ....

69b Re-write the sentences. Use correct punctuation.

0 Jane said my computer's broken   *Jane said, 'My computer's broken.'*

1 I'm sorry to hear that said Ann ....

2 It was working yesterday Tony said ....

3 What's wrong with it asked Ann ....

4 Jane said the mouse isn't working ....

5 Tony asked is the battery OK ....

6 I put in a new battery last week Jane said ....

70 Reported statements

- We use reported speech to report what someone said earlier: *'The train's late,'* *he said.* (direct speech) → *He said that the train was late.* (reported speech)
- We usually change the pronouns and possessive adjectives: *'I'm from Russia,'* *she said.'* → *She said that **she** was from Russia.* *'**Our** son's a dentist,' they said.* → *They said that **their** son was a dentist.*
- After a past tense reporting verb like *said*, the tense of the verb also changes:

Direct speech		Reported speech
Present simple 'I **live** in Brazil,' she said.	→	Past simple She said that she **lived** in Brazil.
Present continuous '**She's shopping**,' they said.	→	Past continuous They said that she **was shopping**.
Present perfect '**They've left**,' he said.	→	Past perfect He said that they **had left**.
Past simple 'I **saw** a film,' she said.	→	Past perfect She said that she **had seen** a film.
Past perfect '**They'd finished**,' he said.	→	Past perfect He said that they **had finished**.
am/is/are going to '**I'm going to stay**,' he said.	→	*was/were going to* He said that he **was going to stay**.
will + infinitive '**I'll help** you,' she said.	→	*would* + infinitive She said that she **would help** me.

⚠️ It is not necessary to use *that*: *She said (**that**) she lived in Brazil.*

PRACTICE

70a Report the statements.

0 'We're worried about Peter,' they said.
They said (that) they were worried about Peter.

1 'I work in an office,' Jane said.
....

2 The weather man said, 'It's going to rain.'
....

3 The motorists said, 'We're driving to a football match.'
....

4 'I've won the lottery!' the old lady said.
....

5 'My friends don't like visiting museums,' Louise said.
....

6   The young boy said, 'People will have holidays in space in the future.'

....

7   James said, 'I broke my leg playing football.'

....

8   'We haven't flown before,' they said.

....

70b   **Re-write the sentences. Use direct speech. See Unit 69 for punctuation.**

0   They said that they would see us soon.   *'We'll see you soon,' they said.*

1   Ed said that he was going to visit his aunt.   ....

2   She said she didn't remember my name.   ....

3   They said they'd bought their car in 1999. ....

4   I said that we hadn't seen the film yet.   ....

5   Sue said she didn't like vegetables.   ....

6   They said their son was studying Biology. ....

70c   **Read the holiday advertisement. Then complete the letter.**

The holiday of your dreams!

A representative of the travel company will meet you at the airport and take you to your hotel. The Hotel Malibu is a four-star hotel. It opened only last year. It has a fabulous swimming pool and restaurant, as well as a bar and disco. There will be a special programme of entertainment this summer and we have organised activities for younger visitors too.

Book now! We are offering you the holiday of your dreams!

We are writing to complain about the holiday we booked at your travel agency. First of all, you told us that a representative (0) ......*would meet*...... us at the airport, but nobody was there. You said that the hotel (1) .... a four-star hotel, but it only has two stars. You told us that the hotel (2) .... last year, but it is at least ten years old. The advertisement said the hotel (3) .... a fabulous pool, but there was no water in it. It said there (4) .... a special programme of entertainment, but we saw the same show every night. The advertisement also said the hotel (5) .... activities for young people, but they only did so at weekends. You told us you (6) .... us the holiday of our dreams, but in fact it was a very great disappointment!

71 Reporting verbs: *say* and *tell*

Say and *tell* are the most common reporting verbs for statements. Notice how they are used:

- *say* (*to someone*) (*that*): She **said to her friend that** she would be late. (Not ~~She said her friend that she would be late.~~)

- *tell someone* (*that*): He **told her that** he didn't mind. (Not ~~He told that he didn't mind~~ OR ~~He told to her that he didn't mind.~~)

 Say and *tell* can come before or after direct speech: **They said,** *'We have a new car.'* *'We're very happy with it,'* **they told us.** However, they usually come before reported speech: **They said that** they had a new car. **They told us** that they were very happy with it.

PRACTICE

71a Circle the correct answer.

  0 Mark *said* / *told* us that he was going on holiday.

  1 'I'm very pleased to meet you,' Ruth *said* / *told*.

  2 The waiter *said* / *told* to me that the table by the window was free.

  3 'You can't park here,' the man *said* / *told* them. 'This is private property.'

  4 Fran *said* / *told* us that she was too busy to come and visit.

  5 Terry and Lesley *said* / *told* they would meet me at the airport.

  6 He *said* / *told*, 'Sally's coming with us.'

  7 The shop assistant *said* / *told* Peter that they didn't have a larger size.

  8 'Take an umbrella,' Carrie *said* / *told* to Peter. 'It's going to rain.'

71b Complete the sentences. Use *said* or *told*.

  0 I ....*told*........ my friends that there was a good film on at the cinema.

  1 'We aren't going to the cinema this weekend,' they ....

  2 'I've already seen that film,' Tania .... me.

  3 Mark and Fiona .... they were going away for the weekend.

  4 'We won't be back until Sunday evening,' they .... us.

  5 Luke .... everyone that he had plans to go to a wedding.

  6 He .... there was a party in the evening after the wedding.

  7 I .... to Tania that I would go with her to see a different film.

  8 But she .... me that that was impossible.

  9 'I've arranged to go out with Will on Saturday,' she ....

  10 So I .... my friends I would go and see the film without them.

72 Reported questions

- Reported questions have the same changes in pronouns, possessive adjectives and tenses as reported statements:
  'Did you enjoy the film?' → I asked them if **they had enjoyed** the film.

▶▶ **For reported statements, see Unit 70.**

- A common reporting verb in questions is *ask*.
- When we report a *Yes/No* question, we use *if* after the reporting verb:
  'Do you like jazz?' → He asked **if I liked** jazz.
- When we report a *Wh*-question, we use the question word:
  'Where did you stay?' Megan asked him **where he had stayed**.
- The word order in reported questions is the same as in statements, and there is no *do/does/did* auxiliary:
  'Are you at home?' → I asked them if **they were** at home.
  'Have you seen the film?' → He asked me if **I had seen** the film.
  'Which song **do you like**?' → She asked me which song **I liked**.
- We do not use a question mark (?) in reported questions.

P R A C T I C E

72a Report the questions.

o 'Are the banks open in the afternoon?'
A couple asked me .... *if the banks were open in the afternoon* .

1 'Do museums close on Sundays?'
A young man asked me ....

2 'Are you waiting for a tourist bus?'
A woman asked me ....

3 'Did the waiter overcharge us?'
Two friends asked me ....

4 'Will a hotel be expensive?'
A couple asked me ....

5 'Has the flight from Bristol arrived?'
A woman asked me ....

6 'Is there a Bureau de Change nearby?'
A man asked me ....

7 'Did you hear the platform number?'
A man at the station asked me ....

8 'Are we going to get a guided tour?'
A woman outside the museum asked me ....

72b **Report the questions.**

0 'Have you been to Egypt before?' She asked ....*if I had been to Egypt before*.... .

1 'What do you think of it?' She asked ....

2 'When did you arrive?' She asked ....

3 'Did you fly to Cairo?' She asked ....

4 'Are you planning to stay long?' She asked ....

5 'What have you seen?' She asked ....

6 'Do you like the food?' She asked ....

72c **Read the conversation. Then complete the diary entry.**

0 A: Where are you from?
B: I'm from Sweden.

1 A: What are you doing at the college?
B: I'm studying Spanish.

2 A: Why did you decide to study Spanish?
B: Because I want to be a translator.

3 A: What other languages do you speak?
B: I speak French and German.

4 A: How long have you been at the college?
B: For three days.

5 A: When do you have classes?
B: Every morning, from nine to one.

6 A: What are you going to do later on?
B: I don't have any plans. Why?

This morning I was sitting in a café having a coffee, when a guy
came and sat next to me and started talking. He asked me
(0) .... *where I was from* ....

I told him and then he asked me (1) ....

I explained and then he asked me (2) ....

He also asked me (3) ....

After we had talked a bit about my plans for the future, he asked me
(4) ....

I told him for three days. He asked me (5) .... ,
and I said I had classes every morning, from nine to one. Then he
asked me (6) .... ,
and I said I didn't have any plans.

73 Reported commands and requests

- We form reported commands and requests with verb + person + *to*-infinitive:
  *She **told me to sit down**. We **asked them to wait**.*

- We often use *tell* to report commands:
  ***'Close** the door.'* → *She **told him to close** the door.*
  ***'Don't be** late!'* → *The teacher **told the students not to be** late.*

- We usually use *ask* to report requests:
  ***'Please don't leave** me!'* → *He **asked us not to leave** him.*
  ***'Please carry** my bag.'* → *His mother **asked him to carry** her bag.*

- For negative requests and commands, we use *not* before the *to*-infinitive:
  ***'Don't touch** the controls!'* → *She told me **not to touch** the controls.*
  ***'Please don't make** a noise.'* → *He asked us **not to make** a noise.*

 We do not use *that* to report a command or request: *A man asked me that I tell him the time.*

 We do not use *say* to report a command: *I said you to clean your shoes.*

PRACTICE

73a **Report the commands.**

0 'Keep your luggage with you at all times.'
They told us .... *to keep our luggage with us at all times* ....

1 'Fasten your seatbelts.'
The flight attendant told us ....

2 'Don't smoke.'
They told us ....

3 'Switch off your mobile phones.'
The pilot told us ....

4 'Don't use any electrical equipment after take-off.'
He told us ....

5 'Don't put bags in the aisle.'
They told us ....

6 'Stay in your seats during the flight.'
The flight attendant told us ....

7 'Don't unfasten your seatbelts.'
They told us ....

8 'Show your passports at immigration control.'
They told us ....

73b **Report the requests.**

o 'Turn down the television, please.'
The mother asked the children ....*to turn down the television*................... .

1 'Please pass me some potatoes.'
He asked someone ....

2 'Please lend me £20.'
The boy asked his sister ....

3 'Be quiet, please!'
The father asked the children ....

4 'Please take me shopping, Mum.'
The girl asked her mother ....

5 'Please help me with my homework.'
The boy asked his brother ....

6 'Stop reading the newspaper, please.'
She asked her brother ....

73c **Report the requests and commands.**

o 'Please open the window for me,' the woman asked the young man.
The woman asked the young man to open the window for her.

1 The manager said to his assistant, 'Don't be late for the meeting.'
....

2 'Bring us the bill, please,' the couple asked the waiter.
....

3 'Open your mouth wide,' the dentist told me.
....

4 'Please turn the music down,' they asked their neighbour.
....

5 'Call me from the airport,' Peter said to Dee.
....

6 I asked my flatmate, 'Please go to the supermarket for me.'
....

7 The mother told her children, 'Don't talk to strangers.'
....

8 'Please look after our cat,' they asked Susie.
....

Check 16 Reported speech

1 Choose the correct answer.

I recently bought a DVD player from your shop on the High Street. The shop assistant told me that it (1) ...... the best model available and that it came with a two-year guarantee. But after a month there was a problem with the sound. I brought it back to the shop and (2) ...... the shop assistant what had happened. He said that they (3) ...... any problems with the DVD before. He asked me when (4) ...... it and if (5) ...... the box. I (6) ...... that I had the receipt, but I had thrown the box away. The shop assistant (7) ...... he couldn't change the DVD without the box. I asked (8) ...... the manager, but he (9) ...... that the manager was in a meeting. So I am writing to ask (10) ...... the DVD or give me a full refund.

1 A is   B was   C will be   D be

2 A told   B said   C told to   D asked to

3 A never have   B never had
  C have never had   D had never had

4 A I buy   B I bought
  C did I buy   D I had bought

5 A do I still have   B did I still have
  C I still had   D I still had had

6 A said him   B told him
  C told   D asked

7 A said me that   B said that
  C said me   D tells that

8 A to fetch   B that he fetch
  C him to fetch   D he fetched

9 A told   B said
  C asked   D told that

10 A you to change   B to change
   C you changed   D had changed

/ 10

2 Re-write the sentences. Use correct punctuation.

11 How long have you been in England she asked him

....

12 He said I arrived six months ago

....

13 She asked do you like living in England

....

14 I don't like the weather in England he said

....

15 But I'm going to stay for a year he said

....

/ 5

3 Complete the second sentence so that it means the same as the first. Use no more than three words.

16 'Does the bus go to the city centre?' Isabel asked the driver.
   Isabel asked the driver if .... to the city centre.

17 The driver said, 'Take the number 66.'
   The driver told .... the number 66.

18 Isabel said, 'I've never seen a number 66 bus.'
   Isabel said she .... a number 66 bus.

19 'Please show me the bus stop,' she asked him.
   She asked him .... the bus stop.

20 He said it was in King Street.
   He .... her it was in King Street.

/ 5

Total: / 20

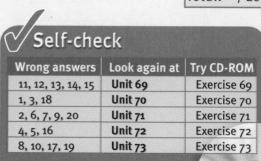

✓ **Self-check**

Wrong answers	Look again at	Try CD-ROM
11, 12, 13, 14, 15	Unit 69	Exercise 69
1, 3, 18	Unit 70	Exercise 70
2, 6, 7, 9, 20	Unit 71	Exercise 71
4, 5, 16	Unit 72	Exercise 72
8, 10, 17, 19	Unit 73	Exercise 73

Now do **Check 16**

74 Indirect questions

- We often use indirect questions to ask politely for information: *Could you tell me what time the train leaves? Do you know if the baker's is open?*

- In indirect questions the word order is the same as in statements and there is no *do/does/did* auxiliary: *Where **is the bus stop**? → Could you tell me where **the bus stop is**? (Not Could you tell me where is the bus stop?)*

- When the direct question is a *Yes/No* question, we use *if* in the indirect question: *Has the bus to Hull left? → Do you know **if** the bus to Hull has left?*

- When the direct question begins with a question word, we use the question word in the indirect question: ***Why** is the supermarket closed? → Could you tell me **why** the supermarket is closed?*

PRACTICE

74a Circle the correct answer.

0 Can you tell me what time (the bus leaves) / does the bus leave?

1 Excuse me. *There's / Is there* a supermarket near here?

2 Do you know when *will be Mr Jones / Mr Jones will be* at home?

3 Could you tell me *do you have this sweater / if you have this sweater* in green?

4 *Has the bank closed / The bank has closed* for the day?

5 How much *do these shoes cost / these shoes cost*?

6 Can you tell me how long *does it take / it takes* to get to Oxford?

7 *Is the station / The station is* far from here?

8 Do you know if *is there / there is* a Bureau de Change near here?

74b Re-write the direct questions as indirect questions.

0 Do you sell maps? Could you tell me ....*if you sell maps*........... ?

1 Is this the right road for Brighton? Can you tell me .... ?

2 Where can I get a bus to Camden Market? Do you know .... ?

3 Will I have to wait long? Could you tell me .... ?

4 How long does the journey take? Can you tell me .... ?

5 Has the film started? Do you know .... ?

6 How much does a ticket cost? Could you tell me .... ?

7 Is there a telephone box near here? Do you know .... ?

8 Does this train go to Oxford? Could you tell me .... ?

75 *Wh*-question words + *to*-infinitive

- We often use a *Wh*-question word and the *to*-infinitive after *decide, explain, forget, know, learn, remember* and *understand*: I don't **know where to go**. We couldn't **decide what to do.**

- After *ask* and *tell* the pattern is: *ask/tell* + person + *Wh*-question word + *to*-infinitive: She **asked me how to use** the washing machine. Nobody **told me what to do.**

PRACTICE

75a Complete the sentences. Use the question words in the box on the left and the *to*-infinitive form of the verbs in the box on the right.

| how | how | how | how | how long |
| what | what | where | ~~which bus~~ | |

| do | drive | empty | get to |
| go | see | ~~take~~ | use | wait |

0 She couldn't remember ....*which bus to take*.... , so she got lost.

1 I'm learning .... , but I haven't got a car yet.

2 We haven't decided .... on our holiday yet. Maybe Italy.

3 Can you explain .... the bag of this vacuum cleaner?

4 Nobody told me .... , so I left after fifteen minutes.

5 My friend doesn't know .... when she leaves university.

6 I've forgotten .... your house. Can you tell me again?

7 You asked me .... in Amsterdam. That's easy: the art galleries.

8 Could you tell me .... this camera, please?

75b Re-write the questions.

0 How do you make a cake?
   I've never learnt ....*how to make a cake*............................... .

1 What shall I wear to the party tonight?
   I can't decide ....

2 How do you use the ticket machine?
   Some tourists asked me ....

3 Who should I speak to about my problem?
   I don't know ....

4 Which button do you have to press to start the DVD?
   I never remember ....

5 What time should we arrive at the party?
   We don't know ....

6 How do you switch on the printer?
   Nobody told me ....

Check 17 Indirect questions

1 Circle the correct answer.

> Do you know if (1) *Amanda can dance / can Amanda dance* salsa? I heard she was taking classes. I'd really like to learn (2) *how I dance / how to dance* too. Can you tell me which dance school (3) *does she go to / she goes to*? The next time I see her, I'm going to ask her (4) *where to go / where do I go*. Do you know (5) where *is she / she is* now?

/ 5

2 Put the words in the correct order.

6 has / you / the salt / where / do / Paul / know / put / ?

....

7 in the dishwasher / could / tell / you / me / if / he / the glasses / puts / ?

....

8 I / asked / leave / where / the neighbours / to / the key

....

9 with the plants / do / me / nobody / what / to / told

....

10 tell / Paul / can / me / coming back / you / is / when / ?

....

/ 5

3 Complete the second sentence so that it means the same as the first. Use no more than three words.

11 Who should I ask for directions?
I don't know .... for directions.

12 Is the shoe department on this floor?
Could you tell me .... the shoe department is on this floor?

13 'How do I pay?' she asked the assistant.
She asked the assistant .... pay.

14 Do you know if I can change these shoes?
Can .... these shoes?

15 Where did the manager go?
Do you know .... went?

/ 5

4 Circle the correct answer.

```
○ ○ ○              New Message              ⬭
```

Hi, Jackie!

I'm arriving at the train station at 4.25 on Friday afternoon. I'm afraid I don't know (16) *how do I get / to get / how to get* to your place. Could you tell me which bus (17) *to take / do I take / take*? Do you know how much (18) *costs / does it cost / it costs* to get to your house?

I'm really looking forward to seeing you. Can you tell me what (19) *is the weather like / does the weather / the weather is like* at the moment? I can't decide what clothes (20) *I bring / to bring / bring*.

See you soon, Irene

/ 5

Total: / 20

119

Relative clauses

76 Defining relative clauses

- We use defining relative clauses to give more information about a person, animal, thing or place, and make it clear which one we are talking about: *This morning I met the boy **who lives next door**.*

- We use these relative pronouns:
  - *who* or *that* for people: **The man who/that** *stole the money was arrested last night.*
  - *which* or *that* for animals and things: *I'd like **a job which/that** pays well.*
  - *where* for a place: *Here's **the factory where** Gary works.*
  - *whose* for possession: *She's **the singer whose** song is Number 1.*

- Compare: *The girl **who** came to your party was nice. The dress **(that) she wore was** pretty.* We can leave out *who*, *which* or *that* when they are followed by a noun or pronoun.

  ⚠ *The girl who came to your party was nice.* (Not ~~The girl who she came to your party was nice.~~) *The dress **(that) she wore** was pretty.* (Not ~~The dress (that) she wore it was pretty.~~)

PRACTICE

76a Complete the sentences. Use *who*, *which*, *whose* or *where*.

- **0** Look at these old photos ......*which*...... I found in a box upstairs.

- **1** This is the house .... we lived when we got married.

- **2** I think that's the woman .... used to live next door to us.

- **3** Yes, she's the one .... dog attacked me in the park.

- **4** That's the friend .... had an apartment in Corfu.

- **5** Yes, and this is the nice couple .... restaurant we liked so much.

- **6** And here's the beach .... we went every day. Paradise!

- **7** Is that the apartment .... we stayed?

- **8** No, that was the apartment .... you wanted to buy!

76b Circle the correct answers. There may be more than one correct answer.

- **0** We went to that new shop (which)/ (that)/ – sells books and CDs.

- **1** It's the kind of shop *where* / *that* / – you could spend a lot of time.

- **2** The game *which* / *that* / – I bought was very cheap.

- **3** I found the book *which* / *that* / – my dad wanted.

- **4** The section *where* / *that* / – you can listen to CDs is amazing.

- **5** I saw an old friend *which* / *that* / – I hadn't seen for ages.

6 The woman *who* / *that* / – served me in the café upstairs was very rude.

7 When we got home, we played the CDs *which* / *that* / – we'd bought.

8 The best one is by the woman *who* / *that* / – sang at the Star Club last week.

76c **Join the sentences. Use relative clauses.**

0 Marie Curie was the scientist. She discovered radium in 1902.
Marie Curie was the scientist who discovered radium in 1902.

1 *Titanic* is the film. It made Kate Winslett famous.

2 Stephen Hawking is a physicist. His books have sold millions of copies.

3 *Robinson Crusoe* is a novel. Daniel Defoe wrote it.

4 Stratford on Avon is the town. Shakespeare was born there.

5 Marco Polo was the explorer. He brought spaghetti to Italy.

6 Van Gogh was the Dutch painter. He painted *Sunflowers*.

7 Saint Helena is the island. Napoleon Bonaparte died there.

8 The electric light bulb was an invention. It changed people's lives.

77 Other ways of identifying people and things

Instead of using a full relative clause, we can give more information about a noun in these ways:

- We can use preposition + noun:
  *The books (**which are**) **on the table** are mine. The girl (**who is standing**) **next to Graeme** is his sister.*
- We can use *with* instead of *who has*: *The man **with** (= who has) **curly hair** is my Uncle James.*
- We can use *in* instead of *who is wearing*: *The girl **in** (= who is wearing) **the green dress** is my sister.*
- We can use an *-ing* clause: *I saw a girl (**who was**) **talking** to Jim.*
- ⚠ We often use an *-ing* clause with *there is/are*: *There were some people (**who were**) **swimming** in the lake.*

PRACTICE

77a **Complete the sentences. Use a preposition.**

o The two girls ......*on*...... the left are talking about the people at the party.

1 The girl .... the witch's costume is explaining who everyone is.

2 The ancient Egyptian .... the table is Alice, my next door neighbour.

3 And I think the queen .... the dog is a friend of hers called Jean.

4 The two Draculas .... the sofa are my twin brothers.

5 The one .... the right is Greg, I think, because he's always eating.

6 My dad is the man .... the pirate costume!

7 But I don't know who the gorilla .... him is.

8 It must be really hot .... a gorilla costume.

77b **Join the sentences. Use an *-ing* clause.**

o My friend Katie sent me a letter. It invited me to visit her in Prague.
My friend Katie sent me a letter ......*inviting me to visit her in Prague*...... .

1 I found a website. It was selling cheap flights to Prague.
I found ....

2 So I booked a flight. It was leaving the following weekend.
So I booked ....

3 At the airport there were hundreds of people. They were queuing to check in.
At the airport there were hundreds of people ....

4 We spent three hours on the plane. We were waiting to take off.
We spent three hours on ....

5 At Prague airport there was a crowd of people. They were waiting to meet friends.
At Prague airport there was a crowd of people ....

6 I finally saw Katie. She was waving excitedly from the back of the crowd.
I finally saw ....

Check 18 Relative clauses

1 Complete the sentences. Use relative pronouns.

A: Who's the girl (1) .... 's standing
next to Kyle?

B: That's Inge. They met at the college
(2) .... Inge's studying English.

A: I don't understand this film. Is that the man
(3) .... stole the money?

B: No, that's the man (4) .... son was
hurt in the accident.

A: I can't find any shoes (5) .... look
nice on my big feet!

B: Jenny knows a place (6) .... they
sell very small and very big sizes. Why don't
you ask her about it?

/ 6

2 Circle the correct answer.

A: I like the puzzle book (7) *who / whose / –*
Ari gave me for my birthday. There's a different
scene on every page with lots of people
(8) *are doing / doing / who* crazy things.
You have to find a boy (9) *who / whose /
wearing* a woolly hat and a red T-shirt. He's
called Wally.

B: Oh yes, the one (10) *with / whose / has* a
backpack and a stick. Let's see. He's here!

A: Where? The boy (11) *by / where / swim* the
lake?

B: No, that boy hasn't got a hat. No, Wally's the
one (12) *who / is sitting / sitting* under the
tree.

/ 6

**3 Read the sentences and complete the
conversation. Use one or two words in each gap.**

13 The girl has red hair.

14 She lived in India.

15 The boy is sitting next to Jan.

16 Those people are dancing energetically.

17 The boy is wearing a purple T-shirt.

18 His sister is in a pop group.

19 Suzie is talking to my brother.

20 I made the pizza.

A: It's a great party, Rose. Do you know all these
people?

B: Yes, most of them. The girl
(13) .... red hair is Jan. She's the
one (14) .... in India for a year.
The boy (15) .... next to her is her
boyfriend, Tariq.

A: And who are those people (16) ....
so energetically?

B: I only know the boy (17) .... the
purple T-shirt. He's called Bob.

A: Oh yes. Isn't he the guy (18) .... is
in a pop group?

B: Yes, that's right. Suzie. She's the girl
(19) .... to my brother.

A: Oh yes! I'd like to meet her. But first, is there
anything to eat?

B: Of course! Come and have some of the pizza
(20) .... I made.

/ 8

Total: / 20

✓ Self-check

Wrong answers	Look again at	Try CD-ROM
1, 2, 3, 4, 5, 6, 7, 14, 18, 20	**Unit 76**	Exercise 76
8, 9, 10, 11, 12, 13, 15, 16, 17, 19	**Unit 77**	Exercise 77

Now do **Check 18**

Linking words and structures

78 Addition: *and, also, too, as well*

- We use *and* to link two words or sentences: We do not need to repeat the same subject or verb after *and*: **We** *went to a department* **store and** *(we)* *bought some new clothes.* **We went to** *the shops* **and** (**we went to**) *the cinema.*

- We can use *also, too* and *as well* with a similar meaning to *and*. We use them to add emphasis.
  - *also* comes before the verb or noun: *We went shopping and (we)* **also saw** *a good film at the cinema. I bought a shirt and (I)* **also** *(bought) a tie.*
  - *too* and *as well* come at the end of a clause: *I bought a shirt. Tom bought one* **too/ as well**. *We went to the shops and the cinema* **too/as well***.*

P R A C T I C E

78a **Join the sentences. Use the words in brackets.**

0 I like classical music. I like opera. (too) *I like classical music and opera too.*

1 We have a dog. We have three cats. (as well) ....

2 They visited London. They visited Paris. (also) ....

3 She's studying Maths. She's studying Music. (as well) ....

4 I can play the guitar. I can play the piano. (too) ....

5 We went to a concert. We went to a party. (also) ....

6 Dick plays tennis. He goes jogging. (as well) ....

7 Jim bought a T-shirt. He bought two comics. (also) ....

8 I had a good time. I made new friends. (too) ....

78b **Complete the e-mail. Use *and, also, too, as* or *well*.**

```
 ○ ○ ○                        New Message                        ▭

 Hi, Lucas!

 I'm having a great time in Oxford. I'm studying English in the morning
 (0) .......and........ working in a restaurant three nights a week
 (1) ..................... . I've made lots of friends! Oxford is very beautiful.
 I've visited some of the university colleges (2) ..................... the
 museum and art gallery (3) ..................... well. I (4) .....................
 went to London with some friends last week. We walked for miles
 (5) ..................... spent all our money on clothes in Oxford Street.
 When we've saved some more money, we'd like to visit Stratford on
 Avon as (6) ..................... .  Everyone says it's fantastic.
```

79 *both ... and, either ... or, neither ... nor*

- We use *both* X *and* Y, *either* X *or* Y and *neither* X *nor* Y to talk about two things or people.
- *Both, either* and *neither* add emphasis: ***Both** Peter **and** Emma are doctors.* ***Either** I've left my phone at home **or** I've lost it.* ***Neither** Lisa **nor** Penny went to the party.*
- *Both ... and* link two similar ideas: ***Both** Anne **and** Lucie are French. I like **both** pop music **and** classical music.*
  We can also say: *Anne **and** Lucie are **both** French. My brother **and** I **both** like classical music.*
- *Either ... or* link two alternatives: *You can **either** have tea **or** coffee. You **either** like techno **or** you hate it.*
  We can also say: *You can have **either** tea **or** coffee. **Either** you like techno **or** you hate it.*
- *Neither ... nor* link two negative ideas: *Harry's **neither** tall **nor** short. **Neither** Pete **nor** Dave drives a car.*

PRACTICE

79a **Complete the conversations. Use** *both ... and, either ... or* **or** *neither ... nor.*

A: What kind of restaurant do you fancy tonight?
B: (0) ...... *Either* ...... Indian .... *or* .... Thai would be really good. Something hot and spicy!

A: Who's coming on the trip?
B: (1) .... Piet .... Greg are definitely coming and Joe might come, but (2) .... Eric .... Lucas can come. They're busy.

A: What's the capital of Australia, Bruce?
B: I'm not sure. I think it's (3) .... Melbourne .... Sydney.

A: Have you decided where to go for your holidays?
B: No, not yet. (4) .... the Cote d'Azur .... Crete are too expensive and (5) .... Lanzarote .... Mallorca has any vacancies, so at the moment it's (6) .... Portugal .... Croatia.

A: I can't decide which T-shirt to get. What do you think?
B: Well, (7) .... the blue one .... the green one suit you.
A: Yes, but I can only buy one!

A: Did you enjoy the film?
B: No, I didn't. It was (8) .... boring .... predictable.

79b **Join the sentences. Use *both ... and, either ... or* or *neither ... nor*.**

0   China has a billion people. India has a billion people too.
    Both China and India have a billion people.
    ....

1   Laos is in Asia. Thailand is also in Asia.
    ....

2   Penguins can't fly. Ostriches can't fly either.
    ....

3   Maybe France won the 2006 World Cup. Perhaps Italy won it.
    ....

4   The Egyptians built pyramids. The Aztecs built pyramids too.
    ....

5   Alfred Hitchcock didn't win an Oscar. Federico Fellini didn't win an Oscar either.
    ....

6   Perhaps Lake Titicaca is in Bolivia. Maybe it's in Peru.
    ....

79c **Complete the article. Use *both ... and, either ... or* or *neither ... nor*.**

(0) ......*Neither*...... Bob (1) .... Janet had ever been to a gym before, so
the experience was new for both of them. There were lots of activities to do. At six
o'clock you could (2) .... do aerobics (3) .... karate and at
seven thirty you could (4) .... go to a yoga class (5) .... try
something called aquagym in the swimming pool. But (6) .... Janet
(7) .... Bob wanted to do aquagym. Bob decided to try karate and Janet
decided to do (8) .... karate (9) .... yoga. After their classes,
Bob and Janet were (10) .... hungry (11) .... thirsty, so they
went to the cafeteria for a cold drink and a snack.

80   Contrast: *but, although/though, however*

We use *but, although, though* and *however* to link two opposite or contrasting ideas:

● *But* comes in the middle of a sentence: *This coat is old,* **but** *(it's) very warm. I like sport,* **but** *my brother hates it.*

● *Although/Though* comes at the beginning or in the middle of a sentence. Notice when we use a comma (,): **Although/Though** *the house was expensive, we bought it. We bought the house* **although/though** *it was expensive.*

● *However* can come in the following positions: *The weather was bad.* **However,** *we got to the top of the mountain. The weather was bad. We got to the top of the mountain,* **however.**

P R A C T I C E

80a Circle the correct answer.

0 (*Although*) / *But* Amaya can drive, she's never bought a car.

1 I looked for my address book, *but / however* I couldn't find it.

2 We tried to book a table. *Though / However*, the restaurant was full.

3 They went for a walk *however / although* it was raining.

4 *Although / However* the train was crowded, we found a place to sit.

5 On Sunday we wanted to play tennis, *but / however* it rained all day.

6 Lots of boys want to be footballers. Very few succeed, *although / however*.

80b Link the sentences. Use the words in brackets.

0 It was cloudy. It didn't rain. (although)
   Although it was cloudy, it didn't rain.

1 They're very rich. They never spend any money. (but)
   ....

2 My grandmother's 81. She's still very active. (though)
   ....

3 The police are looking for the stolen money. They haven't found it yet. (but)
   ....

4 Kip ran fast. He didn't win the race. (although)
   ....

5 I think she's Dutch. She may be Belgian. (but)
   ....

80c Complete the article. Use *but*, *although* or *however*.

BILL GATES became interested in computers at school (0) .....*although*.....
in those days they weren't very common. When he left school, he went
to Harvard University to study law. (1) .... , he spent most of
his time in the computer centre. In 1975, he and his friend Paul Allen
successfully wrote a software program for the first microcomputer, an
Altair, (2) .... they didn't even have one.

Gates was top of his class at Harvard, (3) .... he left without
finishing his degree. Then he and Allen started Microsoft.

In the 1990s, the US government wanted to break up Microsoft because
they said the company was a monopoly. Gates was able to stop them,
(4) .... Today Gates is a billionaire, (5) .... he also
gives millions of dollars to charity.

81 Reason: *because (of), as, since, so, therefore*

- We use *because (of)*, *as* and *since* to introduce a reason for something. They can come at the beginning or in the middle of a sentence. Notice when we use a comma (,): *We got wet **because** it rained. I stayed at home **as** I was really tired. **Since** you won't help me, I'll do it myself.*

 As and *since* are less common than *because*.

- We can also use *because of* + noun: *We couldn't go out **because of the rain**.*
- We use *so* and *therefore* to introduce a result or a consequence.
  - *So* comes in the middle of a sentence: *She was ill, **so** she didn't go to work.*
  - *Therefore* comes in the following positions: *This is a smaller car and **therefore** it uses less petrol. This is a smaller car. **Therefore**, it uses less petrol. This is a smaller car and it **therefore** uses less petrol.*

PRACTICE

81a Complete the sentences. Use *because* or *so*.

   0 I didn't go to the concert ....*because*.......... I hate loud music.

   1 Wilma had toothache, ... she went to the dentist.

   2 .... Aldo only had a small flat, Gianni couldn't stay with him.

   3 Everything was closed .... it was Sunday.

   4 It was quite cold, ... no one wanted to eat outside.

   5 The shops weren't open, ... I couldn't buy any bread.

   6 The road was blocked .... there had been a heavy snowfall.

81b Circle the correct answer.

   0 They were late for work *because of* / (*because*) they got up late.

   1 We missed the bus, *as* / *so* we had to ask my sister to take us to the station.

   2 *Since* / *So* she had nothing to do, Brigitte decided to visit her sister.

   3 Mike went to see his doctor *so* / *as* he kept getting headaches.

   4 Latin is a dead language. *So* / *Therefore*, it isn't popular with most students.

   5 I couldn't sleep last night *since* /*because of* the heat.

   6 The world is getting hotter. *Because* / *Therefore*, deserts are getting bigger.

   7 Emma was bored *as* / *so* all her friends were away that weekend.

   8 *Because* / *So* Paul took us in his car, we got home really quickly.

81c **Complete the sentences. Use one or two words in each gap.**

0 As the weather was good, we went swimming every day.
...*Because of*... the good weather, we went swimming every day.

1 I didn't go to the disco because I hate loud music.
I hate loud music, ... I didn't go to the disco.

2 I've spent all my money, so I can't get a taxi home.
I can't get a taxi home .... I've spent all my money.

3 Since we are both eighteen this month, we've decided to have a big party.
We're both eighteen this month, ... we've decided to have a big party.

4 There will be a lot of traffic, so people should drive carefully.
There will be a lot of traffic and .... people should drive carefully.

5 Kate had never sung in public before. Therefore, she felt extremely nervous.
Kate felt extremely nervous .... she'd never sung in public before.

6 The cost of petrol is very high, so I've decided not to get a car.
I've decided not to get a car .... the high cost of petrol.

82 Purpose: *to, in order to, so that*

- We use (*in order*) *to* + infinitive to explain our purpose for doing something:
  'Why did you come here?' 'I came here to see my cousin.' In order to is more formal.

- The negative is *in order not to* + infinitive: *I spoke quietly in order not to wake the baby.*

- We use (*in order*) *to* to link two sentences when the subject is the same. We use *so (that)* when the subject is the same or different. The pattern after *so (that)* is:
  subject (+ *will/can/could/would*) (+ *not*) + verb: *I came here so (that) I could see my cousin. He phoned his wife so (that) she wouldn't worry about him.*

PRACTICE

82a **Match the sentence halves.**

0	She phoned the dentist	$\boxed{f}$	**a** to ask what films are on.
1	He saved all his money	☐	**b** to buy some fresh fish.
2	We always meet on Saturday night	☐	**c** to go on holiday.
3	I eat lots of fruit	☐	**d** to go dancing.
4	They went to the market	☐	**e** to look smart at the wedding.
5	I'll ring the cinema	☐	**f** to make an appointment.
6	She's bought a new dress	☐	**g** to stay healthy.

82b **Circle the correct answer.**

HOW TO USE YOUR XYZ300 EXERCISE MACHINE

First of all, remove the XYZ from its box carefully (0) *so that not /* (*in order not to*)
break it. Then put in the battery (1) *so that / in order to* the positive end touches
the '+' sign in the machine. (2) *So that / In order to* check that the battery is
working before you use the XYZ, press the red button for five seconds (3) *so that /
in order to* all the lights come on. If they do, the machine is ready to use. If they
don't, start again.

Always start on Speed 1 (4) *so that / in order not to* the machine can warm up
slowly. (5) *So that / In order to* be sure that your XYZ stays in perfect condition,
always follow these instructions. We have a 24-hour emergency telephone hotline
(6) *so that / in order to* answer your questions.

82c **Join the sentences. Use the words in brackets.**

0   Rosa made a list. She wanted to remember what to buy. (so that)
    Rosa made a list so that she would remember what to buy.

1   Gary borrowed Jack's bike. He wanted to go to the library. (to)
    ....

2   The government passed a law. They wanted to stop people smoking at work.
    (in order to)
    ....

3   Yolanda trained a lot. She wanted to run a marathon. (so that)
    ....

4   Some people watch DVDs. They want to practise their English. (to)
    ....

5   I'll leave her a note. She'll know we've gone to the supermarket. (so that)
    ....

6   Companies advertise. They want to sell their products (in order to)
    ....

7   William is going on a diet. He wants to lose weight. (to)
    ....

8   Doctors vaccinate children. They want to prevent diseases. (in order to)
    ....

Check 19 Linking words and structures (1)

1 Complete the sentences. Use the words in the box.

> also although in order to neither so

1 In the Cup Final .... United nor City played well.

2 It's necessary to take a theory exam .... pass your driving test.

3 .... Chris had promised to text Jo, he completely forgot.

4 Alex loves rock music and he .... likes jazz and reggae.

5 Lisa hurt her foot, ... she couldn't dance.

/ 5

2 Choose the correct answer.

Last summer Sue went to visit her friend Ann for the weekend. (6) ...... , when she got there, nobody answered the door. Sue called Ann on her mobile. 'Sorry,' said Ann. 'I won't be home until seven (7) ...... I have to work late, (8) ...... I've left a key with the neighbour (9) ...... you can get into my flat.'

But Ann's neighbour was out (10) ...... ! (11) ...... she'd forgotten about Sue or she'd had to go out. (12) ...... it was only twelve, Sue went to the nearest café (13) ...... have something to eat. She was so hungry that she had a bowl of soup, some spaghetti and a piece of cake (14) .... Then Sue went back to the neighbour's house. Luckily, she was at home, (15) ...... Sue was able to get into Ann's flat.

6	A However	B So that	C Since	D Therefore
7	A because	B but	C as well	D in order to
8	A and	B to	C also	D but
9	A because	B so that	C though	D in order to
10	A so	B either	C too	D however

11	A However	B Neither	C Too	D Either
12	A Neither	B Also	C As	D However
13	A so that	B to	C but	D because
14	A as well	B either	C both	D and
15	A because	B as	C so	D in order to

/ 10

3 Complete the article. Use *and, as, both, or* or *to*.

The new Wizard Console is coming!
Be there!

The Wizard Games Console will be launched at a party in New York next month (16) .... we have ten tickets to give away to the winners of our competition! (17) .... get your ticket, all you have to do is answer the question on page 7 of the magazine. Then either text (18) .... e-mail your answer to us. If you answer correctly, you may win two tickets to the Wizard party. Bring a friend with you and you can (19) .... spend two nights in a five-star hotel. (20) .... the question is so easy, everyone has a chance to be at the party. Enter the competition now!

/ 5

Total: / 20

✓ Self-check

Wrong answers	Look again at	Try CD-ROM
4, 10, 14, 16	Unit 78	Exercise 78
1, 11, 18, 19	Unit 79	Exercise 79
3, 6, 8	Unit 80	Exercise 80
5, 7, 12, 15, 20	Unit 81	Exercise 81
2, 9, 13, 17	Unit 82	Exercise 82

Now do **Check 19**

83 Saying when things happen

We use *when, while, before, after, as soon as* and *until* to say when things happen, often in relation to other events: *I got this bike **when** I lived in London.* ***While** he was shopping, he saw Guy. I always have a shower **before** I go out. **After** you exercise, you need to drink water. **As soon as** she saw him, she recognised him. **Until** they tried it, they never thought horse riding was fun.*

PRACTICE

83a **Choose the correct answer.**

I loved my cat (O) ...... I spotted her. She was so sweet. I saw her (1) ...... I was walking home from the gym. In fact, I heard her (2) ...... I saw her. She was making a terrible noise! I didn't see that her leg was hurt (3) ...... I got close. I think a car had hit her (4) ...... she was crossing the road. But (5) ...... I picked her up, I saw that she wasn't hurt badly. (6) ...... I got home, I washed her leg gently. (7) ...... I'd given her a drink of water, she fell asleep. I never realised how affectionate cats could be (8) ...... I got Mimi. I'm so glad I found her!

	A		B		C		D	
o	A until	B while	Ⓒ as soon as	D before
1	A while	B before	C after	D until
2	A until	B while	C before	D after
3	A until	B after	C as soon as	D while
4	A before	B until	C while	D after
5	A while	B when	C until	D soon
6	A Until	B Before	C While	D As soon as
7	A Soon	B After	C While	D Until
8	A after	B when	C as soon as	D until

83b **Complete the text. Use *when, while, before, after, as soon as* or *until*. There may be more than one possible answer.**

"(0) ......*When*...... I was in town last week, someone said hello to me. He stopped to chat. (1) .... I heard his voice, I realised I knew him. (2) .... we were talking, I tried to remember who he was, but I had no idea (3) .... he asked me about my parents. Then I realised he'd lived near me (4) .... I still lived at home. As he was older, he'd left home (5) .... me. (6) .... we'd chatted for a while, we exchanged phone numbers and we're going to meet again soon."

84 Future time clauses

- We use the present simple, not *will*, in future time clauses with *when, before, after* and *as soon as*: *I'll turn off the lights **when I leave**.* (Not *I'll turn off the lights when I'll leave.*)
- A future time clause can come at the beginning of a sentence or after the main clause. When it comes at the beginning, we put a comma (,) after it: ***When she sees the mess,** she'll be very angry. She'll be very angry **when she sees the mess**.*

P R A C T I C E

84a Circle the correct answer.

0   As soon as I (finish) / 'll finish my work, I go / ('ll go) for a swim.

1   Meg *is* / *will be* at the hotel when I *arrive* / *'ll arrive*.

2   Don't worry. Before I *go* / *'ll go* out, I *wash up* / *'ll wash up*.

3   After I *finish* / *'ll finish* reading this book, I *lend* / *'ll lend* it to you.

4   We *decide* / *'ll decide* which film to see as soon as they *get* / *'ll get* here.

5   I *invite* / *'ll invite* Bianca for dinner before she *goes* / *'ll go* back to Italy.

6   They *pay* / *'ll pay* us for the tickets after we *buy* / *'ll buy* them.

7   When it *stops* / *'ll stop* raining, we *go* / *'ll go* for a walk.

8   The shop *phones* / *will phone* as soon as the DVD player *arrives* / *will arrive*.

84b Complete the sentences. Use the correct form of the verbs in brackets.

A: It's great that you're coming to Geneva. Which campsite are you staying at?

B: I don't know yet. We (0) ....*'ll look*......... (look) for campsites on the Internet before we (1) .... (go). When we (2) .... (see) which ones have got swimming pools, we (3) .... (mark) them on the map. We (4) .... (visit) the ones near the city when we (5) .... (arrive) and choose a nice one.

A: Great! And as soon as you (6) .... (tell) us the address, we (7) .... (come) and find you. We (8) .... (show) you the city and of course we (9) .... (invite) you to our new flat before you (10) .... (leave) for Zermatt.

85 *before/after + -ing*

- We use *before* or *after + -ing* to link two actions if the subject is the same: ***Before coming** to Turkey, Abdul lived in Syria.*
- We cannnot do this if the subject is different: *After **Anna** moved away, **Dawn** was lonely.* (Not *After Anna moving away, Dawn was lonely.*)

PRACTICE

85a **Re-write the sentences. Use *before/after + -ing*.**

o I never leave the house before I check the doors and windows.
I never leave the house before checking the doors and windows.

1 Before you buy a new car, you should go for a test drive.

....

2 I decided to learn Italian after I spent two weeks in Rome.

....

3 Before she moved to London, Lisa lived in a small village.

....

4 After we ate your home-made jam, we decided to make some ourselves.

....

5 Steve and Sue always visit us before they leave their holiday cottage.

....

85b **Decide the order of the actions. Then use *-ing* and the word in brackets to join the sentences.**

o You go to England. You have to get a passport. (before)
Before going to England, you have to get a passport.

1 You buy a plane ticket. You should look for special offers online. (before)

....

2 You have to go through a security check. You get on the plane. (before)

....

3 You go into the departures area. You can buy tax-free products. (after)

....

4 You leave the plane. You should check you have all your hand luggage. (before)

....

5 You can collect your luggage. You go through passport control. (after)

....

6 You arrive in London. You must be careful with your things. (after)

....

7 You see London. You should visit Oxford or Cambridge. (after)

....

86 Sequencers

- We use *first, then, next, after that* and *finally* to show the order of actions.

- We use them for the events or actions in a story. We do not often use commas here: **First** *Joy lived in Bath.* **Then** *she moved to London to study Spanish.* **Next** *she went to Spain for a year.* **After that** *she lived in Peru for ten years.* **Finally** *she came back to London.*

- We also use them to give instructions. Notice the use of commas here: **First**, *press 'Set up' to display the menu options.* **Next**, *select an option using the arrow keys.* **Finally**, *press 'Enter'.*

P R A C T I C E

86a Complete the texts. Use *first, after, after that, next, then* or *finally*.

> We wanted to go for a picnic, so (0) ....*first*........ we got everything ready.
> (1) .... it started to rain, so we decided not to go. But
> (2) .... a while the rain stopped and the sun came out.
> (3) .... we were able to have our picnic.

> OK. I'll show you how to use the photocopier. (4) .... , put the paper in the tray here. (5) .... , key in how many copies you need. And (6) .... , press this green button. It's easy, isn't it?

86b Complete the e-mail. Use one or two words in each gap.

● ● ●	New Message	◯

Hi, Scot!

Just a quick message to tell you my news. I've just passed my motorbike test! Before taking it, I was really nervous, but I started well and (0) ....*after*........ that I relaxed. Of course I can't get a motorbike yet. (1) .... I need to save enough money for the deposit.

I also had my first taekwondo class last week. It was amazing. (2) .... the instructor explained the history of the sport. (3) .... , after we had done some stretching exercises, we tried some of the kicks. It's more difficult than it looks! (4) .... we practised some relaxation techniques. Anyway, I'll let you know how I progress.

Write soon, Lee

Check 20 Linking words and structures (2)

1 Choose the correct answer.

(1) ...... I was sixteen, I learnt to kite surf (2) ...... I was on holiday. (3) ...... going in the sea, you do a short course on the beach with an instructor. (4) ...... you fly a small kite (5) ...... you can do it well. (6) ...... you learn to use a much bigger kite to pull you through the water. (7) ...... you can try to fly the kite with a board on your feet. It's hard at first, but (8) ...... a while I started to feel more confident and I loved it. (9) ...... doing it several times, I've become quite good at it and (10) ...... I have the money, I'll buy my own kite and board.

1 A Next   B Then   C Until   D When

2 A finally B after   C while   D as soon as

3 A Next   B Before   C Then   D As soon as

4 A First   B After   C Then   D When

5 A while   B before   C until   D as soon as

6 A While   B Finally   C Next   D After

7 A Finally B When   C Until   D As soon as

8 A until   B when   C while   D after

9 A Before   B After   C Next   D While

10 A until   B then   C next   D as soon as

/ 10

2 Complete the sentences. Use the words in the box.

after   as soon as   before   when   while

11 Sorry I'm late! I had a problem with the car but I came .... I could.

12 .... watching the DVD, everyone went to bed.

13 .... I go out to the shops, I'll get some more bread.

14 You should always read the instructions .... using a new video game.

15 .... she was walking through the market, she saw an old friend.

/ 5

3 Complete the second sentence so that it means the same as the first. Use no more than three words.

16 Terry's going to ring me to tell me if he's coming to dinner.
I won't know if Terry's coming to dinner until .... me.

17 After finishing work, I'll go to the market to buy some food.
After I .... , I'll go to the market to buy some food.

18 I'll start making dinner immediately after getting home.
I'll start making dinner as soon as .... home.

19 We'll go to the cinema after dinner.
First we'll have dinner and .... we'll go to the cinema.

20 We won't decide what film to see until we arrive at the cinema.
We'll decide what film to see .... arrive at the cinema.

/ 5

Total: / 20

✓ **Self-check**

Wrong answers	Look again at	Try CD-ROM
1, 2, 5, 11, 15	**Unit 83**	Exercise 83
10, 13, 16, 17, 18, 20	**Unit 84**	Exercise 84
3, 9, 12, 14	**Unit 85**	Exercise 85
4, 6, 7, 8, 19	**Unit 86**	Exercise 86

Now do **Check 20**

Conditionals

87 The zero conditional

- We use the zero conditional to talk about something that is always true as a result of a possible action or situation: *If you keep milk in a fridge, it stays fresh longer.*
- To form zero conditional sentences, we use *if/when* + present simple + present simple: ***When** she **gets** home early, she **goes** for a run in the park.*
- The *if/when* clause can come at the beginning of the sentence or after the main clause. When it comes at the beginning, we put a comma (,) after it: ***If I have dinner late**, I don't sleep well. I don't sleep well **if I have dinner late**.*

PRACTICE

87a Match the two parts of the zero conditional sentences.

0	Water turns into steam	**c**	**a**	if you want cheap air tickets.
1	If you want to visit the USA,	☐	**b**	if you have a good Internet connection.
2	You have to book early	☐	**c**	when you heat it to 100°C.
3	When babies are hungry,	☐	**d**	if you drive fast.
4	I get cold feet	☐	**e**	they cry.
5	Cars use more petrol	☐	**f**	if I don't wear woollen socks in winter.
6	Downloading music is quick	☐	**g**	you need a visa.

87b Complete the zero conditional sentences. Use the correct form of the verbs in brackets.

0 When they ....*go*.......... on holiday, a neighbour ....*feeds*........ their cat. (go, feed)

1 He .... early when he .... study a lot. (get up, have to)

2 If I .... late, I usually .... to the college. (not be, walk)

3 What .... if you .... problems getting to sleep? (you / do, have)

4 If James .... to see her, she .... the door. (come, not answer)

5 When I .... advice, I usually .... to my older brother. (need, talk)

6 .... your mobile when you .... in a restaurant? (you / turn off, be)

88 The first conditional

- We use the first conditional to talk about something that may happen in the future, as a result of a possible action or situation: *If it's sunny later, we'll go to the beach.*

- To form first conditional sentences, we use *if* + present simple + *will*/modal verb/ imperative: **If it rains** later, we **won't go out.** **If** your flight **isn't** late, **I can meet** you at the airport. **If you see** Di, **tell** her to ring me.

- The *if* clause can come at the beginning of the sentence or after the main clause. When it comes at the beginning, we put a comma (,) after it: **If it gets colder,** we'll light a fire. We'll light a fire **if it gets colder.**

▶▶   **For future time clauses with when, after, before and as soon as, see Unit 84.**

PRACTICE

88a Circle the correct answer.

0 I *call* / *('ll call)* you if the train *(arrives)* / *will arrive* late.

1 Dr Lee *doesn't* / *can't* see you today if you *don't* / *won't* have an appointment.

2 If we *walk* / *'ll walk* faster, we *get* / *'ll get* to the cinema on time.

3 If you *go* / *'ll go* to the supermarket, *buy* / *you buy* some milk.

4 They *get* / *won't get* lost if they *take* / *'ll take* a map with them.

5 If you *see* / *will see* a snake, you *don't* / *mustn't* touch it!

6 *Don't* / *You don't* tell John where I am if he *asks* / *'ll ask* you.

7 We *catch* / *'ll catch* the last bus home if we *hurry* / *'ll hurry*.

8 If he *doesn't tell* / *not tell* her the truth, she *might be* / *is* very angry.

88b Complete the conversation. Use the correct form of the verbs in brackets.

A: Do you think Tina will be OK in Paris?

B: I'm sure she (0) ....*'ll be*....... (be) happy if she (1) .... (make) friends quickly and if she (2) .... (feel) lonely at first, she (3) .... (can / phone) us.

C: She's going soon. If we (4) .... (not organise) a party now, it (5) .... (might / be) too late.

D: She (6) .... (be) disappointed if she (7) .... (not get) a present from us. If we all (8) .... (give) some money, we (9) .... (can / get) something nice.

A: If you (10) .... (see) her, (11) .... (ask) her if there's anything she needs, but (12) .... (not mention) the party. Then it'll be a surprise!

88c **Write first conditional questions.**

o I / get into / the concert / if / I / not buy / a ticket in advance?
Will I get into the concert if I don't buy a ticket in advance?

1 if / I / phone / you at six o'clock / you / be / at home?

....

2 what / we / do / if / the restaurant / not serve / vegetarian food?

....

3 Jean / be / angry / if / we / not arrive / on time?

....

4 if / I / get / a laptop / where / I / should / buy / it?

....

5 who / you / go / on holiday with / if / you / win / the competition?

....

6 if / you / go away / this weekend / I / can / have / a party in the flat?

....

88d **Match the questions in 88c with the answers.**

a	No, she won't.	☐	**e** They do. I checked.	☐
b	Yes, I will.	☐	**f** On the Internet.	☐
c	Probably with David.	☐	**g** No, you won't.	☐ o
d	No, you can't!	☐		

88e **Complete the conversation. Use the correct form of the verbs in the box.**

| book   do   find   ~~go~~   look   might / find |
| not be able to / stay   not know   spend |

A: Where shall we go this summer?

B: I'd like to go to New York, but it's really expensive. If we (0) ....*go*......... there, we (1) .... very long. How about going round Europe by train?

A: No way! If we (2) .... that, we (3) .... more time travelling than visiting places.

B: What do you suggest?

A: Let me search the Internet. If I (4) .... online, you never know, I (5) .... a cheap flight to somewhere really exciting.

B: But how (6) .... you .... a cheap flight if you (7) .... where we're going?

A: There are websites that have special offers.

B: Well, if you see two cheap flights to New York, (8) .... them! Because that's where I want to go.

89 *unless*

- We can use *unless* in first conditional sentences to mean *if not*: *Your English won't get better **unless** you study more.* (Your English won't get better if you don't study more.)
- We usually use *unless* with an affirmative verb: *They won't let you into the club **unless** you **wear** a tie.*

P R A C T I C E

89a Complete the sentences. Use *if* or *unless*.

0   I won't go to university this year ....*unless*........ I can study medicine.

1   I won't be able to study medicine .... I get good exam results.

2   .... I don't get good exam results, I'll take my exams again next year.

3   I'll have time to go travelling .... I don't go to university.

4   But .... I work this summer, I won't have enough money to go travelling.

5   I won't find a summer job .... I start looking for one soon.

6   .... I contact my uncle, he might give me a job in his company.

7   My uncle won't give me a job .... I do well at school.

8   But .... I do well at school, I'll have good exam results and I won't need a job!

89b Re-write the sentences.

0   She won't believe you if you don't tell her the truth.
She won't believe you unless ....*you tell her the truth*................ .

1   I won't come to the barbecue if you don't invite my boyfriend as well.
I won't come to the barbecue unless ....

2   Unless we get to the airport early, we won't get a window seat on the plane.
If .... , we won't get a window seat on the plane.

3   Frozen food can be bad for you unless you cook it very well.
Frozen food can be bad for you if ....

4   If he doesn't listen to people, he'll never have many friends.
Unless .... , he'll never have many friends.

5   That plant will die if she doesn't water it more often.
That plant will die unless ....

6   If you don't phone to say sorry, Helen will never forgive you.
Unless .... , Helen will never forgive you.

7   We'll never finish unless we get some help.
We'll never finish if ....

90 The second conditional

- We use the second conditional to talk about:
  - the result of an action or situation that is imaginary or impossible: *If he **was** younger, he'**d get** the job.* (This is impossible; he cannot become younger.)
  - an action that is not likely to happen in the present or future: *If I **won** the lottery, I'**d buy** a house.* (This is not likely. I probably won't win the lottery.)
- To form second conditional sentences, we use *if* + past simple + *would*: *If she **knew** the answer, she **would tell** us.*
- In formal English, we use *were* after *if* instead of *was*: *If he **were** younger, he'**d get** the job.*
- We can use *if I were you* to give advice: *If I **were you**, I'**d tell** the truth.*
- The *if* clause can come at the beginning of the sentence or after the main clause. When it comes at the beginning, we put a comma (,) after it: *If I knew the answer, I'd tell you. I'd tell you if I knew the answer.*

PRACTICE

90a Circle the correct answer.

A: I've got a problem. John lent me his MP3 player and I've lost it. What (0) *did /* ⟨*would*⟩ you do if you (1) *were /* '*d be* me?

B: I (2) *bought /* '*d buy* him a new one.

A: What about you, Danny? (3) *Would / Did* you buy him a new one?

C: No, I (4) *didn't / wouldn't*. I (5) *told /* '*d tell* him what happened and wait to see what he said first.

_____

A: If you (6) *found /* '*d find* a wallet in the street, what (7) *did / would* you do?

B: If it (8) *had / would have* identification in it, I (9) *took /* '*d take* it to the police.

A: And if it (10) *didn't / wouldn't* have any, (11) *did / would* you keep the money?

B: Yes, I (12) *did / would*. Why do you ask?

A: I've just found one and I don't know what to do.

90b Complete the conversations. Use the correct form of the verbs in brackets.

A: I feel exhausted. I don't sleep at night.

B: I think you'd sleep better if you (0) ....*did*............ (do) some exercise during the day. And if you (1) .... (sleep) better, maybe you (2) .... (not be) so irritable!

_____

A: Becky's not doing well at school.

B: She (3) .... (get) better marks if she (4) .... (not watch) so much TV. Then she (5) .... (be able to) study whatever she wanted at university.

_____

A: I don't know what to do. If I (6) .... (have) some money, I (7) .... (go away) in August, but I spend all the money I get.

B: If I (8) .... (be) you, and if I (9) .... (need) some money to go on holiday, I (10) .... (ask) my parents to lend me some.

90c Write second conditional questions.

0 if / you / find / someone's diary / what / you / do?
   A: *If you found someone's diary, what would you do?*   **B:** I'd read it.

1 if / you / see / a ghost / you / be / frightened?
   A: ....   **B:** Yes, I would!

2 if / Sarah / have / a problem / who / she / talk to?
   A: ....   **B:** She'd talk to you.

3 Marc / come / to the party / if / I / ask / him?
   A: ....   **B:** No, he wouldn't.

4 what / you / do / if / you / be / in Kate's position?
   A: ....   **B:** I'd tell the truth.

5 if / you / can / go / anywhere / where / you / go?
   A: ....   **B:** I'd go to Cuba.

90d Re-write the sentences.

0 I'm busy, so I'm not going to the party tonight.
   If ....*I wasn't busy, I'd go to the party tonight*............... .

1 Toni doesn't want to see us, so he doesn't phone us.
   If ....

2 We don't eat out because it's so expensive.
   If ....

3 You won't get in the football team because you don't come to training sessions.
   If ....

4 The students enjoy your lessons, so they come to every class.
   If ....

5 She practises every day, so she's very good.
   If ....

6 I won't win the lottery, so I'll carry on working.
   If ....

Check 21 Conditionals

1 Circle the correct answer.

A: This plant's dying and I don't know why.

B: Do you water it a lot? Some plants (1) *will die / die / died* when you (2) *'ll give / give / 'd give* them too much water.

A: No, I don't. Just a couple of times a week.

B: In that case it's the light. Unless you (3) *move / don't move / 'll move* it to a place with more light, it (4) *survives / doesn't survive / might not survive.*

A: If I (5) *have / had / 'd have* a balcony or a garden, I (6) *'ll put / put / 'd put* it there, but this is the best place for it.

B: Why don't you get a plant that can survive with less light? I (7) *'ll tell / tell / 'd tell* Jenny to give you a ring if I (8) *'ll see / see / saw* her. She knows a lot about plants.

/ 8

2 Complete the e-mail. Use the correct form of the verbs in brackets.

```
○○○              New Message              ⬭

Hi, Jean!
You asked for my advice about Kevin
and the money you lent him. If I
(9) ....................... (be) you, I
(10) ....................... (not get) angry
about it. He's preparing for his driving
test and everyone (11) .......................
(forget) things when they
(12) ....................... (have) a lot to think
about. If you remind him about the
money after his test, I'm sure he
(13) ....................... (pay) you back.
And if he (14) ....................... (not
pay) you back then, you'll have a good
reason to be angry!

Does that help? Robert
```

/ 6

3 Complete the second sentence so that it means the same as the first one. Use no more than three words.

15 Don't visit Cornwall in August because it's impossible to find a hotel room.
If you visit Cornwall in August, you .... a hotel room.

16 We don't have a spare room, so you can't stay here.
If we .... a spare room, you could stay here.

17 If I'm not at work, I'll meet you at the station.
Unless I .... , I'll meet you at the station.

18 I'm very busy during the week, so I won't see you much.
If I wasn't so busy during the week, I .... you more.

19 If the weather isn't bad at the weekend, we'll go for a walk.
Unless .... bad at the weekend, we'll go for a walk.

20 Bring your swimming costume and we can go to the beach.
If .... your swimming costume, we can go to the beach.

/ 6

Total: / 20

✓ Self-check

Wrong answers	Look again at	Try CD-ROM
1, 2, 11, 12	Unit 87	Exercise 87
4, 7, 8, 13, 14, 15, 20	Unit 88	Exercise 88
3, 17, 19	Unit 89	Exercise 89
5, 6, 9, 10, 16, 18	Unit 90	Exercise 90

Now do **Check 21**

Prepositions

91 Prepositions of place

We use prepositions of place to talk about where things or people are.

*The post office is **under** the travel agency. There is a flag **on top of** the building. The bank is **between** the post office and the library. My flat is **above** the bank. My flat is **near** the park. The park is **behind** the library. There are picnic tables **among** the trees. The library is **next to** the bank. There is a clock **on** the wall of the library. There is a car **in front of** the library. There is a family **in** the car. The bus stop is **opposite** the bank. There are some people **at** the bus stop.*

⚠️ We use *at* when the exact position is not important: *He was waiting **at** the station.*

PRACTICE

91a **Complete the article. Use prepositions.**

This is a picture of a girl's bedroom. There's a bed (0) ......*between*...... two tables, and there's a poster (1) .... the wall (2) .... the bed. There's an alarm clock (3) .... one of the tables (4) .... the bed. There are some shoes (5) .... the bed.

There's a desk with a computer (6) .... it. There's a lamp (7) .... the computer. There's a wastepaper bin (8) .... the desk. (9) .... the desk there's a large kite and (10) .... the desk there's a chair. (11) .... the window there's a wardrobe with some clothes (12) .... it. There's a collection of dolls (13) .... a shelf. They're (14) .... a photo and some books.

91b **Complete the sentences. Use prepositions.**

o My cat spends a lot of time hiding ......*under*...... the bed.

1 Victor is .... the sports centre this morning. He's playing squash.

2 We live .... the fourth floor. My parents live .... us .... the fifth floor.

3 On a plane, I like sitting .... the window. I hate sitting .... two strangers.

4 We waited for ages .... the tourist office. The man .... us had a lot of questions. The couple .... us were getting impatient.

5 Ours is the only new house .... a lot of old houses.

6 It's raining, so the children are playing .... their room.

7 I live .... my school. I only have to cross the road in the morning.

8 There's a big television aerial .... my block of flats.

92 Prepositions of movement

We use prepositions of movement to describe where things or people move.

*Clive walked **out of** his house and **down** the steps.*

*He walked **along** the pavement and **across** the street.*

*He went **to** a market and walked **round** the stalls.*

*He walked **away from** the market and **towards** the park.*

*He walked **past** a pond. A plane was flying **over** the park.*

*He jumped **off** a wall and walked **through** the wood.*

*He walked **under** a bridge and **up** some steps.*

*He went **into** the theatre.*

*He walked **onto** the stage.*

PRACTICE

92a Circle the correct answer.

0 You should never walk *over* / *under* a ladder – it's bad luck.

1 At the weekend we enjoy walking *through* / *along* the woods near our home.

2 The man got *out of* / *down* his car and locked the door.

3 We rested after walking *into* / *up* the hill. Then we walked *down* / *under* again.

4 They drove *towards* / *through* the station, but turned left before they got there.

5 One day I'd like to sail *past* / *across* the Pacific Ocean.

6 If you go *along* / *onto* this street, you'll see a café on the right.

7 We drove *round* / *over* the Golden Gate Bridge in San Francisco.

8 It was cold, so we went *into* / *out of* a café to have a hot drink.

9 The London tour bus goes *across* / *past* the London Eye and Big Ben.

10 We climbed *onto* / *up* the roof of our building to watch the procession.

11 I felt very sad as we drove *away from* / *off* our old home.

12 Clare bumped into the table and some glasses fell *off* / *out of* and broke.

92b Complete the text. Use the prepositions in the box.

across	down	~~into~~	out of	over	past	round	through	up

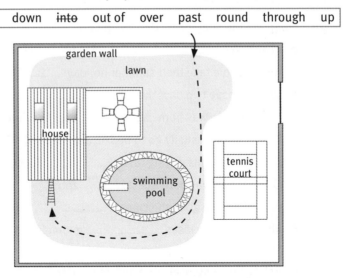

I know how the thief got (0) ......**into**........ my house because I saw his tracks. First he climbed (1) .... the garden wall. Then he walked (2) .... the lawn, (3) .... the tennis court and (4) .... the swimming pool to the back of the house. There, he climbed (5) .... a ladder and (6) .... one of the upstairs windows. He took my jewellery and went (7) .... the stairs and (8) .... the house. Then his tracks disappeared.

93 Prepositions of time (1)

We use prepositions of time to say when something happens.

- We use *on* with days or dates: ***on** Wednesday(s)* ***on** 6th July* ***on** my birthday*
- We use *in* with parts of the day, months, seasons, years and centuries: *in the afternoon* ***in** September* ***in** the summer* ***in** 1999* ***in** the eighteenth century*
- We use *at* with clock times: ***at** five past nine* ***at** midday* ***at** midnight* ***at** lunchtime*
- We use *at about* if the time is not exact: *I got up **at about** eleven.*
- We also say: ***at** night* ***at** the weekend* ***at** Christmas* ***at** Easter* ***at** the moment*
- We can use *before/after* + noun/pronoun/clause/-*ing* to talk about the order of two events or actions: *I arrived **after Sam and June**. I arrived **after them**. I arrived **after the party had started**. I danced **before leaving**.*

⚠ We say ***in** the morning*, but ***on** Monday morning*.

▶▶ *For more on before and after, see Units 83, 84 and 85.*

P R A C T I C E

93a **Complete the sentences. Use *on*, *in* or *at*.**

0   I can't go out ....*on*......... Saturday because I have a family dinner.

1   Most people take their summer holiday .... July or August.

2   We only have two days' holiday .... Easter.

3   Shakespeare was born .... 23rd April 1564.

4   Their children usually go to bed .... half past nine.

5   Matt is taking his driving test .... Tuesday morning.

6   Our first son was born .... 2002.

7   A lot of people go to the cinema .... the weekend.

8   The restaurant closes .... midnight.

93b **Complete the sentences. Use *before* or *after*.**

0   Please turn off the lights ....*before*...... you leave the house.

1   It's a good idea to answer e-mails as soon as possible .... you receive them.

2   I usually read .... going to sleep at night.

3   We left .... the film finished, so I can't tell you what happened in the end.

4   A lot of students do one or two hours of homework every evening .... school.

5   I'd like to visit The British Museum .... I leave London.

6   .... finishing work, I went out for a coffee with my friends.

93c **Complete the article. Use *on, in, at, before* or *after*.**

The *Burning of the Clocks festival* in Brighton, England takes place (0) ....*in*.......... winter and celebrates the shortest day of the year. The festival only started (1) .... 1993 and is now celebrated (2) .... 21st December every year. The festival takes place (3) .... night. It starts (4) .... six o'clock (5) .... the evening with a procession of enormous paper clocks. (6) .... the festival people spend weeks making the clocks. These are then burnt on a big fire (7) .... about seven o'clock. (8) .... the fire there are fireworks and music and dancing on the beach.

94 Time expressions with no preposition

We do not use a preposition before:

- time expressions with *last, this, next* and *all*: *Some friends came to dinner **last Saturday**.* (Not ~~on last Saturday~~) *I'm on holiday **this week**.* (Not ~~in this week~~) *He's going to start an Italian course **next July**.* (Not ~~in next July~~) *I haven't stopped **all morning**.* (Not ~~in all morning~~)

- *today, tonight, yesterday, tomorrow*: *I was tired **yesterday**. I'm going to go to bed early **tonight**.*

- expressions with *yesterday* and *tomorrow*: *I got up at six o'clock **yesterday morning** to meet my sister at the airport. My university course starts **the day after tomorrow**. I saw them **the day before yesterday**.*

 We say *yesterday morning, yesterday afternoon* and *yesterday evening*, but *last night*.

PRACTICE

94 **Re-write the sentences. Use the time expressions in the box.**

> all day   ~~last Monday~~   last night   next week   the day after tomorrow
> the day before yesterday   this week   tomorrow evening
> yesterday afternoon

Today is Thursday 13th July.

0 I had to meet my tutor at university on Monday 10th July.
I had to meet my tutor last Monday.
....

1 I'm going to the cinema on Friday 14th July at 7pm.
....

2 We had an interesting lecture on 11th July.
....

3 I've been at university since eight this morning and I'm still here at six o'clock.
....

4 I'm going to meet my friends to go shopping on Saturday 15th July.
....

5 I went to bed at midnight on 12th July.
....

6 I have to do an exam on Wednesday 19th July.
....

7 I've been to the gym every morning from 10–13th July.
....

8 I worked in the library from 2– 6pm on 12th July.
....

95 Prepositions of time (2)

- We use *from ... to ...* to say how long an action or event lasts: *I work **from** Monday **to** Friday. I lived in South Africa **from** 2001 **to** 2003.*
- We use *until* or *till* to say when an action or event finishes: *He's staying in Rome **until** Friday.* (He leaves on Friday.) *I stayed in bed **until** ten o'clock today.*
- We can use *by* to mean 'not later than': *You must finish this report **by** Friday.*
- We can use *for* to talk about a period of time: *I exercise **for** an hour a day. I worked as a waiter **for** a year. I'm going away **for** the weekend.*
- We use *during* to mean 'at some time in a period of time': *I often wake up **during** the night. His mobile phone rang three times **during** the meal.*

⚠ Compare *during* and *while*:
- *during* + noun: *Don't talk **during the film**.*
- *while* + clause: *Don't talk **while we're watching the film**.*

PRACTICE

95a **Complete the sentences. Use *from, to, by, until, for* or *during*.**

0 Paul studied computer engineering ....*from*......... 2000 to 2003.

1 After he graduated, he went on holiday to Spain. He stayed there .... the summer was over.

2 When he returned, he worked for his father .... the beginning of September .... the end of the year.

3 After that, Paul decided to go to the United States .... a while.

4 .... his time in the States, he started his own computer business.

5 .... the end of the year, Paul was a millionaire.

95b **Complete the article. Use *from, to, by, until, for* or *during*.**

Yesterday morning I went shopping with mum (0) ......*for*...... a couple of hours. We came home and I helped her clean the house from twelve (1) .... two. After lunch I read in my room, but (2) .... about four o'clock I was bored, so I called Fran and we arranged to go out. We met at a café and stayed there (3) .... six to seven. Then we went dancing at a club. (4) .... the evening I met Tim, an old friend of mine, and we chatted (5) .... half an hour. Fran and I stayed at the club (6) .... it closed and then got a taxi home.

96 *with, by*

- We use *with* + noun/pronoun to talk about the instrument we use to do something: *In China people eat **with chopsticks**.* (They use chopsticks to eat.) *I clean my teeth **with an electric toothbrush**. Do you know where the scissors are? I want to cut some paper **with them**.*

- We use *by* + *-ing* to talk about how we do something: *I keep fit **by going** to the gym every day. She learnt French **by talking** to French people. You turn on the DVD **by pressing** this button.*

P R A C T I C E

96a Circle the correct answer.

0   Most children learn to eat (with)/ *by* a knife and fork when they're about five.

1   The best way to stay cool in summer is *with* / *by* having cool showers.

2   You can learn a lot *with* / *by* watching documentaries on TV.

3   You play cricket *with* / *by* a bat and a very hard ball.

4   Before you get dressed, dry yourself *with* / *by* a towel.

5   Children learn to speak *with* / *by* repeating what their parents say.

6   You can only open that tin of cat food *with* / *by* a tin opener.

7   Some thieves got into my flat *with* / *by* breaking a window.

8   Do you dry your hair *with* / *by* a hairdryer?

96b Complete the sentences. Use *with* or *by* and the words in the box.

> a digital camera   a ruler   a vacuum cleaner   an electric razor
> chatting online   ~~going on a diet~~   listening to songs in English
> looking it up   working hard

0   He tried to lose weight ......*by going on a diet*...... .

1   A lot of students learn English vocabulary ....

2   You can only draw a really straight line ....

3   Nowadays, a lot of people make friends ....

4   The best way to clean this carpet is ....

5   You can find out what a word means .... in a dictionary.

6   I took all my holiday photos ....

7   The only way to become really successful is ....

8   All the men I know shave ....

97 *like*

- We use *like* + noun/pronoun to mean 'similar to': *Your coat is **like mine**.*
- We use *be/look/sound/smell/taste like* to ask for and give descriptions of people and things: ***'What's** your flat **like**?' 'It's quite big and modern.'*
  ***'What does** her cousin **look like**?' 'He's very good-looking!'* (Not *He looks like very good-looking.*)   ***'What did** the noise **sound like**?' 'It sounded like a car alarm.'*

P R A C T I C E

97a Write questions. Use *What + be + ... + like?* and the words in the box.

> <del>Oxford</del>   the accommodation   the buildings   the nightlife
> the other students   the teachers   the weather

0 A: *What's Oxford like?* .... **B:** It's a lovely place. I liked it a lot.

1 A: .... **B:** They're old but very beautiful.

2 A: .... **B:** It was fine. We stayed in college rooms.

3 A: .... **B:** They were good. I learnt a lot.

4 A: .... **B:** They were nice – from all over the world.

5 A: .... **B:** It's good. There's lots to do at night.

6 A: .... **B:** It was warm and sunny. It didn't rain once!

97b Write questions. Use *What do/does/did ... look/sound/smell/taste like?*

0 A: .... *What do* ..... the twins .... *look like* .... ? **B:** They've got long hair.

1 A: .... the music .... ? **B:** It sounded terrible.

2 A: .... her perfume .... ? **B:** It smells lovely.

3 A: .... your meal .... ? **B:** It tastes delicious.

4 A: .... these trousers .... ? **B:** They look great!

5 A: .... the noise .... ? **B:** It sounded like thunder.

6 A: .... Kelly .... ? **B:** She's got curly hair.

7 A: .... curry .... ? **B:** It tastes hot and spicy.

8 A: .... incense .... ? **B:** It smells fragrant.

9 A: .... the songs .... ? **B:** They were all right.

10 A: .... the new CD .... ? **B:** It sounds fantastic!

11 A: .... the coat .... ? **B:** It looked too small.

12 A: .... the medicine .... ? **B:** It tasted awful!

Check 22 Prepositions

1 **Complete the sentences. Use the words in the box. You do not need all of them.**

> between into like look like
> next to off on with

1 Ben paid for the ticket and put his wallet back .... his pocket.

2 Where's the corkscrew? I want to open this bottle of wine .... it.

3 Most people have an alarm clock .... their bed.

4 What's their new car .... ?

5 The theatre is .... the bank on the left and the book shop on the right.

/ 5

2 **Complete the second sentence so that it means the same as the first. Use no more than three words.**

6 Two days ago, I decided that I needed to get fit.
The .... yesterday, I decided that I needed to get fit.

7 I want to get fit no later than July.
I want to get fit .... July.

8 A friend told me that she ran every day to keep fit.
A friend told me that she kept fit .... every day.

9 So yesterday I finished work and then I put on my shorts and trainers.
So yesterday, ... finishing work, I put on my shorts and trainers.

10 I went to the park and ran, but I stopped when I was exhausted.
I went to the park and ran .... I was exhausted.

/ 5

3 **Circle the correct answer.**

(11) *On / In / At* August I visited Reykjavik in Iceland. What (12) *does / did / was* it like? Well, I was only there (13) *during / in / for* two days, but I had a fantastic time. When I arrived, I walked (14) *along / over / round* the city. I found a church in a little side street and got an amazing view of the whole city (15) *by / with / for* climbing onto the roof. I spent (16) *last / all / during* day sightseeing, so in the evening I was tired. However, I couldn't sleep because in summer it's still light (17) *in / on / at* night. (18) *The next / In the next / On next* day I decided to explore the countryside, so I strolled (19) *through / between / out of* some beautiful woods (20) *near / along / from* Reykjavik. It was a short walk, but I felt refreshed when I got back to town.

/ 10

Total: / 20

Prepositional phrases

98 Prepositional phrases: time

We can use *at*, *in* and *on* in time expressions. We say:

- *at first, at present, at once, at the same time, at last, at the latest: Learning a new language is hard **at first**. (= at the beginning) The Browns are decorating their new flat **at present**, so they're busy. (= at this moment/at this point in time) The boss wants to see you **at once**. (= immediately) She can talk and type **at the same time**. (= simultaneously) You're here **at last**! (= at the end of a long wait) We'll need your answer by Friday **at the latest**. (= not later than Friday)*

- *in advance, in time, in the end: Let us know **in advance** if you're coming to the party. (= before the party) I ran to catch the train, but didn't arrive **in time**. (= before the train left) We didn't move to Scotland **in the end**. (= finally, after considering it)*

- *on time: It's a surprise party, so please arrive **on time**. (= at the time arranged)*

P R A C T I C E

98a Circle the correct answer.

  0 If you're coming to the wedding, let me know by the 25ᵗʰ *at* / *in* / *on* the latest.

  1 I met Sophie at a party and I knew *at* / *in* / *on* once that we'd be good friends.

  2 You never arrive *at* / *in* / *on* time! You're always at least ten minutes late!

  3 University students often have to work and study *at* / *in* / *on* the same time.

  4 He hated Maths *at* / *in* / *on* first, but *at* / *in* / *on* the end he found it very easy.

  5 John's arrived *at* / *in* / *on* last, so we'll be at the restaurant in fifteen minutes.

  6 I'd like to get home *at* / *in* / *on* time to see the news.

98b Complete the article. Use the words in the box.

| at first | ~~at last~~ | at the latest | in advance | in the end | in time | on time |

After months of preparations, I was in London (0) ......*at last*...... . However, things didn't go very well (1) .... I hadn't booked a hotel (2) .... because I was sure that my flight would arrive (3) .... for me to find somewhere to stay. 'Even if it's late,' I thought, 'I'll be in London by six o'clock (4) ....' My flight didn't arrive (5) .... , though, and I found myself at the airport with nowhere to go. I considered sleeping there, but (6) .... I decided to get a room at one of the extremely expensive hotels nearby. Things could only get better!

99 Prepositional phrases: place and activity

We often use *at/in/on* + noun to say where someone is or what they are doing. We say:

- *at home, at school, at work, at college, at university, at lunch, at the door, at my desk*: *If Jerry's not **at home**, ring him on his mobile. I'll be **at lunch** from 1.30 to 2.30.*
- *in bed, in class, in hospital, in prison, in a meeting, in traffic*: *She's **in bed** with a bad cold. I can't talk now, I'm **in a meeting**.*
- *on a cruise, on an excursion, on a journey, on a trip, on my way, on business, on holiday, on strike, on the phone*: *We'll be **on holiday** for two weeks. I always take a book to read **on** long **journeys**.*

PRACTICE

99a Complete the conversation. Use *at, in* or *on*.

John: Hi, Tony.
Tony: Hi, John. Where are you? Are you (0) ....*at*......... home?
John: I'm (1) .... my way home. Why?
Tony: Well, I'm still (2) .... school. The problem is, Jayne's just phoned.
        She can't get here because the trains are (3) .... strike. I'm
        (4) .... class till seven o'clock, so I can't do her class and Tom's
        away (5) .... a Mediterranean cruise, as you know. Could you
        possibly come back to do Jayne's class?
John: OK, but if I get stuck (6) .... traffic, it might take half an hour to
        get there.
Tony: Don't worry. I'm just happy you can help out.

99b Complete the conversation. Use the words in the box.

| bed desks door holiday lunch meeting phone trip ~~work~~ |

A: Where is everyone? They're meant to be at (0) ....*work*....... , so why aren't
    they at their (1) .... working?
B: They are working, Mr Crenshaw, but it's one o'clock. Gina's still at
    (2) .... , but she normally gets back at about 1.30. Then remember
    that Sarah's away on (3) .... till Friday. Martin's gone to pick up his
    daughter – she's been on a school (4) .... Brenda's in
    (5) .... with flu. She phoned this morning to say she wasn't coming
    in. Sally's in a (6) .... with a new customer and Bill's on the
    (7) .... in the next room.
A: And where's Margaret?
B: That's her at the (8) .... I'll go and let her in.

100 Other prepositional phrases

We use *by/in/on* + noun in a number of expressions.

- Some common expressions with *by* are: *by bus/car/plane/train/boat/bike, by road/ sea/air, by accident, by credit card, by e-mail, by mistake: Can I pay **by credit card**? We usually go to the shops **by bike**.*

 *We paid for the things **in cash**.* (Not ~~by cash~~) *They went to the train station **on foot**.* (Not ~~by foot~~)

- Some common expressions with *in* are: *in a hurry, in danger, in good condition, in love, in stock, in trouble: I can't stop, I'm **in a hurry**. Is the new iPod **in stock**?*

- Some common expressions with *on* are: *on a diet, on offer, on sale: Olive oil's **on offer** this week.*

P R A C T I C E

100a Circle the correct answer.

    0 Dennis is very happy at the moment. Do you think he's *by /(in)/ on* love?

    1 Oh, no! I think Sheila's taken my mobile phone *by / in / on* mistake.

    2 No cake for me, thanks. I'm *by / in / on* a diet.

    3 Most goods in Europe are transported *by / in / on* road.

    4 Simon's been *by / in / on* trouble at school again. We have to see the head.

    5 I found this *by / in / on* accident when I was cleaning your room. What is it?

    6 Human activity is putting many animals round the world *by / in / on* danger.

    7 I can't talk to you now because I'm *by / in / on* a hurry. What about tomorrow?

    8 He normally goes to work *by / in / on* bus, but today he's going *by / in / on* foot.

100b Complete the advertisement. Use the words in the box.

cash	condition	credit card	e-mail	offer	~~sale~~	stock

The new Techtron P90 is now on (0) ....*sale*........... in all our shops!

The P90 will be on (1) .... at a 10% discount for the next seven days, so buy one today! You'll get an extra 5% discount if you pay in (2) .... and if you buy the P90 from our website and pay by (3) .... , you'll get an extra 8% discount.

We're also selling the last twenty P80s that we have in (4) .... These have been on display in our shops, but are in excellent (5) .... and cost just 59.99€!

For further details contact us by (6) .... at: info@e-electronics.com

Check 23   Prepositional phrases

1 **Complete the sentences. Use the words in the box.**

> advance car foot last my way strike time

1 There you are at .... ! I've been here for forty minutes!

2 I decided to come by .... , but the traffic was terrible.

3 The bus drivers are on .... , so there are no buses running.

4 I was already on .... when I remembered about the strike.

5 I parked my car about a kilometre away and finished the journey on ....

6 We won't arrive at the theatre on .... unless we hurry.

7 It's a good thing we bought tickets in .... !

/ 7

2 **Complete the conversation. Use *at, by, in* or *on*.**

A: Jackie? Have you got a moment?

B: I'm (8) .... a bit of a hurry. I have to be (9) .... class in fifteen minutes.

A: Can we talk afterwards?

B: What's up? Are you (10) .... some kind of trouble?

A: It's John. I read an e-mail (11) .... accident. It was to a woman called Jackie – like you. Who is she?

B: She's probably just someone he sees (12) .... work or someone he knew (13) .... university.

A: That's what I thought (14) .... first, but he said you're the only Jackie he knows. But I don't believe him. Sometimes he's (15) .... the phone to someone, but he stops talking when he sees me.

B: Actually, he's been talking to me. We're organising a surprise for your birthday!

/ 8

3 **Complete the second sentence so that it means the same as the first. Use no more than three words.**

16 I recently used a credit card to pay for some CDs I bought online.
I recently paid .... for some CDs I bought online.

17 The music shop said they would send the CDs immediately, so I was pleased.
The music shop said they would send the CDs at .... , so I was pleased.

18 They promised that the CDs would arrive no later than Friday.
They promised that the CDs would arrive on Friday .... latest.

19 I wanted them to arrive before a friend's birthday.
I wanted them to arrive in .... for a friend's birthday.

20 But the shop made a mistake and sent the CDs to the wrong address.
But the shop sent the CDs to the wrong address .... mistake.

/ 5

Total: / 20

✓ Self-check

Wrong answers	Look again at	Try CD-ROM
1, 6, 7, 14, 17, 18, 19	**Unit 98**	Exercise 98
3, 4, 9, 12, 13, 15	**Unit 99**	Exercise 99
2, 5, 8, 10, 11, 16, 20	**Unit 100**	Exercise 100

Now do **Check 23**

Words that go together

101 Adjective + preposition

- We use a preposition after some adjectives: *They're **proud of** their children. I'm **terrible at** singing!*
- Many of these adjectives describe feelings: *Is she **angry with** us?*
- We use *good/brilliant/bad/terrible at* to talk about ability: *She's **good at** athletics.*
- The pattern is adjective + preposition + noun/pronoun/-ing: *They're **excited about** their holiday. Our neighbours are very **kind to us**. I'm **bored with doing** nothing all day.*

⚠ Notice the pattern: *it + be + nice/kind/cruel + of + someone + to-*infinitive: ***It was nice of you to visit** me. **It was cruel of them to say** such things!*

▶▶ **See Appendix 12: Adjective + preposition, page 173.**

PRACTICE

101a Circle the correct answer.

A: Mary was excited (0) *(about)/ to* going to America, but she was worried (1) *with / about* the journey.

B: Why? Is she afraid (2) *about / of* flying?

A: Yes, but the flight attendants were very kind (3) *with / to* her, so she was fine in the end.

A: New York was great! It was so different (4) *from / of* anywhere we'd been before. We were tired (5) *about / of* always going to the beach.

B: I'm glad. And thanks for this T-shirt. It was nice (6) *at / of* you to buy me a present!

101b Complete the conversations. Use a preposition and the *-ing* form of the verbs in brackets.

A: You're really good (0) ....*at playing*......... (play) the saxophone.

B: Yes, but I'm bored (1) .... (practise) every day. And no one is interested (2) .... (form) a band with me.

A: I'm sorry (3) .... (forget) your CD. I'll bring it tomorrow.

B: Don't worry! So, are you excited (4) .... (go) to university?

A: Not really. I'm angry (5) .... (not get) on the course I wanted. I'm also worried (6) .... (waste) my time on a course I don't really like.

B: Is Izzy interested (7) .... (do) the climbing course?

A: Izzy? No! Izzy's frightened (8) .... (go) onto his balcony!

102 Verb + preposition

- We use a preposition after some verbs: *She **apologised for** not making lunch.*

- The pattern is verb (+ object) + preposition + noun/pronoun/-ing: *Do you **believe in ghosts**? Her friends know they can **depend on her**. He **accused her of taking** the money.*

- Some prepositional verbs have an idiomatic meaning: *Please **look after** the baby for me.* (= take care of) *Who do you **take after**, your mother or your father?* (= resemble)

▶▶ **See Appendix 13: Verb + preposition, pages 173–174.**

P R A C T I C E

102a Complete the questions. Use prepositions.

0	**A:** What was Sonia telling you ......*about*...... ?	**B:** Oh, nothing!
1	**A:** How much did Davy pay .... his mobile?	**B:** It was a present.
2	**A:** What kind of music do you listen .... ?	**B:** Heavy metal.
3	**A:** What's everyone looking .... ?	**B:** A street artist.
4	**A:** What time did they arrive .... the party?	**B:** Eight thirty.
5	**A:** What does the training consist .... ?	**B:** I don't know yet.
6	**A:** Are you still waiting .... Delia?	**B:** Yes! She's late!

102b Re-write the sentences.

0 'Can I have another cup of coffee?' said Kate.
   Kate asked ....*for another cup of coffee*............. .

1 Her parents think her new friends are nice.
   Her parents approve ....

2 You should answer that e-mail at once!
   You should reply .... !

3 'I'm sorry I'm late,' said Robin.
   Robin apologised ....

4 Whose is that MP3 player?
   Who does that MP3 player belong .... ?

5 'I must pay for the ice cream,' said Sue.
   Sue insisted ....

6 The police are investigating the crime.
   The police are looking ....

7 'I love the present, Luke,' said Emma.
   Emma thanked ....

8 'Yes, I think so too, Ben,' said Loli.
   Loli agreed ....

103   Phrasal verbs

- Most phrasal verbs have two parts: verb + adverb: *The plane **took off** at nine.*
- Often the meaning of the verb changes when we add the adverb: ***Come on**, we'll be late.* (= hurry)
- There are two main patterns for phrasal verbs:
  - phrasal verbs with no object: *The thief **ran away**.*
  - phrasal verbs with an object. If the object is a noun, it can come after the adverb or between the verb and the adverb: *The firemen **put out the fire**. The firemen **put the fire out**.*
    If the object is a pronoun, it can only come between the verb and the adverb: *The firemen **put it out**.* (Not *The firemen put out it.*)

▶▶   **See Appendix 14: Common phrasal verbs, page 174.**

P R A C T I C E

103a Re-write the sentences. Use pronouns.

   0 **A:** Can you turn down the music?   **B:** Yes, I'll ....*turn it down*.... in a minute.

   1 **A:** Please tidy up your room.   **B:** I'm busy. I'll .... later.

   2 **A:** Put away those clothes!   **B:** OK, I'll .... after lunch.

   3 **A:** Did you make up the story?   **B:** No, Sue ....

   4 **A:** When are you going to ring up Peter?   **B:** I'll .... tomorrow.

   5 **A:** You didn't switch off the computer.   **B:** I'll .... in a minute.

   6 **A:** Why did you turn down the offer?   **B:** I didn't .... !

103b Complete the sentences. Use the correct form of the phrasal verbs in the box.

> check in   go out   grow up   join in   ~~look up~~
> put on   take off   ~~turn down~~   wake up

   0 Can you ....*turn down*........ the radio, please?
       I'm ......*looking up*...... phrasal verbs in the dictionary!

   1 **A:** Did you .... in Manchester?
       B: No, I'm from a small village.

   2 **A:** Are you .... to the shops?
       B: Perhaps later. It's still early and I've only just .... !

   3 He .... his coat and left the house.

   4 The airport was so busy that it took us ages to ....

   5 We were worried about missing the plane, but in the end it .... an hour late.

   6 What a concert! When he sang his big hits, everyone ....

104 *make, do, have, get*

- We can use *make* to mean 'create' or 'produce': ***make** a cake*   ***make** a mess*   ***make** a list*   ***make** a noise*   ***make** a mistake*
- We can use *do* to talk about work or activities in general: ***do** a sport*   ***do** a course* ***do** an exam*   ***do** a job*   ***do** housework*   ***do** homework*

⚠ To ask what job somebody does, we can say: *What **do** you **do**?*

- We can use *get* to mean:
  – 'obtain' or 'receive': *I **got** my car in 2006. She **gets** about fifty e-mails a day.*
  – 'arrive': *He **got** home at six o'clock.*
  – 'become': *Sorry we're late, but we **got** lost.*
- We can use *have* or *have got*:
  – to talk about possession: *Matt **hasn't got**/**doesn't have** a car.*
  – to describe somebody: *They**'ve got**/**have** black hair.*
  – to talk about illnesses: ***Have** you **got**/**Do** you **have** a headache?*
- We can use *have*, but not *have got* to talk about food and drink, events and activities: *Are they **having** a party on Saturday?*

PRACTICE

104 **Complete the conversations. Use the correct form of *make, do, have (got)* or *get*.**

  A: Are you (o) ....*doing*........ anything on Friday night? I'm (1) .... a birthday party. Would you like to come?
  B: I'd love to. Shall I (2) .... a chocolate cake?

  ─────────────────────────

  A: I (3) .... a strange dream last night.
  B: Really? What was it about?
  A: I dreamt that I had a job interview and I (4) .... really nervous. But when I (5) .... there, they said I'd (6) .... a mistake.

  ─────────────────────────

  A: Whose turn is it to (7) .... the washing up?
  B: Not mine! I've (8) .... enough housework today!

  ─────────────────────────

  A: Shall we (9) .... lunch? I'm (10) .... hungry!
  B: I don't want any lunch. I (11) .... a stomach ache.

  ─────────────────────────

  A: What do you (12) .... ?
  B: I'm not working at the moment. I (13) .... a degree in Philosophy, but I can't (14) .... a job, so now I'm (15) .... a computer course.

  ─────────────────────────

  A: I (16) .... cold and wet in the rain!
  B: Well, (17) .... a hot shower when you (18) .... home.

Check 24 Words that go together

1 Complete the sentences. Use the words in the box. You do not need all of them.

about after at in like on to with

1 I sometimes look .... my neighbour's children.

2 She says I'm very good .... making them behave.

3 And she insists .... paying me.

4 I do it because my neighbour is always so kind .... me.

5 And of course I'm crazy .... children.

/ 5

2 Complete the sentences. Use prepositions or adverbs.

6 Do you listen .... the radio very often?

7 Why do you get so angry if I don't agree .... you?

8 Can you switch .... the lights before you go to bed?

9 I think you should apologise .... breaking my clock.

10 Someone always rings us .... when we're having dinner.

/ 5

3 Choose the correct answer.

Last Sunday we (11) ...... a picnic at Blagdon Lake. We (12) ...... lots of sandwiches to take with us. We were very excited (13) ...... our first summer excursion. Until we got (14) ...... in the morning, we didn't know if we could go. Everything depended (15) ...... the weather, but it was a beautiful day. We cycled and we (16) ...... there in an hour. We were really hot, so we all (17) ...... a swim in the lake. On the way back we (18) ...... lost and we had to ask someone (19) ...... directions. It was a lovely day and now we're looking (20) ...... a good place to go on our next excursion.

11	A got	B made	C had	D did
12	A did	B made	C ate	D put
13	A for	B on	C to	D about
14	A to	B over	C up	D away
15	A on	B at	C with	D for
16	A had	B made	C got	D made
17	A got	B had	C had got	D did
18	A got	B had	C did	D made
19	A from	B about	C with	D for
20	A at	B for	C from	D to

/ 10

Total: / 20

✓ Self-check

Wrong answers	Look again at	Try CD-ROM
2, 4, 5, 13	**Unit 101**	Exercise 101
1, 3, 6, 7, 9, 15, 19, 20	**Unit 102**	Exercise 102
8, 10, 14	**Unit 103**	Exercise 103
11, 12, 16, 17, 18	**Unit 104**	Exercise 104

Now do **Check 24**

Word formation

105 Adjectives ending in -ed and -ing

- We use -ed adjectives to describe a person's feelings: *Kieran felt **excited** about going to the amusement park. Fay is **frightened** of dogs.*
- We use -ing adjectives to describe something that makes us feel a certain way: *Kieran thought the amusement park was **exciting**. Fay thinks dogs are **frightening**.*

PRACTICE

105a Circle the correct answer.

In my first job I worked in an office, but I was (0) (bored) / boring, so I trained as a nurse. My present job is always (1) interested / interesting though after a long day I'm usually very (2) tired / tiring. Being in hospital can be (3) frightened / frightening for people, so we try to help them feel more (4) relaxed / relaxing when they arrive. Some people think being a nurse is (5) depressed / depressing, but I disagree. It's great to help people get better. In fact, I think it's a very (6) rewarded / rewarding job.

105b Complete the second sentence in each pair. Use -ed or -ing adjectives.

0 The instructions for the DVD player are confusing.
I'm ...*confused*... by the instructions for the DVD player.

1 We thought the football match was boring.
We were .... by the football match.

2 I was fascinated by a programme I saw about the history of chocolate.
I saw a .... programme about the history of chocolate.

3 Climate change is very worrying, I think.
I'm very .... about climate change.

4 Everyone thought it was surprising that Andy failed his university course.
Everyone was .... when Andy failed his university course.

5 I felt embarrassed when I accepted the prize because I didn't know what to say.
Accepting the prize was .... because I didn't know what to say.

6 Visiting New York was exciting.
I felt .... when I visited New York.

7 I'm interested in books about other cultures because they teach us a lot.
I think books about other cultures are .... because they teach us a lot.

8 People were terrified by the film!
People thought it was a .... film!

163

106 Negative prefixes

A prefix is a group of letters that we add to the beginning of a word to form a new word. We can make some adjectives negative by adding the prefixes *un-*, *in-*, *im-*, *il-* and *ir-*:

- *un-*: **un**comfortable   **un**expected   **un**happy   **un**kind   **un**popular
- *in-*: **in**accurate   **in**considerate   **in**efficient   **in**expensive   **in**sensitive
- *im-*: **im**mature   **im**moral   **im**perfect   **im**personal   **im**possible   **im**polite
- *il-*: **il**legal   **il**legible   **il**literate   **il**logical
- *ir-*: **ir**rational   **ir**regular   **ir**relevant   **ir**responsible

P R A C T I C E

106a Complete the sentences. Use negative adjectives.

0   That's not an important detail. In fact, it's completely ......*unimportant*...... .

1   You said Fred was a considerate person, but in fact, he's very ....

2   They said the bed was comfortable, but it was really ....

3   He said driving without insurance is legal here, but I'm sure it's ....

4   His argument isn't rational. It's completely ....

5   Kay said she was responsible with money, but I think she's totally ....

6   I asked if it was possible to change my ticket, but he said it was ....

106b Complete the texts. Use the negative form of the adjectives in the boxes.

| happy   kind   mature   perfect   ~~popular~~   sensitive |

The novel is about a very (0) ......*unpopular*...... boy who doesn't have any friends. This is because he's (1) .... to other people's feelings: he's (2) .... to everyone and he criticises everything they do. He's also quite (3) .... for his age and his family life is very (4) .... , but when he finds an injured dog in the street, his life changes. I like this story because it makes you realise that although we live in an (5) .... world, things can get better.

| correct   legible   relevant |

When you write a composition in an exam, you should plan it to make sure you don't say anything (6) .... or repetitive. You will lose marks if your writing is (7) .... or difficult to read. When you finish writing, check your work for (8) .... spelling or grammar.

107 Forming adjectives

A suffix is a group of letters that we add to the end of a word to form a new word. We can form some adjectives by adding a suffix to a noun:

- *-able* = having (a quality): *comfort**able*** *valu**able***
- *-ous* = having or full of (a quality): *danger**ous*** *mysteri**ous***
- *-ful* = having or full of: *beauti**ful*** *care**ful*** *harm**ful*** *success**ful***
- *-less* = without: *care**less*** *harm**less*** *home**less*** *pain**less*** *use**less***
- *-y* = having (a quality): *cloud**y*** *dirt**y*** *luck**y*** *nois**y*** *rain**y*** *thirst**y***
- *-al* = related to: *environment**al*** *financi**al*** *mechanic**al*** *person**al***

⚠️ Notice the changes in spelling: *beaut**y*** → *beauti**ful*** *adventur**e*** → *adventur**ous*** *financ**e*** → *financi**al***.

P R A C T I C E

107a Complete the sentences. Use the correct form of the words in brackets.

0 Having my tooth out was ....*painless*...., but later my mouth was very ....*painful*.... . (pain, pain)

1 Even the most .... companies can have .... problems if they aren't managed well. (success, finance)

2 Melanie's so .... that she broke three plates yesterday. (care)

3 You're .... to live in such a .... place. (luck, beauty)

4 The weather tomorrow will be .... and .... (cloud, rain)

5 The dog looks fierce, but it's completely .... (harm)

107b Complete the texts. Use the correct form of the words in the box.

care	comfort	danger	~~environment~~
mechanic	mystery	noise	person	value

Many people are against nuclear power because it causes (o) ...*environmental*... problems. They say that the risk of explosion or contamination makes nuclear power very (1) ....

If you get a (2) .... phone call saying you've won a (3) .... prize, be (4) .... ! It might be a trick!

The travellers wanted to hire a large, (5) .... car. They also employed their own (6) .... driver. Unfortunately, the car had a (7) .... engine and it developed a (8) .... fault which took two days to repair.

108 Forming nouns

- We can add *-ness* to some adjectives: *happiness   sadness   illness*
- We can add *-er* or *-or* to some verbs: *driver   worker   actor   sailor*
- We can add *-ment* to some verbs: *advertisement   agreement   enjoyment*
- We can add *-tion, -ation, -ition* or *-ion* to some verbs: *introduction   imagination   opposition   invention*

⚠ Notice the changes in spelling: *produce → production*
examine → examination   communicate → communication

P R A C T I C E

108a Complete the sentences. Use nouns that end in *-er* or *-or*.

0   She paints portraits. She's a ..... *painter* ..... .

1   I act a lot on television. I'm an ....

2   We're visiting some friends. We're ....

3   He drives a lorry. He's a lorry ....

4   I clean offices. I'm a ....

5   He directs a company. He's a company ....

6   We build houses. We're ....

108b Complete the sentences. Use the correct form of the words in brackets.

0   Have you seen this .....*advertisement*..... ? It's very clever! (advertise)

1   Thank you for your .... and help. (kind)

2   After long negotiations they finally reached an .... (agree)

3   The cinema is still a popular form of .... (entertain)

4   What's the cause of his .... ? (sad)

5   This country needs a new .... ! (govern)

6   The restaurant is under new .... (manage)

108c Write nouns that end in *-tion, -ation, -ition* or *-ion*.

0   a great .....*invention*..... (invent)

1   exam .... (prepare)

2   a theatre .... (produce)

3   a hotel .... (reserve)

4   a lot of .... (imagine)

5   a strong .... (react)

6   a police .... (investigate)

7   a university .... (educate)

8   a heart .... (operate)

9   a useful .... (suggest)

10   a long .... (introduce)

11   a painting .... (compete)

109 Compound nouns

- Compound nouns have two parts: noun + noun. The first noun usually gives more information about the second noun: *a film star* (a star who is in films) *a fire alarm* (an alarm that tells you if there's a fire)
- We write some compound nouns as two words, and others as one word: *a toothbrush*   *a bus stop*
- To make a compound noun plural, we add *-s* to the second noun, not the first noun: *a shoe shop → shoe shops* (Not ~~shoes shop~~)

P R A C T I C E

109a Complete the sentences. Use the words in the box.

alarm   credit   door   hand   ~~music~~   sun   taxi   tooth   traffic

0   I'd like to buy some CDs. Is there a ......*music*...... shop near here?

1   That was the .... bell. Who's there?

2   His father's a(n) .... driver. He often works at weekends.

3   Jean's got terrible .... ache. Do you know a good dentist?

4   Don't forget to set the .... clock. We mustn't wake up late.

5   Can I pay for the clothes by .... card?

6   You'll need to put on .... cream if you go to the beach.

7   You can only take one piece of .... luggage onto the plane.

8   We're sorry we're late. We got stuck in a(n) .... jam.

109b Complete the article. Use one word from each box in each gap.

| ~~car~~   city   phone   police   post |
| seat   shoe   traffic   travel |

| agency   belt   call   centre   lights |
| office   officer   ~~park~~   shop |

On Saturday morning I went to do some shopping. I parked the car in a (0) ....*car park*............ in the (1) .... and walked to the shops. I bought some stamps at the (2) .... , some trainers in a (3) .... , and I asked about summer holidays in a (4) .... On my way home, I was waiting in my car at some (5) .... when I decided to make a (6) .... Suddenly, I heard a knock on the window. It was a (7) .... He gave me a fine for talking on my mobile and another one because I wasn't wearing my (8) .... !

110   Compound adjectives

- Compound adjectives are formed from two words and are usually joined by a hyphen: *We eat **low-fat** yoghurt. The city centre's a **two-mile** walk from here.*
- The first word gives more information about the second: *a **home-made** cake* (a cake made at home)   *a **six-storey** building* (a building with six storeys)   ***slow-moving** traffic* (traffic that moves slowly)
- The following word combinations are common in compound adjectives:
  - adjective/number + noun: *a **long-distance** flight*   *a **twenty-page** report*
  - adjective/number + noun-*ed*: *an **old-fashioned** photograph*   *a **one-sided** argument*
  - adjective/adverb/noun + past participle: *a **low-paid** job*   *a **well-known** person*   ***handmade** shoes*
  - adjective/adverb/noun + -*ing* form: *a **good-looking** man*   *a **never-ending** meeting*   ***record-breaking** temperatures*
  - noun + adjective: *a **world-famous** actor*   ***lead-free** petrol*

PRACTICE

110a   Complete the sentences. Use the words in the box.

distance   fashioned   going   hand   known   ~~minute~~   way

0   There are lots of last-......*minute*...... travel offers on the Internet.

1   This bicycle looks new, but it's actually second-...................... .

2   She's very easy-...................... . She gets on well with everybody.

3   I'd like a one-...................... ticket to Sydney, please. I'm not coming back.

4   He's very old-...................... . He always wears a suit when he goes out.

5   The Taj Mahal in India is a very well-...................... building.

6   What's the cheapest way to make a long-...................... phone call?

110b   Complete the sentences. Use compound adjectives.

0   A person who normally uses their right hand is ......*right-handed*...... .

1   A story that never ends is a .... story.

2   A car with five doors is a .... car.

3   A toy that is made by hand is a .... toy.

4   A runner who breaks a record is a .... runner.

5   A job that pays well is a .... job.

6   A person that looks good is a .... person.

7   A student who behaves badly is a .... student.

8   Ice cream that's low in fat is .... ice cream.

Check 25 Word formation

1 Choose the correct answer.

A: What did you think of the film?

B: It was a thriller, so I expected it to be (1) ...... , but it wasn't. It wasn't even (2) ...... ! Also, the plot was (3) .... By the end, I was really (4) ...... , to be honest. Luckily, the seats were very (5) ...... , or I'd have fallen asleep!

A: Really? I thought it was good (6) .... The ending was really (7) .... I had no idea who the killer was! They were very (8) ...... not to give you too many clues.

B: Well, I've heard that they had serious (9) ...... problems when they were making the film and I think that shows. In my opinion, it was a (10) ...... film!

1 A excite   B excited
   C exciting   D excitement

2 A enjoyed   B enjoying
   C enjoyable   D enjoyment

3 A never-moving   B slow-moving
   C slowly-moving   D moving

4 A bored   B boring
   C bore   D boredom

5 A comfortable   B comforting
   C uncomfortable   D comforted

6 A entertainer   B entertained
   C entertaining   D entertainment

7 A surprised   B surprising
   C unsurprising   D unsurprised

8 A caring   B careless
   C careful   D cared

9 A finance   B financial
   C financed   D financing

10 A well-made   B home-made
   C handmade   D badly-made

/ 10

2 Complete the text. Use the words in the box.

centre drivers lights tempered way

"I wouldn't drive to the city (11) .... if I were you. You have to stop at traffic (12) .... every two minutes. The centre's full of one- (13) .... streets too. Even taxi (14) .... can get lost! And drivers get bad- (15) .... in heavy traffic, so it can be stressful."

/ 5

3 Complete the letter. Use the correct form of the words in brackets.

Dear Sir or Madam,

I am writing this note because the (16) .... (manage) was not there on the evening I had a meal in your restaurant.

To start with, the menu was so badly printed that it was (17) .... (legible). Also, the service was (18) .... (efficient) and we waited for an hour for our meal. The food was cold and the plates were (19) .... (dirt). Now I understand why the restaurant is so (20) .... (popular)!

/ 5

Total: / 20

✓ Self-check

Wrong answers	Look again at	Try CD-ROM
1, 4, 7	Unit 105	Exercise 105
5, 17, 18, 20	Unit 106	Exercise 106
2, 8, 9, 19	Unit 107	Exercise 107
6, 16	Unit 108	Exercise 108
11, 12, 14	Unit 109	Exercise 109
3, 10, 13, 15	Unit 110	Exercise 110

Now do **Check 25**

Appendices

1 Spelling rules for plural nouns

Noun	Rule	Examples
most nouns	add -s	student → students cake → cakes
nouns ending in consonant + -y	change -y to -i and add -es	baby → babies cherry → cherries
nouns ending in vowel + -y	add -s	boy → boys day → days
nouns ending in -ch, -sh, -ss, -s or -x	add -es	match → matches brush → brushes dress → dresses box → boxes
nouns ending in -o	add -s or -es	video → videos photo → photos potato → potatoes tomato → tomatoes
nouns ending in -f or -fe	change -f to -v and add -es	shelf → shelves knife → knives

2 Spelling rules for comparative and superlative adjectives

Adjective	Rule	Examples
most adjectives	add -er or -est	old → older → oldest short → shorter → shortest
adjectives ending in -e	add -r or -st	nice → nicer → nicest safe → safer → safest
adjectives ending in -y	change -y to -i and add -er or -est	easy → easier → easiest happy → happier → happiest
adjectives ending in one vowel + consonant	double the final consonant* and add -er or -est	big → bigger → biggest hot → hotter → hottest

* But we do not double -w: slow → slower → slowest

3 Spelling rules for adverbs

To make an adverb, we often add -ly to an adjective.

Adjective	Rule	Examples
most adjectives	add -ly	beautiful → beautifully safe → safely
adjectives ending in -y	change -y to -i and add -ly	angry → angrily easy → easily
adjectives ending in -le	take away the -e and add -y	terrible → terribly simple → simply
adjectives ending in -ic	add -ally*	automatic → automatically tragic → tragically

* But to form the adverb of public, we ad -ly: public → publicly

4 Spelling rules for present simple verbs (*he, she, it*)

Verb	Rule	Examples
most verbs	add -*s*	read → read**s** sleep → sleep**s**
verbs ending in consonant + -*y*	change -*y* to -*i* and add -*es*	fl**y** → fl**ies** stud**y** → stud**ies**
verbs ending in vowel + -*y*	add -*s*	bu**y** → buy**s** pla**y** → play**s**
verbs ending in -*ch*, -*sh*, -*ss*, -*s* or -*x*	add -*es*	wat**ch** → watch**es** fini**sh** → finish**es** mi**ss** → miss**es** fi**x** → fix**es**
verbs ending in -*o*	add -*es*	g**o** → go**es** d**o** → do**es**

5 Spelling rules for verbs + -*ing*

Verb	Rule	Examples
most verbs	add -*ing*	sleep → sleep**ing** work → work**ing**
verbs ending in -*e*	take away the -*e* and add -*es*	liv**e** → liv**ing** danc**e** → danc**ing**
verbs ending in -*ee*	add -*ing*	s**ee** → see**ing** agr**ee** → agree**ing**
verbs ending in -*ie*	change -*ie* to -*y* and add -*ing*	l**ie** → l**ying** d**ie** → d**ying**
verbs ending in one vowel + consonant	double the final consonant* and add -*ing*	st**op** → sto**pping** sw**im** → swi**mming**
verbs ending in two vowels + consonant	add -*ing*	r**ain** → rain**ing** r**ead** → read**ing**

* But we do not double the final consonant if the last part of the word is not stressed:
begin → beginning BUT *open → opening*
And we do not double -*w*: *snow → snowing*

6 Spelling rules for verbs + -*ed*

Verb	Rule	Examples
most verbs	add -*ed*	ask → ask**ed** help → help**ed**
verbs ending in -*e* or -*ee*	add -*d*	arriv**e** → arrive**d** agr**ee** → agree**d**
verbs ending in consonant + -*y*	change -*y* to -*i* and add -*ed*	stud**y** → stud**ied** tr**y** → tr**ied**
verbs ending in vowel + -*y*	add -*ed*	pla**y** → play**ed** enjo**y** → enjoy**ed**
verbs ending in one vowel + consonant	double the final consonant* and add -*ed*	st**op** → sto**pped** pl**an** → pla**nned**
verbs ending in two vowels + consonant	add -*ed*	r**ain** → rain**ed** rep**eat** → repeat**ed**

* But we do not double the final consonant if the last part of the word is not stressed:
prefer → preferred BUT *answer → answered*

7 State verbs

be	have	like	need	see	think	wish
believe	hear	love	prefer	smell	understand	
hate	know	mean	remember	taste	want	

8 Verbs followed by *-ing* form

avoid	continue	finish	keep	mind	recommend	suggest
begin	enjoy	hate	like	miss	start	
consider	feel like	imagine	love	prefer	stop	

9 Verbs followed by *to*-infinitive

agree	can't afford	expect	hope	offer	promise	want
arrange	can't wait	forget	learn	plan	refuse	would like
ask	decide	help	need	prepare	try	

10 Verbs followed by object + *to*-infinitive

(a) Verbs that need an object before the *to*-infinitive

advise	order	invite	tell
allow	persuade	remind	warn
encourage	force	teach	

(b) Verbs that can have an object before the *to*-infinitive

ask	need	would prefer
expect	want	
help	would like	

11 Irregular verbs

Infinitive	Past simple	Past participle
be	was/were	been
beat	beat	beaten
become	became	become
begin	began	begun
bite	bit	bitten
blow	blew	blown
break	broke	broken
bring	brought	brought
build	built	built
buy	bought	bought
catch	caught	caught
choose	chose	chosen
come	came	come
cost	cost	cost
cut	cut	cut

Infinitive	Past simple	Past participle
do	did	done
draw	drew	drawn
dream	dreamed/dreamt	dreamed/dreamt
drink	drank	drunk
drive	drove	driven
eat	ate	eaten
fall	fell	fallen
feel	felt	felt
fight	fought	fought
find	found	found
fly	flew	flown
forget	forgot	forgotten
forgive	forgave	forgiven
get	got	got
give	gave	given

Infinitive	Past simple	Past participle
go	went	gone
grow	grew	grown
hang	hung	hung
have	had	had
hear	heard	heard
hide	hid	hidden
hit	hit	hit
hold	held	held
hurt	hurt	hurt
keep	kept	kept
know	knew	known
learn	learned/learnt	learned/learnt
leave	left	left
lend	lent	lent
let	let	let
lie	lay	lain
lose	lost	lost
make	made	made
mean	meant	meant
meet	met	met
pay	paid	paid
put	put	put
read	read	read
ride	rode	ridden
ring	rang	rung
run	ran	run
say	said	said

Infinitive	Past simple	Past participle
see	saw	seen
sell	sold	sold
send	sent	sent
set	set	set
show	showed	shown
shut	shut	shut
sing	sang	sung
sit	sat	sat
sleep	slept	slept
smell	smelled/smelt	smelled/smelt
speak	spoke	spoken
spell	spelled/spelt	spelled/spelt
spend	spent	spent
stand	stood	stood
steal	stole	stolen
swim	swam	swum
take	took	taken
teach	taught	taught
tear	tore	torn
tell	told	told
think	thought	thought
throw	threw	thrown
understand	understood	understood
wake	woke	woken
wear	wore	worn
win	won	won
write	wrote	written

12 Adjective + preposition

afraid of
angry about (something)
angry with (someone)
bad at
bored with
brilliant at
careful with
crazy about

different from
excited about
famous for
fed up with
frightened of
full of
good at
interested in

kind to
married to
nice to (someone)
nice of (someone) to
 (do something)
pleased with/about
polite to
proud of

ready for
rude to
sorry about/for
sure of
surprised at/by
terrible at
tired of
worried about

13 Verb + preposition

agree with (something)
agree with (someone) about (something)
apologise to (someone) for (something)
approve of (something/someone)
argue with (someone) about (something)
arrive at (a place)
ask (someone) about (something)
believe in (something/someone)

belong to (someone/an organisation, club etc.)
communicate with (someone)
complain about (something/someone)
consist of (something)
depend on (something/someone)
disagree with (something/someone)
dream about (something/someone)
feel like (something/doing something)

forget about (something/someone)
hear about (something/someone)
insist on (doing something)
know about (something/someone)
listen to (something/someone)
look after (something/someone)
look for (something/someone)
look at (something/someone)
look like (something/someone)

pay for (something/someone)
reply to (something/someone)
suffer from (an illness)
talk to (someone) about (something)
tell (someone) about (something)
thank (someone) for (something/doing
think about (something/someone)
wait for (something/someone)
worry about (something/someone)

14 Common phrasal verbs

break down = if a car or machine breaks down, it stops working

carry on = to continue doing something

check in = to go to the check-in desk at the airport to get a boarding card

come back = to return

come round = to visit someone

drive off = if a car drives off, it leaves

find out = to get information about something

get back = to return

get off = to leave a bus, train, plane etc.

get on = to walk onto a bus, train, plane etc.

get up = to wake up and get out of bed

give up = to stop doing something

go away = to leave a place or person

go back = to return

go on = to continue doing something

go out = to leave your house to do something you enjoy

grow up = to go from a baby into a child and then an adult

hurry up = to do something more quickly

join in = to do what everyone else is doing, like a game or activity

keep on = to continue doing something

lie down = when you lie down, your body is flat on a bed, on the floor etc.

look forward to = to expect with pleasure

look out = used to warn someone of danger

look up = to find information in a book, on a computer etc.

put on = to put clothes on your body

run away = to escape from a situation or person by running

ring up = to telephone someone

set off = to leave and start going somewhere

sit down = to lower yourself down so that you are sitting

stand up = to get up so that you are standing after you have been sitting or lying down

stay in = to stay in your home and not go out

stay up = to not go to bed

take off = to remove something

throw away = to get rid of something that you do not want

try on = to put on a piece of clothing to find out if it fits or if you like it

turn down = to make a machine produce less heat, sound etc.

turn off = to make a machine, light etc. stop working

turn on = to make a machine, light etc. start working

turn up = to make a machine produce more heat, sound etc.

wake up = to stop sleeping, or to make someone stop sleeping

wash up = to wash the plates, dishes etc. after a meal

write down = to write something on a piece of paper, especially so that you do not forget it

Index

The numbers in this index are unit numbers (not page numbers).

A

(a) few	4
(a) little	4
a bit	22
a little	20
a lot of/lots of	4
a lot	20
a/an	12, 15
adjective + preposition	101
adjectives ending in *-ed* and *–ing*	105
adjectives	16–18, 101, 105–107, 110
adjectives and adverbs	18
comparative adjectives	17
compound adjectives	110
order of adjectives	16
superlative adjectives	17
adverbs	18–22
adverbs of frequency	21
adverbs of manner	18
comparative adverbs	19
superlative adverbs	19
after	40–41, 83–85
all	5
already	36, 40
also	78
although	80
and	78
any	2
anybody, anything etc.	11
articles	12–15
definite article	12–15
indefinite article	12, 15
zero article	13–15
as ... as	23
as soon as	83–84
as well	78
as	81

B

be able to	45
be allowed to	46
be going to	42–43
because of	81
because	81
before	40–41, 83–85, 87

both ... and	79
but	80
by	40–41, 67, 95–96, 100

C

can	45–46, 49–50
can't	48, 52
causative	68
commands, reported	73
comparative adjectives	17
comparative adverbs	19
comparative structures	23–25
compound adjectives	110
compound nouns	109
conditional sentences	87–90
first conditional	88
second conditional	90
zero conditional	87
could	45–47, 49–50
countable nouns	2–3

D

definite article	12–15
determiners	2–6
di-lexical verbs	104
direct object	55
direct speech, punctuation	69
do	104
don't have to	53
don't need to	53

E

each	6
either ... or	79
either	61
enough	24
ever	37, 40
every	6
everybody, everything etc.	11
extremely	22

F

fairly	22
first conditional	88
for	38

future forms

future forms	42–44
be going to	42–43
will	42
present continuous	43–44
present simple	44
future time clauses	84

G

gerunds: see *-ing* forms	
get	104

H

have something done	68
have to	51, 53
have	104
how about ... ?	50
however	80

I

if	72, 74, 87–88, 90
in order to	82
indefinite article	12, 15
indefinite pronouns	11
indirect object	55
indirect questions	74–75
infinitive of purpose	82
infinitive	64–65
-ing forms	63–64, 85
irregular verbs	31, 35–41
it is	56

J

just	36, 40

L

let's	50
like	97
linking words and structures	78–86

M

make	104
many	4
may	47
might	47

modal verbs | 45–54
more | 17, 19
most | 5
much | 4, 20
must | 48, 51–52, 54
mustn't | 52

N

need to | 51, 53
negative prefixes | 106
neither ... nor | 79
neither/nor | 61
never | 21, 37, 40
no | 2
nobody, nothing etc. | 11
none | 5
not as ... as | 23
not be allowed to | 52
nouns | 1–3
countable nouns | 2–3
singular and plural nouns | 1
uncountable nouns | 2–3

O

object pronouns | 7
one, ones | 10
order of adjectives | 16
ought to | 54

P

passive | 66–67
form and use | 66
passive + by | 67
past continuous | 32–33
past perfect simple | 40–41
past simple: irregular verbs | 31
past simple: regular verbs | 30
phrasal verbs | 103
plural nouns | 1
possessive 's | 8
possessive of | 8
possessive pronouns | 7
prepositions | 77, 85, 91–93, 95–97
prepositions at the end of questions | 59
prepositions of movement | 92
prepositions of place | 91
prepositions of time | 93, 95
like | 97
with, by | 96
prepositional phrases | 98–100

present continuous | 27–28
present continuous (for future) | 43–44
present perfect | 35–39
form and use | 35
with ever, never | 37
with for, since | 38
with just, already, yet | 36
present simple | 26, 28
present simple (for future) | 44
pronouns | 7, 9–11

Q

question tags | 60
questions | 57–60, 74–75
questions, reported | 72
quite | 22

R

really | 22
reduced relative clauses | 77
reflexive pronouns | 9
relative clauses, defining | 76
relative pronouns | 76
reported speech | 70–73
commands | 73
requests | 73
questions | 72
statements | 70
reporting verbs | 71
requests, reported | 73

S

's | 8
say | 71
second conditional | 90
sequencers | 86
shall we ... ? | 50
short responses | 61–62
should | 54
since | 38, 81
singular and plural nouns | 1
slightly | 20
so ... that | 25
so that | 82
so | 61, 81
some | 2, 5
somebody, something etc. | 11
state verbs | 29
statements, reported | 70
subject pronouns | 7
such (a/an) ... that) | 25

suffixes, adjective | 107
suffixes, noun | 108
superlative adjectives | 17
superlative adverbs | 19

T

tell | 71
than | 17, 19
that | 76
the most | 17, 19
the | 12, 14, 15
there is | 56
therefore | 81
though | 80
time expressions | 94
to (infinitive of purpose) | 82
to-infinitive: see infinitive
too | 24, 61, 78

U

uncountable nouns | 2–3
unless | 89
until | 83
used to | 34

V

verb + preposition | 102
very | 22, 24

W

what about ... ? | 50
when | 33, 41, 83–84, 87
where | 76
which | 76
while | 32–33, 83
who | 76
whose | 76
why don't we ... ? | 50
will | 42, 50
with | 77, 96
would | 49

Y

yet | 36, 40

Z

zero article | 13–15
zero conditional | 87

Answer key

Unit 1

1a

Singular	Plural	Singular	Plural
teacher	*teachers*	person	people
potato	potatoes	bus	buses
secretary	secretaries	thief	thieves
beach	beaches	box	boxes
half	halves	student	students
disco	discos	foot	feet
dress	dresses	place	places
sheep	sheep	day	days

1b

1 keys   2 sandwiches   3 tomatoes   4 glasses, dishes
5 dictionaries, shelves   6 children   7 fish   8 messages

Unit 2

2a

friend	C	music	U	butter	U
bread	U	DVD player	C	furniture	U
rice	U	money	U	flat	C
book	C	plate	C	oil	U
sugar	U	cheese	U	sand	U
car	C	information	U	banana	C
office	C	bag	C	shampoo	U
soup	U	vegetable	C	tea	U

2b

1 a   2 some   3 an   4 a   5 some   6 a

2c

1 some   2 an, a   3 any   4 some   5 any   6 any   7 no   8 any
9 a, some   10 any

2d

1   There's no milk in the fridge.
2   There aren't any shops open today.
3   He hasn't got any friends at work.
4   There are no buses after midnight.
5   I've got no free time tomorrow.
6   There isn't any sugar in my coffee.

2e

1 any   2 a   3 no   4 some   5 some   6 any   7 some   8 a

Unit 3

3a

1 slice   2 tin   3 bar   4 jar   5 loaf   6 carton   7 tube

3b

1 grams   2 piece   3 tube   4 piece   5 litres   6 piece

Unit 4

4a

1 many   2 much   3 many   4 much   5 many   6 much   7 many
8 much

4b

1 a few   2 a little   3 a little   4 a few   5 a few   6 a little
7 a little   8 a few

4c

1 a lot of, little   2 little, a lot of   3 a lot of, few   4 little, a lot of
5 a lot of, little   6 a lot of, few

4d

1 How many   2 lots of   3 a little   4 much   5 how much
6 a little

Unit 5

5a

1 some   2 Some   3 All   4 Most   5 Most   6 Most, some   7 All
8 Some   9 Some   10 All

5b

1 of   2 –   3 of   4 of   5 of   6 –   7 of   8 –

5c

1 all of   2 Some   3 most of   4 All   5 some of   6 None of

5d

1   Most of my friends like going to the cinema.
2   Some people work at night.
3   None of these mobiles has/have a camera.
4   Are all (of) your brothers and sisters vegetarian?
5   My brother spends all (of) his free time reading comics.
6   Most young people get some of their music from the
    Internet.

Unit 6

6a

1 each   2 every   3 Every   4 each   5 each   6 Every   7 each
8 Each

6b

1 each   2 every/each   3 each   4 each   5 each   6 every/each
7 every   8 each

Check 1

1

1 many   2 None   3 every   4 each   5 no

2

6 c   7 d   8 b   9 e   10 a

3

11 A   12 D   13 C   14 A   15 D   16 B   17 C   18 C   19 A   20 D

Unit 7

7a

1 We, them 2 you, us 3 our, Their, ours 4 mine, hers
5 it, her 6 my, yours

7b

1 you 2 My 3 its 4 I 5 my 6 His 7 He 8 him 9 She
10 her 11 they 12 us 13 their 14 yours

Unit 8

8a

1 Sam's room is next to my parents' room.
2 The twins' playroom is down the hall.
3 My uncles' names are David and Mark.
4 David's wife's name is Sheila.
5 Their children's names are Pat and Clare.
6 Pat and Clare's room is on the right.

8b

1 top of the building 2 grandparents' house 3 walls of the
bathroom/bathroom walls 4 capital of Australia 5 Lisa's
teacher 6 women's changing rooms 7 kitchen light
8 end of the street

Unit 9

9a

1 yourselves 2 himself 3 itself 4 herself 5 myself
6 themselves

9b

1 each other 2 themselves 3 each other 4 yourselves
5 each other 6 themselves

Unit 10

10a

1 ones 2 one 3 one 4 ones 5 one 6 ones

10b

1 one, The one 2 The (white) ones 3 one, The one
4 one, The one 5 ones, the ones 6 ones, The ones

Unit 11

11a

1 something 2 somewhere 3 anybody 4 nowhere
5 anything 6 no one 7 anywhere 8 someone

11b

1 don't have anywhere 2 saw no one/nobody 3 's nowhere
4 doesn't know anything 5 doesn't listen to anybody/anyone
6 can tell you nothing 7 's nobody/no one 8 ate nothing

11c

1 Everybody 2 Nowhere 3 Something 4 Nobody
5 Everything 6 Somewhere 7 Nobody 8 Something
9 Everywhere 10 Somebody

11d

1 somewhere 2 anything 3 Everywhere 4 something
5 everybody/everyone 6 Nobody/No one

Check 2

1

1 them 2 themselves 3 each other 4 their 5 they

2

6 end of the film 7 car keys 8 children's bedroom
9 back of the car 10 parents' house

3

11 yours 12 ones 13 somewhere 14 herself
15 nobody/no one

4

16 us 17 Everything 18 ones 19 yourself 20 each other

Unit 12

12a

1 The 2 the 3 a 4 a, a, The, the 5 the 6 an, a

12b

1 a 2 the 3 a 4 the 5 the 6 a 7 the 8 the 9 the 10 the
11 the 12 The

Unit 13

13a

the			–	
Amazon	Indian Ocean	*Asia*	Istanbul
Andes	Philippines	Canada	Park Avenue
Caribbean Sea	Rhine	Chile	Lake Como
Dominican Republic	Sahara Desert	Europe	Mount Fuji

13b

1 The 2 – 3 The, the 4 The, the, –, –, – 5 –, – 6 the 7 –, the
8 The 9 –, – 10 –, the

Unit 14

14a

1 – 2 – 3 the 4 the 5 – 6 the

14b

1 the supermarket 2 a 3 university 4 work 5 a 6 the disco

14c

1 – 2 the 3 – 4 – 5 a 6 – 7 the 8 the 9 – 10 the 11 a
12 the

Unit 15

15a

1 the 2 – 3 an 4 the, – 5 a 6 The 7 – 8 –, – 9 – 10 –
11 a 12 – 13 the 14 a 15 the 16 –

15b

1 a 2 – 3 – 4 a 5 a 6 a 7 – 8 the

Check 3

1

1 a 2 the 3 a, a, The 4 the 5 the

2

6 the 7 The 8 – 9 The 10 the

3

11 – 12 a 13 a 14 the 15 – 16 the 17 – 18 the 19 a 20 a

Unit 16

16a

1 a dark blue cotton scarf 2 a huge stone building 3 some red paper bags 4 a horrible little plastic dinosaur 5 some new black leather boots 6 some large Italian ceramic plates

16b

1 some long Indian cotton curtains 2 four comfortable black metal chairs 3 a beautiful Dutch oil painting 4 an enormous wooden wardrobe 5 a lovely little round carpet
6 a colourful square Peruvian bedcover

Unit 17

17a

1 hotter 2 the best 3 the quietest 4 more entertaining
5 the earliest 6 more useful 7 the worst 8 funnier
9 more interesting 10 the heaviest

17b

1 the busiest 2 slower than/less fast than 3 are less 4 the least 5 less crowded than

17c

1 more pairs of trainers, the most pairs of trainers
2 more, the most gold metals
3 more MP3s, the most MP3s

17d

1 less popular 2 the best 3 the least populated 4 quieter
5 easier 6 more welcoming

Unit 18

18a

1 safely 2 beautifully 3 nervously 4 hard 5 automatically
6 heavily 7 comfortably 8 easily

18b

1 stressful 2 quietly 3 good 4 politely 5 happily 6 happy
7 well 8 lucky

18c

1 He thinks quickly. 2 I sing well. 3 She eats noisily.
4 You work hard. 5 He drives carefully. 6 They run fast.

18d

1 fluent 2 immediately 3 tiring 4 international 5 good
6 easily 7 bad 8 slowly

Unit 19

19a

1 more carefully 2 better 3 harder 4 more slowly 5 worse
6 more efficiently 7 more easily 8 faster

19b

1 the most imaginatively 2 the most creatively 3 the hardest
4 the most heavily 5 the best 6 the most loudly 7 the worst
8 the fastest

19c

1 the most fluently 2 more carefully 3 more slowly than
4 the hardest 5 more simply than 6 the fastest

Unit 20

20a

1 a little heavier than silver 2 slightly faster than boys
3 a bit more popular than golf 4 far better than CDs
5 a bit more safely than men 6 far friendlier than cats
7 a lot easier than karate 8 much better than videos

20b

1 a lot more powerful 2 a bit harder 3 slightly larger
4 much worse 5 a little faster 6 far more comfortable
7 a lot bigger 8 a bit more quietly

Unit 21

21a

1 We are always tired in the evening.
2 He almost never goes to the cinema.
3 They rarely watch TV.
4 She seldom writes letters.
5 I hardly ever stay up late.
6 The trains are almost always on time.
7 We don't often eat fish.
8 She never cooks for herself.

21b

1 Does he always get up early?
2 She never sees her brother.
3 My parents don't often phone me.
4 You always make the same mistakes.
5 They are hardly ever at home.
6 We don't usually drive to work. / Usually we don't drive to work. / We don't drive to work usually.
7 Do you often play tennis? / Do you play tennis often?
8 She is rarely late for class.

21c

1 twice a week 2 every 3 Sometimes 4 usually
5 hardly ever 6 once a year 7 never 8 always

Unit 22

22a

1 These chairs are quite cheap.
2 Sonia walks fairly slowly.
3 He drives very dangerously.
4 We live in quite a big flat.
5 I'm feeling a bit tired.
6 The film was extremely long.
7 It's quite an old computer.
8 You eat really unhealthily.

22b

1 a very 2 a bit 3 really 4 quite 5 very 6 quite a 7 fairly
8 extremely

Check 4

1

1 He bought a big Mexican hat.
2 We are usually tired in the evening. / Usually we are tired in the evening. / We are tired in the evening usually.
3 This chair is much more comfortable than that one.
4 There's a horrible square glass building in the city centre.
5 I don't often eat chocolate. / I don't eat chocolate often.
6 That's quite a good restaurant.
7 Is he the best student in the class?

2

8 safely   9 really   10 Usually   11 good   12 very   13 most
14 slightly   15 less

3

16 well   17 less expressively than   18 more brilliantly than
19 enthusiastic   20 warmer than

Unit 23

23a

1 as well as   2 as badly as   3 as tired as   4 as well as
5 as good as   6 as carefully as

23b

1 as sensitive as   2 as noisy as   3 as hard as   4 as badly as
5 as exciting as   6 as easy as

Unit 24

24a

1 too tired   2 not clean enough   3 too small   4 not big enough
5 too late   6 not well enough

24b

1 He's too short to reach that shelf.
2 We aren't in Rome long enough to see the whole city.
3 The man was too angry to speak.
4 They aren't old enough to drive yet.
5 The music at the disco was too loud for us to have a conversation.
6 Dan doesn't play the guitar well enough to become a musician.

Unit 25

25a

1 so   2 such   3 such a   4 so   5 so   6 such   7 such a   8 so

25b

1 so   2 such   3 so   4 such   5 so   6 so

Check 5

1

1 too   2 so   3 such a   4 pretty   5 smart enough

2

6 as good as   7 so crowded   8 as loud as   9 enough
10 such a

3

11 B   12 C   13 A   14 C   15 A   16 D   17 D   18 B   19 A   20 B

Unit 26

26a

1 work, don't relax   2 goes, doesn't do   3 lives, often spends
4 don't go, listen   5 comes, doesn't speak   6 don't drive, usually catch

26b

1 Does Tim go, he does   2 Do they go, they don't   3 Does Sue always wear, she does   4 Do you play, I don't   5 Do they live, they do   6 Does she come, she doesn't

26c

1 do (you) travel   2 don't use   3 drive   4 walks   5 catches
6 do (you) recycle   7 put   8 do (you) borrow

Unit 27

27a

1 're playing   2 'm not reading   3 're having   4 isn't working
5 're saving   6 isn't running

27b

1 Are you enjoying, are, 're having   2 are you doing, 'm waiting
3 Is Holly using, isn't, isn't doing   4 Are they watching, aren't, 're preparing

27c

1 're having   2 'm learning   3 Is Gary taking   4 isn't
5 isn't doing   6 Are you getting   7 are   8 Are you enjoying
9 'm not   10 isn't raining

Unit 28

28a

1 Do tigers live   2 have   3 don't eat   4 's calling   5 're making
6 goes   7 's cooking   8 usually buy

28b

1 'm buying   2 play   3 are you doing   4 'm still studying
5 'm working   6 go   7 dance   8 start

Unit 29

29a

1 're staying   2 belongs   3 has   4 's making   5 smells   6 love
7 don't know   8 don't want

29b

1 aren't dancing, hate   2 know, don't remember   3 are you doing, have, need   4 think, don't see   5 Is he writing, wants

Check 6

1

1 doesn't understand   2 're trying   3 have   4 Does Ellie want
5 Are you reading

2

6 What time does the museum close on Sundays?
7 Someone's singing a song.
8 People don't eat late at night in Britain.
9 She carries a briefcase to work every day.
10 Are you sitting on them?

3
11 's working 12 doesn't have 13 goes 14 tries 15 want

4
16 Do you want 17 is my computer making 18 Is mum cooking 19 does it belong 20 are those people putting

Unit 30
30a
1 arrived 2 didn't travel 3 chatted 4 didn't play 5 studied 6 stayed 7 didn't want 8 loved 9 stopped 10 didn't clean 11 didn't like 12 carried

30b
1 decided 2 waited 3 didn't arrive 4 tried 5 didn't answer 6 missed 7 started 8 arrived 9 didn't believe 10 shouted

30c
1 danced 2 talked 3 did (the party) finish 4 walked 5 Did (you) live 6 worked 7 travelled 8 did (you) move 9 started 10 hated

Unit 31
31a
1 saw 2 took 3 slept 4 ate 5 met 6 bought

31b
1 drove 2 did 3 was 4 didn't remember 5 was 6 spent 7 didn't find 8 felt 9 rang 10 didn't get 11 told 12 caught 13 went 14 found

31c
1 did the concert begin, began, came 2 did your parents give, didn't give 3 were you, was, didn't hear 4 did you break, fell 5 did your brother wear, wore, cost

Unit 32
32a
1 was raining, was thinking 2 was surfing 3 wasn't looking 4 was advertising 5 were travelling 6 were having 7 wasn't sitting, was flying 8 were waiting

32b
1 was Karl going, was wearing 2 Were you using, was, was chatting 3 were making, were celebrating, were trying 4 were they doing, was driving, was working 5 were you talking, were discussing 6 were digging, were you digging

32c
1 was doing 2 was planting 3 was working 4 were having 5 were talking 6 was sleeping

Unit 33
33a
1 while 2 When 3 While 4 when 5 While 6 when

33b
1 Your mother rang while you were having a bath.
2 When we saw them, they were buying food for the party.
3 While she was shopping, she met an old friend.
4 We were parking our car when we had the accident.
5 What were you reading when I came into the room?
6 While I was chopping the onions, I cut my finger.

33c
1 was flying 2 got 3 took off 4 sat 5 was wearing 6 landed 7 was waiting 8 decided 9 looked 10 wasn't

Unit 34
34a
1 used to be 2 used to live 3 didn't use to worry 4 used to go 5 didn't use to have

34b
1 Did he use to go swimming every week?
2 Did they use to have a smaller car?
3 What did she use to do for a living?
4 Did you use to do sports at school?
5 Did it use to be more expensive to fly?

34c
1 did you use to do 2 used to like 3 didn't use to have 4 Did you use to go 5 didn't use to give 6 did your parents use to come 7 used to come

34d
1 used to play 2 didn't do 3 used to work, became 4 didn't use to eat 5 didn't have 6 rained

Check 7
1
1 Were 2 wasn't 3 did 4 didn't 5 did

2
6 was listening 7 when 8 didn't go 9 went 10 When

3
11 studied 12 was driving 13 broke 14 didn't read 15 were you going

4
16 used to 17 was snowing 18 went 19 phoned 20 knocked

Unit 35
35a
1 's forgotten 2 haven't done 3 's moved 4 hasn't replied 5 have borrowed 6 've left 7 hasn't stopped 8 've made

35b
1 Have (you) bought 2 Has (he) hurt 3 Have (your parents) planned 4 Have (you) tried 5 Has (your sister) started 6 Has (Kate) arrived

35c
a has, 6 b haven't, 1 c have, 3 d haven't, 0 e has, 2 f haven't, 4 g hasn't, 5

35d
1 have you done 2 've cleaned 3 's painted 4 hasn't finished 5 've made 6 Has Steve repaired 7 haven't had 8 Have you bought 9 have given 10 's put up

Unit 36
36a
1 've just bought 2 's just heard 3 've just left 4 's just stolen 5 've just had 6 've just started

36b

1 Sarah and Jane haven't done the washing up yet.
2 Has Mark taken out the rubbish yet?
3 Paul's already tidied the living room.
4 Have Martin and Bill put the furniture back yet?
5 Sue hasn't thrown away the old magazines yet.
6 Have you tidied the CDs yet?

36c

1 haven't unpacked our suitcases yet 2 's already met 3 've just sent 4 haven't visited St Mark's Square yet 5 've already seen 6 Have you booked your holiday yet?

Unit 37
37a

1 He's never written a poem.
2 Have they ever hear a podcast?
3 She's never broken a bone.
4 Have you ever found money in the street?
5 I've never spoken in public.
6 They've never stayed in a five-star hotel.
7 Has he ever eaten octopus?
8 We've never seen the sea.
9 Has she ever visited an Asian country?
10 Have you ever met anyone famous?

37b

1 gone 2 gone 3 been 4 been 5 been 6 gone

37c

1 Have you seen 2 haven't 3 's played 4 hasn't toured 5 's seen 6 Have you ever been 7 've bought 8 haven't heard

Unit 38
38a

1 They haven't watched television for two weeks.
2 Chris has lived here since he was a child.
3 I haven't read a newspaper since Monday.
4 It hasn't rained for months.
5 I've known Sam for three years.
6 Sarah 's been married for ten months.

38b

1 How long has Chris known Nora?
2 How long have you liked football?
3 How long have they owned a shop?
4 How long has she lived in her flat?
5 How long have the children been asleep?
6 How long has Tom had his guitar?

38c

1 for 2 since she was 3 've liked 4 since 5 's lived 6 for 7 for ten 8 've worked

Unit 39
39a

1 's lived 2 's never travelled 3 knows 4 reads 5 's been 6 gets up 7 goes 8 doesn't want 9 've visited 10 look forward 11 tells 12 've ever met

39b

1 have 2 've been 3 was 4 have you visited 5 went 6 have you travelled 7 haven't 8 've had 9 did you go 10 were

39c

1 is 2 began 3 started 4 kept 5 appeared 6 included 7 has changed 8 became 9 have started 10 write

Check 8
1

1 just 2 never 3 yet 4 already 5 for

2

6 How long has he lived in France?
7 Where have you been?
8 Have they arrived yet?
9 Have you ever written a short story?
10 Has Alison tidied her room?

3

11 haven't been/'ve never been 12 for 13 have been 14 the first time 15 hasn't arrived

4

16 opened 17 since 18 doesn't stop 19 was 20 has appeared

Unit 40
40a

1 hadn't prepared 2 'd spent 3 hadn't booked 4 'd had 5 hadn't ridden 6 had washed up 7 had told 8 hadn't met

40b

1 'd left 2 had never had 3 had already won 4 'd beaten 5 hadn't done 6 'd also collected

40c

1 had 2 'd never been 3 had recommended 4 'd read 5 Had he ever played 6 hadn't 7 'd never heard 8 hadn't seen

Unit 41
41a

1 First the train left.
2 First the film finished.
3 First I turned off my phone.
4 First the restaurant closed.
5 First they sold all the tickets.

41b

1 When we saw them, they hadn't finished decorating their house.
2 Lou had already tried on ten suits when he bought the white one.
3 When I went to Argentina, I'd never flown before.
4 He'd already written his first novel by the time he was twenty-two.
5 When Kelly joined the army, she hadn't had a job before.
6 They'd already found work by the time they finished university.

41c
1 happened 2 arrived 3 hadn't started 4 introduced
5 didn't know 6 started 7 'd met 8 compared 9 'd done
10 remembered 11 'd been 12 'd come

Check 9

1
1 I'd never been to a wedding before.
2 We arrived late because we hadn't brought the address with us.
3 The ceremony had already begun by the time we got there.
4 The groom looked nervous because he'd forgotten the ring.
5 By the time the wedding was over, it had started to rain.

2
6 Had he taken 7 'd already failed 8 hadn't practised
9 'd had 10 'd just broken up

3
11 spent 12 'd never seen 13 hadn't invented 14 was
15 had bought

4
16 'd won three World Cups 17 hadn't read your e-mail (yet)
18 'd done all her homework 19 Kim had just left university
20 had (already) sold a million copies

Unit 42

42a
1 'll 2 's going to 3 's going to 4 'll 5 are going to 6 won't

42b
1 'm going to take, 'll come 2 Is Felix going to look for, 'll find
3 's going to make, won't have 4 're going to arrive, won't
start 5 isn't going to go, won't go

Unit 43

43a
1 going to start 2 going to get 3 seeing 4 going to do
5 coming 6 going to be 7 going 8 going to come

43b
1 're going to travel 2 are you doing 3 's going to study
4 'm taking 5 are going to live 6 's driving

Unit 44

44a
1 're playing 2 'm going 3 lasts 4 starts 5 doesn't arrive
6 's buying

44b
1 is 2 starts 3 finishes 4 are (you) doing 5 'm meeting
6 'm flying 7 does (your flight) leave 8 'm not doing

Check 10

1
1 're taking 2 'm going to visit 3 'll do 4 leaves 5 gets
6 are you doing 7 's going to rain 8 'll walk

2
9 going to 10 meeting 11 will not/won't find 12 are going
13 are/'re going to

3
14 Will they enjoy 15 does the shop open 16 are you doing
17 is Georgina going to call 18 will ordinary people have
19 are you going to study 20 Is/Are Moira's group playing

Unit 45

45a
1 Bob wasn't able to read until he was six.
2 We're able to see the sea from our window.
3 Not many people are able to drive a bus.
4 We were able to speak to them in English.
5 They weren't able to dance or sing.
6 I wasn't able to understand the film.

45b
1 ~~could~~ 2 both 3 both 4 ~~could~~ 5 both 6 both

45c
1 was able to find 2 couldn't do 3 can't dance
4 'm able to dance

Unit 46

46a
1 allowed, not 2 could/can, aren't 3 to 4 can 5 Were
6 Can/Could, course, can 7 can 8 can/could, can

46b
1 Can we swim 2 are allowed to stay up 3 could go
4 were allowed to take 5 can come 6 you allowed to take
7 could feed 8 can play

Unit 47

47a
1 might be 2 could see 3 may not have 4 might not go
5 may not want 6 could be

47b
1 might do 2 may work 3 might not have 4 might ask
5 may not be 6 could meet

Unit 48

48a
1 can't 2 must 3 must 4 must 5 can't 6 can't

48b
1 must collect 2 must have 3 can't own 4 can't belong
5 must be 6 can't have 7 can't be

Unit 49

49a
1 can you pass 2 would you phone 3 could you bring
4 can you help 5 Could you lend 6 Would you pay

49b
1 Can/Could you lend me (your DVD of) *Lord of the Rings* tonight?
2 Could/Would you translate this song for me?
3 Can/Could you lend me your camera for a week?

4 Could/Would you turn the music down?
5 Can you look at my computer?
6 Could/Would you speak more slowly?

Unit 50
50
1 We can take sandwiches with us.
2 Shall I lend you a good pair of walking shoes?
3 How about going to the Lake District?
4 We could get there by bus.
5 I'll find out the bus times, if you like.
6 Why don't we stay the weekend?
7 Shall we take a tent and camp?
8 What about staying in a youth hostel?
9 Let's stay in the youth hostel.

Check 11
1
1 could   2 can't   3 I'll   4 How   5 could   6 Shall
2
7 couldn't   8 must   9 was able to   10 are allowed to   11 Could   12 could
3
13 was able to   14 was allowed to   15 must have   16 may win
4
17 can't   18 can   19 can   20 could

Unit 51
51a
1 have to   2 had to   3 need to   4 have to   5 need to   6 must
51b
1 has to buy   2 had to find   3 must go   4 Do (we) need to leave   5 must clean   6 did (you) have to pay
51c
1 needed to   2 had to   3 have to   4 have to   5 Does   6 must

Unit 52
52a
1 mustn't swim   2 aren't allowed to talk   3 mustn't touch   4 couldn't enter   5 can't use   6 weren't allowed to smoke
52b
1 aren't allowed to listen   2 mustn't talk   3 aren't allowed to do   4 couldn't have   5 wasn't (even) allowed to drink   6 can't leave

Unit 53
53a
1 f   2 a   3 e   4 d   5 c   6 g
53b
1 don't need to   2 didn't have to   3 don't usually have to   4 didn't have to   5 mustn't   6 didn't need to

53c
1 didn't need to get   2 doesn't have to train   3 didn't need to give   4 don't have to wear   5 didn't have to walk   6 doesn't need to buy   7 don't need to paint   8 didn't have to cook

Unit 54
54a
1 You must try the new kebab restaurant.
2 Should I eat more vegetables?
3 She shouldn't go out every night.
4 I think they ought to join a gym.
5 Do you think I should get a haircut?
6 You oughtn't to watch so much TV.
54b
1 ought to drink   2 shouldn't do   3 should I   4 ought to talk   5 should also try   6 mustn't

Check 12
1
1 'm not allowed   2 mustn't   3 don't have to   4 didn't need to   5 don't have to
2
6 wasn't allowed to   7 have to   8 had   9 didn't have to   10 needed to
3
11 has to   12 can't/aren't allowed to   13 aren't allowed   14 have to   15 allowed to
4
16 shouldn't eat   17 must get   18 must see   19 ought to eat   20 mustn't tell

Unit 55
55a
1 The bank won't lend them any money.
2 She didn't tell me her name.
3 Have you paid them the deposit?
4 We gave Sue a watch for her birthday.
5 I made all the family lunch.
6 Could you fetch me some milk?
7 I bought the child an expensive toy.
8 Have they offered him the job?
55b
1 Did Matt get a drink for you?
2 Will you show your photos to me?
3 Can you pass the salt to Bill?
4 I've made a cake for Laura.
5 The waiter brought our food to us.
6 They haven't given the bill to me.
7 She didn't buy a ticket for me.
8 I often take flowers to my grandmother.
9 He taught the words of the song to the class.
10 Please could you send a photo to me?
55c
1 She fetched a newspaper for her father.
2 She took her aunt some library books.

3 She cooked some lunch for her brother.
4 She sent her grandmother a birthday card.
5 She bought her friend a present.
6 She made her neighbour a cup of tea.
7 She brought her uncle a hot drink.
8 She got some fruit for her sister.
9 She taught a new trick to her dog.
10 She told a bedtime story to her brother.

Unit 56
56a
1 are there 2 is there 3 there are 4 There's 5 there are
6 there isn't 7 there aren't

56b
1 They're 2 There's 3 There isn't 4 there's 5 It's 6 There's
7 it isn't 8 there isn't 9 There are 10 They aren't

56c
1 It was Paul's birthday yesterday.
2 It's six kilometres to the airport.
3 It's half past eleven.
4 It was cloudy yesterday.
5 It's a long way from London to Edinburgh.
6 It was Tuesday yesterday.

Unit 57
57a
1 Are we going for a picnic tomorrow?
2 Is Pat a good cook?
3 Can Mary type fast?
4 Did you see the football match yesterday?
5 Does she have/Has she got a lot of work to do?
6 Will they be here soon?
7 Has Andy gone to the post office?
8 Should he speak to the director?
9 Do they watch TV most evenings?
10 Is it snowing heavily?

57b
1 Whose dictionary did you borrow?
2 Why was he crying?
3 Where have they gone?
4 What time is she arriving?
5 Which (one) do you prefer?
6 Who are you meeting tonight?

57c
1 How often do they go to the gym? e
2 How much does a room cost? c
3 How big is your flat? d
4 How do you usually get to work? b
5 How long did you study last night? a
6 How tall are you? i
7 How many cousins do you have/have you got? h
8 How far is it to the bus stop? g

57d
1 How long have you lived there?
2 Do you like it?
3 Why did you go there?

4 Is it interesting?
5 What are you going to do (when you finish?)
6 Where would you like to go?

Unit 58
58a
1 What does Dee do every Friday?
2 What might happen tonight?
3 Who did you meet for lunch yesterday?
4 What can you see over there?
5 Who's left a message?
6 Who are they going to visit?

58b
1 did Dr Baird invent 2 did they beat 3 happened 4 wrote
5 did Nelson Mandela win 6 wrote

Unit 59
59a
1 Who were you speaking to?
2 Which hotel did they stay at?
3 What is Peter good at?
4 What was Lisa angry about?
5 Who is Paula married to?
6 Which pizza did you ask for?
7 What were they looking at?
8 What are you thinking about?

59b
1 (What) are you afraid of?
2 (Who) did he go on holiday with?
3 (What) were they talking about?
4 (What) are you interested in?
5 (Who) does this dog belong to?
6 (Who) did she give the money to?
7 (What) are you listening to?
8 (Who) is she waiting for?

Unit 60
60a
1 hasn't 2 did 3 were 4 can 5 doesn't 6 is 7 won't 8 had
60b
1 do you 2 have we 3 wasn't she 4 didn't they 5 hadn't you
6 is he 7 couldn't we 8 will you

Unit 61
61a
1 e 2 i 3 f 4 b 5 c 6 a 7 g 8 h
61b
1 Neither/Nor did (Joe.) 2 (Yours) isn't either. 3 Neither/Nor
was (Lynn.) 4 (They) could too. 5 So have (mine.) 6 (I) am
too. 7 (Neither) had (you.) 8 (So) will (I.)

Unit 62
62a
1 I hope so. 2 I don't think so. 3 I hope not. 4 I think so.
5 I hope not. 6 I don't think so.

62b

1 (I) hope not. 2 (I) hope not. 3 (I) hope so. 4 (I) don't think so. 5 (I) think so. 6 (I) hope so. 7 (I) hope not. 8 (I) don't think so.

Check 13

1

1 happened   2 the bicycle to me   3 don't think so   4 so do I
5 do bicycles cost

2

6 It   7 There   8 so   9 they   10 either

3

11 Julie made dinner for us last night.
12 He told Sarah the address.
13 Where did those flowers come from?
14 Are you listening to me?
15 Who did you give the letter to?

4

16 didn't   17 did you go with   18 isn't   19 paid for it
20 did you stay (there)

Unit 63

63a

1 Using   2 Sitting   3 Working   4 Recycling   5 Lying
6 Travelling

63b

1 Studying   2 Taking   3 relaxing   4 Drinking   5 eating   6 Doing
7 Walking   8 sleeping

Unit 64

64a

1 getting   2 to build   3 to travel   4 becoming   5 to stay
6 not to tell   7 going   8 not to do

64b

1 to take   2 having to   3 listening   4 to play   5 living   6 seeing
7 to hear   8 to reply

Unit 65

65a

1 him   2 –   3 them   4 –   5 –   6 her

65b

1 Laura to come   2 Harry to get   3 you to call   4 us to stay
5 them (to) move

Check 14

1

1 to come   2 Being   3 seeing   4 Not understanding
5 to speak   6 to take

2

7 to move   8 to do   9 to help   10 painting   11 decorating
12 you to come   13 us to finish   14 them to come

3

15 to get   16 Driving   17 making   18 to travel   19 to arrive
20 to take

Unit 66

66a

1 The new bridge will be finished next year.
2 The new drug hasn't been tested yet.
3 Spaghetti is made from wheat.
4 Paper was invented in China.
5 500 student flats were built last year.
6 The winner will be announced tomorrow.
7 The invitations have already been sent.
8 Pineapples are grown in hot countries.

66b

1 Has (the house next door) been sold   2 weren't given
3 Are (these grapes) grown   4 hasn't been found   5 was (the Internet) created   6 will be sent

66c

1 were invited   2 were awarded   3 are held   4 will be staged
5 has already been started   6 will be finished

66d

1 (Nowadays, albums) are released on CDs.
2 (The CD) was developed in the 1980s.
3 (CDs) are used to store music or computer software.
4 (CDs) are made from plastic and aluminium.
5 (Billions of CDs) have been sold in the last twenty years.
6 (Maybe one day all music) will be downloaded from the Internet.
7 (But probably CDs) will be bought for a few years to come.

Unit 67

67a

1 Three languages are spoken in Switzerland.
2 The FIFA World Cup was once stolen.
3 Penicillin was discovered by Alexander Fleming.
4 Everest has been climbed by about 1,500 people.
5 The Nobel Peace Prize is awarded every year.
6 Water has been discovered on Mars.

67b

1 (What languages) are spoken in Switzerland?
2 (Who) was the FIFA World Cup stolen by?
3 (How) was penicillin discovered?
4 (When) was Everest climbed (for the first time)?
5 (In which city) is the Nobel Peace Prize awarded?
6 (How) was water discovered on Mars?

Unit 68

68a

1 (She) had her CD player repaired.
2 (They) have their photo taken once a year.
3 (I) had my head shaved.
4 (Leah) has her clothes made.
5 (We) have our house cleaned.
6 (I) had my living room painted.

7 (They) had their shoes polished.

8 (I) have my newspaper delivered every day.

68b

1 had it fixed 2 do you have your hair cut 3 get my nails manicured 4 did she get her passport photo taken
5 had it developed 6 had a short story published

Check 15

1

1 was made 2 was directed 3 star 4 will be filmed
5 has been chosen

2

6 will be married 7 had 8 have been invited 9 by
10 had the house redecorated 11 hasn't been sold

3

12 by 13 were used 14 was opened 15 is visited by
16 is known

4

17 The Eiffel Tower is/was/has been used as a radio transmitter.

18 No one was killed during its construction.

19 The Eiffel Tower is painted every seven years.

20 Every year millions of people have their photo taken in front of the Eiffel Tower.

Unit 69

69a

1 Max said, 'We won't get to work on time.'

2 'What shall we do?' Peter asked.

3 'Here's the bus now,' Max said.

4 Max said, 'There are lots of people on it.'

5 Peter said, 'It isn't going to stop.'

69b

1 'I'm sorry to hear that,' said Ann.

2 'It was working yesterday,' Tony said.

3 'What's wrong with it?' asked Ann.

4 Jane said, 'The mouse isn't working.'

5 Tony asked, 'Is the battery OK?'

6 'I put in a new battery last week,' Jane said.

Unit 70

70a

1 Jane said (that) she worked in an office.

2 The weather man said (that) it was going to rain.

3 The motorists said (that) they were driving to a football match.

4 The old lady said (that) she had won the lottery.

5 Louise said (that) her friends didn't like visiting museums.

6 The young boy said (that) people would have holidays in space in the future.

7 James said (that) he had broken his leg playing football.

8 They said (that) they hadn't flown before.

70b

1 Ed said, 'I'm going to visit my aunt.'/'I'm going to visit my aunt,' Ed said.

2 She said, 'I don't remember your name.'/'I don't remember your name,' she said.

3 They said, 'We bought our car in 1999.'/'We bought our car in 1999,' they said.

4 I said, 'We haven't seen the film yet.'/'We haven't seen the film yet,' I said.

5 Sue said, 'I don't like vegetables.'/'I don't like vegetables,' Sue said.

6 They said, 'Our son is studying Biology.'/'Our son is studying Biology,' they said.

70c

1 was 2 had opened 3 had 4 would be 5 had organised
6 were offering

Unit 71

71a

1 said 2 said 3 told 4 told 5 said 6 said 7 told 8 said

71b

1 said 2 told 3 said 4 told 5 told 6 said 7 said 8 told
9 said 10 told

Unit 72

72a

1 if museums closed on Sundays

2 if I was waiting for a tourist bus

3 if the waiter had overcharged them/us

4 if a hotel would be expensive

5 if the flight from Bristol had arrived

6 if there was a Bureau de Change nearby

7 if I had heard the platform number

8 if we/they were going to get a guided tour

72b

1 what I thought of it 2 when I had arrived 3 if I had flown to Cairo 4 if I was planning to stay long 5 what I had seen
6 if I liked the food

72c

1 what I was doing at the college

2 why I had decided to study Spanish

3 what other languages I spoke

4 how long I had been at the college

5 when I had classes

6 what I was going to do later on

Unit 73

73a

1 to fasten our seatbelts 2 not to smoke 3 to switch off our mobile phones 4 not to use any electrical equipment after take-off 5 not to put bags in the aisle 6 to stay in our seats during the flight 7 not to unfasten our seatbelts 8 to show our passports at immigration control

73b

1 to pass him some potatoes 2 to lend him £20
3 to be quiet 4 to take her shopping 5 to help him with his homework 6 to stop reading the newspaper

73c

1 The manager told his assistant not to be late for the meeting.
2 The couple asked the waiter to bring them the bill.
3 The dentist told me to open my mouth wide.
4 They asked their neighbour to turn the music down.
5 Peter told Dee to call him from the airport.
6 I asked my flatmate to go to the supermarket for me.
7 The mother told her children not to talk to strangers.
8 They asked Susie to look after their cat.

Check 16

1

1 B 2 A 3 D 4 D 5 C 6 B 7 B 8 C 9 B 10 A

2

11 'How long have you been in England?' she asked him.
12 He said, 'I arrived six months ago.'
13 She asked, 'Do you like living in England?'
14 'I don't like the weather in England,' he said.
15 'But I'm going to stay for a year,' he said.

3

16 the bus went 17 her to take 18 'd never seen 19 to show her 20 told

Unit 74

74a

1 Is there 2 Mr Jones will be 3 if you have this sweater
4 Has the bank closed 5 do these shoes cost 6 it takes
7 Is the station 8 there is

74b

1 if this is the right road for Brighton 2 where I can get a bus to Camden Market 3 if I'll have to wait long 4 how long the journey takes 5 if the film has started 6 how much a ticket costs 7 if there's a telephone box near here 8 if this train goes to Oxford

Unit 75

75a

1 how to drive 2 where to go 3 how to empty 4 how long to wait 5 what to do 6 how to get to 7 what to see 8 how to use

75b

1 what to wear to the party tonight 2 how to use the ticket machine 3 who to speak to about my problem 4 which button to press to start the DVD 5 what time to arrive at the party 6 how to switch on the printer

Check 17

1

1 Amanda can dance 2 how to dance 3 she goes to 4 where to go 5 she is

2

6 Do you know where Paul has put the salt?
7 Could you tell me if he puts the glasses in the dishwasher?

8 I asked the neighbours where to leave the key.
9 Nobody told me what to do with the plants.
10 Can you tell me when Paul is coming back?

3

11 who to ask 12 if 13 how to 14 I change 15 where the manager

4

16 how to get 17 to take 18 it costs 19 the weather is like 20 to bring

Unit 76

76a

1 where 2 who 3 whose 4 who 5 whose 6 where
7 where 8 which

76b

1 where 2 which/that/– 3 which/that/– 4 where
5 that/– 6 who/that 7 which/that/– 8 who/that

76c

1 *Titanic* is the film which/that made Kate Winslett famous.
2 Stephen Hawking is a physicist whose books have sold millions of copies.
3 *Robinson Crusoe* is a novel (which/that) Daniel Defoe wrote.
4 Stratford on Avon is the town where Shakespeare was born.
5 Marco Polo was the explorer who/that brought spaghetti to Italy.
6 Van Gogh was the Dutch painter who/that painted *Sunflowers*.
7 Saint Helena is the island where Napoleon Bonaparte died.
8 The electric light bulb was an invention which/that changed people's lives.

Unit 77

77a

1 in 2 near/next to 3 with 4 on 5 on 6 in 7 near/next to/behind 8 in

77b

1 a website selling cheap flights to Prague
2 a flight leaving the following weekend
3 queuing to check in
4 the plane waiting to take off
5 waiting to meet friends
6 Katie waving excitedly from the back of the crowd

Check 18

1

1 who/that 2 where 3 who/that 4 whose 5 which/that
6 where

2

7 – 8 doing 9 wearing 10 with 11 by 12 sitting

3

13 with 14 who/that lived 15 sitting 16 dancing 17 wearing/with/in 18 whose sister 19 talking 20 which/that

Unit 78
78a
1 We have a dog and (we have) three cats as well.
2 They visited London and (they) also (visited) Paris.
3 She's studying Maths and (she's studying) Music as well.
4 I can play the guitar and (I can play) the piano too.
5 We went to a concert and (we) also (went to) a party.
6 Dick plays tennis and (he) goes jogging as well.
7 Jim bought a T-shirt and (he) also (bought) two comics.
8 I had a good time and (I) made new friends too.

78b
1 too   2 and   3 as   4 also   5 and   6 well

Unit 79
79a
1 Both (Piet) and (Greg)   2 neither (Eric) nor (Lucas)   3 either (Melbourne) or (Sidney)   4 Both (the Cote d'Azur) and (Crete)   5 neither (Lanzarote) nor (Mallorca)   6 either (Portugal) or (Croatia)   7 both (the blue one) and (the green one)   8 both (boring) and (predictable)

79b
1 Both Laos and Thailand are in Asia.
2 Neither penguins nor ostriches can fly.
3 Either France or Italy won the 2006 World Cup.
4 Both the Egyptians and the Aztecs built pyramids.
5 Neither Alfred Hitchcock nor Federico Fellini won an Oscar.
6 Lake Titicaca is either in Bolivia or (in) Peru.

79c
1 nor   2 either   3 or   4 either   5 or   6 neither   7 nor   8 both   9 and   10 both   11 and

Unit 80
80a
1 but   2 However   3 although   4 Although   5 but   6 however

80b
1 They're very rich, but they never spend any money.
2 Though my grandmother is 81, she's still very active. / My grandmother is 81 though she's still very active.
3 The police are looking for the stolen money, but they haven't found it yet.
4 Although Kip ran fast, he didn't win the race. / Kip ran fast although he didn't win the race.
5 I think she's Dutch, but she may be Belgian.

80c
1 However   2 although   3 but   4 however   5 but

Unit 81
81a
1 so   2 Because   3 because   4 so   5 so   6 because

81b
1 so   2 Since   3 as   4 Therefore   5 because of   6 Therefore   7 as   8 Because

81c
1 so   2 because/as/since   3 so   4 therefore/so   5 because/as/since   6 because of

Unit 82
82a
1 c   2 d   3 g   4 b   5 a   6 e

82b
1 so that   2 In order to   3 so that   4 so that   5 In order to   6 in order to

82c
1 Gary borrowed Jack's bike to go to the library.
2 The government passed a law in order to stop people smoking at work.
3 Yolanda trained a lot so that she could run a marathon.
4 Some people watch DVDs to practise their English.
5 I'll leave her a note so that she'll know we've gone to the supermarket.
6 Companies advertise in order to sell their products.
7 William is going on a diet to lose weight.
8 Doctors vaccinate children in order to prevent diseases.

Check 19
1
1 neither   2 in order to   3 Although   4 also   5 so
2
6 A   7 C   8 D   9 B   10 C   11 D   12 C   13 B   14 A   15 C
3
16 and   17 To   18 or   19 both   20 As

Unit 83
83a
1 A   2 C   3 A   4 C   5 B   6 D   7 B   8 D

83b
1 As soon as/When   2 While   3 until   4 when   5 before   6 After/When

Unit 84
84a
1 will be, arrive   2 go, 'll wash up   3 finish, 'll lend   4 'll decide, get   5 'll invite, goes   6 'll pay, buy   7 stops, 'll go   8 will phone, arrives

84b
1 go   2 see   3 'll mark   4 'll visit   5 arrive   6 tell   7 'll come   8 'll show   9 'll invite   10 leave

Unit 85
85a
1 Before buying a new car, you should go for a test drive.
2 I decided to learn Italian after spending two weeks in Rome.
3 Before moving to London, Lisa lived in a small village.
4 After eating your home-made jam, we decided to make some ourselves.
5 Steve and Sue always visit us before leaving their holiday cottage.

85b

1 Before buying a plane ticket, you should look for special offers online. / You should look for special offers online before buying a plane ticket.
2 Before getting on the plane, you have to go through a security check. / You have to go through a security check before getting on the plane.
3 After going into the departures area, you can buy tax-free products. / You can buy tax-free products after going into the departures area.
4 Before leaving the plane, you should check you have all your hand luggage. / You should check you have all your hand luggage before leaving the plane.
5 After going through passport control, you can collect your luggage. / You can collect your luggage after going through passport control.
6 After arriving in London, you must be careful with your things. / You must be careful with your things after arriving in London.
7 After seeing London, you should visit Oxford or Cambridge. / You should visit Oxford or Cambridge after seeing London.

Unit 86

86a

1 Then 2 after 3 Finally 4 First 5 Then/Next/After that
6 finally/after that/then

86b

1 First 2 First 3 Then/Next 4 Next/Then/After that/Finally

Check 20

1

1 D 2 C 3 B 4 A 5 C 6 C 7 A 8 D 9 B 10 D

2

11 as soon as 12 After 13 When 14 before 15 While

3

16 he rings 17 finish work 18 I get 19 then
20 after/when we

Unit 87

87a

1 g 2 a 3 e 4 f 5 d 6 b

87b

1 gets up, has to 2 'm not, walk 3 do you do, have 4 comes, doesn't answer 5 need, talk 6 Do you turn off, 're

Unit 88

88a

1 can't, don't 2 walk, 'll get 3 go, buy 4 won't get, take
5 see, mustn't 6 Don't, asks 7 'll catch, hurry 8 doesn't tell, might be

88b

1 makes 2 feels 3 can phone 4 don't organise 5 might be
6 'll be 7 doesn't get 8 give 9 can get 10 see 11 ask
12 don't mention

88c

1 If I phone you at six o'clock, will you be at home?
2 What will we do if the restaurant doesn't serve vegetarian food?
3 Will Jean be angry if we don't arrive on time?
4 If I get a laptop, where should I buy it?
5 Who will you go on holiday with if you win the competition?
6 If you go away this weekend, can I have a party in the flat?

88d

a 3 b 1 c 5 d 6 e 2 f 4 g 0

88e

1 won't be able to stay 2 do 3 'll spend 4 look 5 might find
6 will (you) find 7 don't know 8 book

Unit 89

89a

1 unless 2 If 3 if 4 unless 5 unless 6 If 7 unless 8 if

89b

1 you invite my boyfriend as well 2 we don't get to the airport early 3 you don't cook it very well 4 he listens to people
5 she waters it more often 6 you phone to say sorry
7 we don't get some help

Unit 90

90a

1 were 2 'd buy 3 Would 4 wouldn't 5 'd tell 6 found
7 would 8 had 9 'd take 10 didn't 11 would 12 would

90b

1 slept 2 wouldn't be 3 'd get 4 didn't watch 5 'd be able to
6 had 7 'd go away 8 were 9 needed 10 'd ask

90c

1 If you saw a ghost, would you be frightened?
2 If Sarah had a problem, who would she talk to?
3 Would Marc come to the party if I asked him?
4 What would you do if you were in Kate's position?
5 If you could go anywhere, where would you go?

90d

1 (If) Toni wanted to see us, he'd phone us.
2 (If) it wasn't/weren't so expensive, we'd eat out.
3 (If) you came to training sessions, you'd get in the football team.
4 (If) the students didn't enjoy your lessons, they wouldn't come to every class.
5 (If) she didn't practise every day, she wouln't be very/so good.
6 (If) I won the lottery, I wouldn't carry on working.

Check 21

1

1 die 2 give 3 move 4 might not survive 5 had 6 'd put
7 'll tell 8 see

2

9 were 10 wouldn't get 11 forgets 12 have 13 'll pay
14 doesn't pay

3
15 won't find   16 had   17 'm at work   18 'd see   19 the weather
is   20 you bring

Unit 91
91a
1 on   2 above   3 on   4 next to   5 under   6 on   7 near   8 next
to   9 Behind   10 in front of   11 Next to/Near   12 in   13 on
14 between

91b
1 at   2 on, above, on   3 next to, between   4 at/in, in front of,
behind   5 among   6 in   7 near/opposite   8 on

Unit 92
92a
1 through   2 out of   3 up, down   4 towards   5 across   6 along
7 over   8 into   9 past   10 onto   11 away from   12 off

92b
1 over   2 across   3 past   4 round   5 up   6 through   7 down
8 out of

Unit 93
93a
1 in   2 at   3 on   4 at   5 on   6 in   7 at   8 at

93b
1 after   2 before   3 before   4 after   5 before   6 After

93c
1 in   2 on   3 at   4 at   5 in   6 Before   7 at   8 After

Unit 94
94
1 I'm going to the cinema tomorrow evening.
2 We had an interesting lecture the day before yesterday.
3 I've been at university all day.
4 I'm going to meet my friends to go shopping the day after
   tomorrow.
5 I went to bed at midnight last night.
6 I have to do an exam next week.
7 I've been to the gym every morning this week.
8 I worked in the library yesterday afternoon.

Unit 95
95a
1 until   2 from, to/until   3 for   4 During   5 By
95b
1 to/until   2 by   3 from   4 During   5 for   6 until

Unit 96
96a
1 by   2 by   3 with   4 with   5 by   6 with   7 by   8 with
96b
1 by listening to songs in English   2 with a ruler   3 by chatting
online   4 with a vacuum cleaner   5 by looking it up   6 with a
digital camera   7 by working hard   8 with an electric razor

Unit 97
97a
1 What are the buildings like?
2 What was the accommodation like?
3 What were the teachers like?
4 What were the other students like?
5 What's the nightlife like?
6 What was the weather like?

97b
1 What did (the music) sound like?
2 What does (her perfume) smell like?
3 What does (your meal) taste like?
4 What do (these trousers) look like?
5 What did (the noise) sound like?
6 What does (Kelly) look like?
7 What does (curry) taste like?
8 What does (incense) smell like?
9 What did (the songs) sound like?
10 What does (the CD) sound like?
11 What did (the coat) look like?
12 What did (the medicine) taste like?

Check 22
1
1 into   2 with   3 next to   4 like   5 between
2
6 day before   7 by   8 by running   9 after   10 until
3
11 In   12 was   13 for   14 round   15 by   16 all   17 at   18 The
next   19 through   20 near

Unit 98
98a
1 at   2 on   3 at   4 at, in   5 at   6 in
98b
1 at first   2 in advance   3 in time   4 at the latest   5 on time
6 in the end

Unit 99
99a
1 on   2 at   3 on   4 in   5 on   6 in
99b
1 desks   2 lunch   3 holiday   4 trip   5 bed   6 meeting
7 phone   8 door

Unit 100
100a
1 by   2 on   3 by   4 in   5 by   6 in   7 in   8 by, on
100b
1 offer   2 cash   3 credit card   4 stock   5 condition   6 e-mail

Check 23
1
1 last   2 car   3 strike   4 my way   5 foot   6 time   7 advance

2

8 in   9 in   10 in   11 by   12 at   13 at   14 at   15 on

3

16 by credit card   17 once   18 at the   19 time   20 by

Unit 101

101a

1 about   2 of   3 to   4 from   5 of   6 of

101b

1 with practising   2 in forming   3 about forgetting   4 about going   5 about not getting   6 about wasting   7 in doing 8 of going

Unit 102

102a

1 for   2 to   3 at   4 at   5 of   6 for

102b

1 of her new friends   2 to that e-mail at once   3 for being late 4 to   5 on paying for the ice cream   6 into the crime   7 Luke for the present   8 with Ben

Unit 103

103a

1 tidy it up   2 put them away   3 made it up   4 ring him up 5 switch it off   6 turn it down

103b

1 grow up   2 going out, woken up   3 put on   4 check in 5 took off   6 joined in

Unit 104

104

1 having   2 make   3 had   4 got   5 got   6 made   7 do 8 done   9 have   10 getting   11 've got/have   12 do   13 've got/have   14 get   15 doing   16 got   17 have   18 get

Check 24

1

1 after   2 at   3 on   4 to   5 about

2

6 to   7 with   8 off   9 for   10 up

3

11 C   12 B   13 D   14 C   15 A   16 C   17 B   18 A   19 D   20 B

Unit 105

105a

1 interesting   2 tired   3 frightening   4 relaxed   5 depressing 6 rewarding

105b

1 bored   2 fascinating   3 worried   4 surprised 5 embarrassing   6 excited   7 interesting   8 terrifying

Unit 106

106a

1 inconsiderate   2 uncomfortable   3 illegal   4 irrational 5 irresponsible   6 impossible

106b

1 insensitive   2 unkind   3 immature   4 unhappy   5 imperfect 6 irrelevant   7 illegible   8 incorrect

Unit 107

107a

1 successful, financial   2 careless   3 lucky, beautiful   4 cloudy, rainy   5 harmless

107b

1 dangerous   2 mysterious   3 valuable   4 careful 5 comfortable   6 personal   7 noisy   8 mechanical

Unit 108

108a

1 actor   2 visitors   3 driver   4 cleaner   5 director   6 builders

108b

1 kindness   2 agreement   3 entertainment   4 sadness 5 government   6 management

108c

1 preparation   2 production   3 reservation   4 imagination 5 reaction   6 investigation   7 education   8 operation 9 suggestion   10 introduction   11 competition

Unit 109

109a

1 (door)bell   2 (taxi) driver   3 (tooth)ache   4 (alarm) clock 5 (credit) card   6 (sun) cream   7 (hand) luggage   8 (traffic) jam

109b

1 city centre   2 post office   3 shoe shop   4 travel agency 5 traffics lights   6 phone call   7 police officer   8 seatbelt

Unit 110

110a

1 (second-)hand   2 (easy-)going   3 (one-)way 4 (old-)fashioned   5 (well-)known   6 (long-)distance

110b

1 never-ending   2 five-door   3 handmade   4 record-breaking 5 well-paid   6 good-looking   7 badly-behaved   8 low-fat

Check 25

1

1 C   2 C   3 B   4 A   5 C   6 D   7 B   8 C   9 B   10 D

2

11 centre   12 lights   13 way   14 drivers   15 tempered

3

16 manager   17 illegible   18 inefficient   19 dirty   20 unpopular